AF588445

School of the South

School of the South

The Colonial Roots of French Theory

ONUR ERDUR

Translated by Andrew Brown

polity

First published in German as *Schule des Südens. Die kolonialen Wurzeln der französischen Theorie* © MSB Matthes & Seitz Berlin Verlagsgesellschaft mbH, Berlin 2024. All rights reserved.

This English translation © Polity Press, 2026.

The translation of this book was supported by a grant from the Goethe-Institut.

Polity Press Ltd.
65 Bridge Street
Cambridge CB2 1UR, UK

Polity Press Ltd.
111 River Street
Hoboken, NJ 07030, USA

All rights reserved. Except for the quotation of short passages for the purpose of criticism and review, no part of this publication may be reproduced, stored in a retrieval system or transmitted, in any form or by any means, electronic, mechanical, photocopying, recording or otherwise, without the prior permission of the publisher.

ISBN-13: 978-1-5095-6934-2 – hardback

A catalogue record for this book is available from the British Library.

Library of Congress Control Number: 2025950461

Typeset in 11 on 14pt Warnock Pro
by Fakenham Prepress Solutions, Fakenham, Norfolk NR21 8NL
Printed and bound by CPI Group (UK) Ltd, Croydon

The publisher has used its best endeavours to ensure that the URLs for external websites referred to in this book are correct and active at the time of going to press. However, the publisher has no responsibility for the websites and can make no guarantee that a site will remain live or that the content is or will remain appropriate.

Every effort has been made to trace all copyright holders, but if any have been overlooked the publisher will be pleased to include any necessary credits in any subsequent reprint or edition.

For further information on Polity, visit our website:
politybooks.com

To the memory of Frieder

Becoming stranger to oneself, to one's language and nation, is not this the peculiarity of the philosopher and philosophy, their 'style,' or what is called a philosophical gobbledygook?
Gilles Deleuze and Félix Guattari, *What is Philosophy*?

By telling in a different way, I tell something different.
Pierre Bourdieu, *Algerian Sketches*

Contents

INTRODUCTION
In the South of Theory

Algiers, 1955. He could right now have simply been doing his military service somewhere in the French provinces. Instead, the young philosopher Pierre Bourdieu is boarding a ship that takes him to Algeria. What he sees in that war-torn country shocks him: an uprooted Algerian society, its members locked up in camps by the French. He sees his own situation and presence there as a moral problem, as the 'original sin of the intellectual from the land of the colonial rulers'.[1] He decides to stay in the country after his military service, intent on doing something useful in the midst of the Algerian War; he starts on sociological research to bear witness to the injustice that surrounds him. These Algerian experiences will shape Bourdieu's entire academic work. His famous theory of the 'habitus' stems from his experience in Algeria.

Paris, 1957. In contrast to most left-wing intellectuals of his generation, who support the Algerian struggle for independence, Albert Camus, born in Algeria, avoids taking clear sides. His desire to mediate, his advocacy of a peaceful coexistence between French and Algerians, has already been denigrated as 'liberal'. Caught between the colonialism of the right, the anti-colonialism of the left, and the terror of the Algerian National Liberation Front (FLN), he deliberately chooses to remain silent. In Sweden, two days after being awarded the Nobel Prize for Literature, he is confronted by students over his silence. In the heat of the moment he answers, 'I have always condemned terrorism, and I must condemn a terrorism that works blindly in the streets of Algiers and one day might strike at my mother and my family. I believe in justice, but I will defend my mother before justice.'[2] It will be a long time before Camus the moralist is forgiven for these sentences.

Tunis, 1968. Michel Foucault has been living in the picturesque coastal village of Sidi Bou Said for two years. It is a magical place for him. On one of his walks along the beach he at last comes up with a definition of the concept of 'discourse' that has so far eluded him, and he later produces the idea of 'the other spaces'. Tunisia in general seems to be an inspiring backdrop: on one of his earlier stays in the Club Méditerranée, Foucault, on the beach in Djerba, had thought up the famous sentence from *The Order of Things:* 'one can certainly wager that man would be erased, like a face drawn in sand at the edge of the sea.'[3] Foucault is teaching philosophy at the University of Tunis, but he is mainly preoccupied with himself. He resolves to become a little more athletic and to improve his tan every day. He tells the *Presse de Tunisie*: 'I came because of the mythical image that all Europeans have of Tunisia: the sun, the sea, the great dry expanse of Africa.'[4] Foucault never comments, not a single time, on the neo-colonial conditions in the country, which has been independent for some ten years, or on the bloody French colonial rule in North Africa in general.

These three scenes could not be more different. They are about three intellectuals who each gained their own experiences and made decisions in three different places and in three different life situations. Despite all the differences, the scenes have certain things in common: these are what I will be exploring. My focus will be on the personal confrontation between French intellectuals and colonial spaces and situations. What applies to Bourdieu, Camus, and Foucault also applies to many other leading French philosophers and intellectuals of the second half of the twentieth century: they all have a 'colonial background'. Many of them come directly from French colonies: for example, in addition to Camus, Louis Althusser, Hélène Cixous, Jacques Derrida, and Jacques Rancière were born in Algeria, while Marguerite Duras was born in French Indochina and Alain Badiou in Morocco. Others, however, spent lengthy periods of time in the colonies or their successor states, for a variety of reasons – including Roland Barthes in Morocco, Bruno Latour in Ivory Coast, and Étienne Balibar, Simone de Beauvoir, and Jean-François Lyotard in Algeria. One could easily add other prominent names and places to this list. The basic tenor would remain the same: colonialism was an undeniable biographical reality for all of them. The only question is why this quite remarkable colonial setting of French thought has remained unnoticed for so long.

This book is an exploratory journey to the south of French Theory. Almost all its protagonists associated their stays in the colonies and post-colonies with key events, both liberating and traumatic, which had a decisive influence on their personal lives, their political attitudes, and their theoretical works. In order to gauge the extent of these influences, we need to track them back to specific historical locations – to the colonial period, to the Algerian War, to the former protectorates of Morocco and Tunisia, to independent Algeria, but also, again and again, to Paris, the metropolis of the empire and its intellectuals.[5] We need to search for clues: how did intellectuals end up in these colonial situations? What drove them? How did they behave there? And above all: how did the spatial experiences of colonial life affect their scholarly works and theoretical concepts? I am interested in the question of the connection between experience and theory: how can human experience be brought so close to intellectual theory that we can see the one sliding into the other? How does theory emerge? Like no other movement of the twentieth century, French Theory in particular developed a style of thinking that opposed identity and stood for difference, that was against the centre and for the periphery, against the hegemonic and for the minority. This book traces how this style of thinking emerged not in Parisian libraries, but on the beach in Tunis and in the streets of Algiers.

I am also interested in the questions of morality and justice that flash up in these three scenes, and in the responsibility of intellectuals in times of colonialism. We are dealing with classic experiments in intellectual self-definition and moral testing. Since at least Émile Zola, intellectuals have always been exponents of morality, even in peaceful times. But what happens to their public convictions when they are confronted with colonial reality? Regardless of whether the intellectuals sought out these encounters or not, whether they were based in the colonies or in the metropolis, whether they took up a political position immediately or only thirty years later, whether they belonged to the 'Sartre' generation or the 'Foucault' generation – they were all confronted in one way or another with the moral question of how they should react to the political and cultural injustice of colonialism, while being at the same time representatives of the French state, the military, the educational system, or the European colonial population. This motif of the colonial dilemma runs like a thread through the debates of these intellectuals. Some took concrete action, some struggled with themselves, while others preferred to remain silent; but they all tried to occupy a position. If you like, their specific ways of dealing with the colonial question are nothing more than variations on this one leitmotif of guilt and atonement. How they dealt with it in particular cases, and what ensued – that is also the subject of this book. One could speak of a doctrine of the virtues of the mind in the face of colonial injustice.

Let me clearly state the basic assumptions and theses of this book: I am convinced that the emergence of theories (and the adventure of thinking in general) is inseparably linked to the lived experience of their creators. By this, I do not mean to say that theory and thinking can be reduced to biographical life stories, or that thinkers are mechanically determined by social and political circumstances. But it is also clear that theory does not emerge in the abstract or in a vacuum, but always in local, historical, and individually grasped social contexts. As witnesses and actors of their time, intellectuals capture and shape the world around them, but they are just as strongly involved in the history of their societies, and are thus imbued with that history. What makes them special (and makes them interesting, in my view) has less to do with the supposed uniqueness of their life stories and experiences than it does with the way in which they take up these lived experiences, how they interpret their past and their social environment, and how they ultimately incorporate these interpretations into their theoretical and political projects.[6]

For French intellectuals in the second half of the twentieth century, a considerable part of their historical reality consisted of the experience of decolonization. In general, decolonization is understood to mean the global decoupling and formal independence of European colonies after the end of the Second World War. For France, decolonization was the longest conflict of the twentieth century: an extended and bloody historical process in the course of which the country lost most of its colonies (four-fifths of its territories), became involved in gruelling and ultimately unsuccessful wars (Indochina, Algeria), and experienced a profound government crisis that sealed the end of the Fourth Republic in 1958 and brought with it conditions similar to civil war, until Algeria gained independence in 1962.[7] With the decline of the colonial empire, the centuries-old universalistic cultural model of the 'civilizing mission' also collapsed: this was the political idea, very powerful in French republicanism since the French Revolution, that France was tasked with educating and civilizing the subjugated indigenous populations by exporting Western institutions, values, and culture to the wider world, thus advancing the progress of humanity – an ideology that was also shaped and supported by large parts of the political and intellectual left until 1962.[8]

The beginnings of French Theory fall precisely into this era of decolonization. It flourished immediately after the end of the Algerian War. In philosophy – in Foucault, Derrida, Deleuze, and Lyotard, for instance – this was a moment in which the certainties of traditional (some would say Western) reason began to falter, and its internal contradictions (some would say differences) became apparent. These writers questioned traditional notions of identity, power, knowledge, and language, just as they rejected the cultural hegemony claimed by the *Grande Nation* of France. The posture of this critical thinking was always anti-hegemonic, whether in the form of a poststructuralism that attacked long-established self-evident truths such as the idea of the stable meaningfulness of the world and emphasized the complexity, contingency, and subversion of meaning, or in the form of a postmodernism that diagnosed the decline of grand narratives, political ideologies of progress, and universally binding values, and sought to move beyond modernity.

I argue that some of these theoretical innovations were related to the attempt to reflect and understand the collapse of a certain political and cultural order in French society. In order to shed light on this connection and examine it historically, we need to take a look back at the beginnings of French Theory – to when, in the 1950s and 1960s (that is, in the middle of the Algerian War and the phase of decolonization), biographical fates, political awareness, and theoretical questions shaped each other mutually. In this collective space of experience, a colonial 'formatting' of thought emerged, one that impacted on different theories and across the generations. It influenced poststructuralists and postmodernists as well as deconstructionists and Marxists, and permeated deep into the formation of concepts and theories. In its simplest form, my argument is that central slogans and works of French Theory cannot be understood unless we take into account the way their protagonists experienced colonial borders and differences.

The chapters of this book aim to support this thesis with regard to particular cases. The colonial roots of French Theory are explored through individual essays, each of which focuses on a person, a place, and a theoretical crystallization of the colonial situation. I have selected and highlighted those actors who are paradigmatic for a certain intellectual attitude, and who cover a specific set of topics in an emblematic way. The geographical focus is (with a few exceptions) on Algeria, due to historical circumstances and the relevant biographies. The chapters not only offer portraits of intellectuals in colonial contexts, but also provide, as contextualization, insights into the history of French colonial rule. The fact that the chapters stand alone and can be read independently of each other is mainly due to the conviction that the differences between colonial and postcolonial settings, between individual theories, between places, and between times, are far too great to be simply absorbed into a homogenizing narrative. I think it makes a difference if some thinkers are confronted with a colonial situation and others with a barely postcolonial one – and if the Algerian setting for Hélène Cixous, the daughter of Jewish-German emigrants, is completely different from that of, say, Jacques Rancière, who as a child of French-Algerian parents (*pieds-noirs*) was born in Algiers but grew up in Paris. The lives and theories of the protagonists have their own character and their own momentum – and this is worth emphasizing.

Nevertheless, within this broad field of different intellectual itineraries, there are also commonalities and similarities that I do not wish to ignore, as they can provide the reader with an overall orientation. The chapters can be divided into four pairs with particular characteristics and focal points. The first two chapters focus on two figures, Pierre Bourdieu (1930–2002) and Jean-François Lyotard (1924–98), who both lived in Algeria in the 1950s. Their early life experiences there directly determined their later careers, their political attitudes, and their theories. In chapters three and four we follow Roland Barthes (1915–80) and Michel Foucault (1926–84) to Morocco and Tunisia respectively. The former French protectorates provided the two close friends with a setting for hedonistic lifestyles, erotic adventures, and new creative ideas. Chapters five and six are devoted to Jacques Derrida (1930–2004) and Hélène Cixous (1937–), the Algerian-born stars of that brand of deconstruction that had Jewish roots. Both had ambiguous and even traumatic experiences growing up in colonial Algeria, experiences that were etched into their identity, but also into their ways of philosophizing and writing. Chapters seven and eight are devoted to two younger representatives of French Theory, Étienne Balibar (1942–) and Jacques Rancière (1940–). Both experienced their political awakening as Parisian students protesting against the Algerian War (after which Balibar left for independent Algeria). Although their respective political philosophies did not take shape until much later, their ideas were nourished by events during and after the Algerian War.

These eight main protagonists – seven men and one woman – are among the guiding lights of French Theory. Even though they pursued very different and indeed conflicting approaches (structuralism, poststructuralism, deconstruction, postmodernism) and worked in different disciplines (sociology, philosophy, history, literary studies), they all shared a basic education in philosophy and a passionate penchant for theoretical thinking. Their intransigence on theoretical questions and the fact that they belonged to the generation of 'French Theory' make them obvious subjects for investigation. My focus on this generation of theorists does, of course, result in a certain limitation: other thinkers such as Jean-Paul Sartre, Simone de Beauvoir, Albert Camus, Frantz Fanon, Germaine Tillion, and Raymond Aron also have their say in my book, or make an appearance now and again, but no separate chapter is dedicated to them.

These days, the heyday of French Theory seems to be over. After winning global recognition in the second half of the twentieth century, in the form of structuralism, poststructuralism, deconstruction and postmodernism, it is now falling more and more out of favour. One major criticism, primarily from the postcolonial side, is that it never really overcame the problem of Eurocentrism that it had itself originally raised, and that questions of colonialism played little or no role in it. The French philosophers may have spoken theoretically of identity, difference, and alterity, but they simply overlooked real injustice, or blithely ignored anti-racist movements.[9] This criticism is to some extent aimed at ignorant white French colonialists. It has a kernel of truth, but it is also misguided. I do not agree with many of these negative appraisals because they are too simplistic and do not stand up to historical scrutiny, but I will discuss them whenever the criticism arises and is directed at the person I am discussing.

French Theory, however, faces a completely different form of criticism in the features pages of newspapers and in contemporary political debates. For some time now, both the right and the left have been accusing it of being ideologically responsible for current phenomena such as 'cancel culture', 'wokeness', and 'identity politics'. The main representatives of French Theory, such as Derrida and Foucault, are seen as being to blame for the dogmatism of identity politics because they launched ideas and concepts subsequently used by 'woke' activists from the fields of postcolonialism, gender studies, queer theory, and critical race theory – activists who censor speaking and thinking.[10] In my opinion, this criticism is an absurd, but politically very effective, distortion. A separate chapter at the end of the book is devoted to this.

One final comment on topicality. The chapters of this book deal on a general scale with issues that concern us (again) today: questions of national, cultural, and linguistic identity (and its appropriation), as well as questions of colonialism, racism, exoticism, and sexism. In this respect, they provide us with historical material in both positive and negative respects, but can also guide us through the maze of several of our contemporary concerns, as, for example, when we realize that some of the structures and events of the colonial period or the Algerian War were not settled long ago, but just repressed for decades in a kind of colonial amnesia, and continue to shape large areas of French society and politics – witness the colonial revisionism of the extreme right, the blindness to the grievances of those living in the *banlieue*, and police violence against the descendants of immigrants from the colonies.[11]

But we do not become topical merely by uncovering genealogies and latent trends. It is precisely the above-mentioned doctrine of the virtues of the mind that poses the most crucial question for dialogue with the present: what can we learn, both good and bad, from the colonial experiences of French intellectuals? They travelled and wrote a great deal, constantly examined their own role as intellectuals in colonial society, and reflected on the corrupting effect of colonialism, the decay of values, the loss of political legitimacy, and the limits of Eurocentrism. Even if some of them did this more than others, a moral demand can be perceived in the dynamics of their confrontations with the colonial world: not to be blind to existing injustice, or to the suffering and sacrifices that colonialism has exacted, and at the same time to find a concrete way in which this historical experience can be directed into theoretical and political channels. I do not think that this automatically makes them role models for the present, or moral compasses – some of their reactions, blind spots, entanglements, and masculinist fantasies are too problematic for that, and I will not refrain from criticism in the following pages (whenever I feel it is necessary). Nevertheless, I take the view that, in their debates about colonialism, French intellectuals arrived at theoretical insights and political positions that are worth documenting and narrating. Today they help us understand what it means to philosophize in times of colonial injustice.

PIERRE
BOURDIEU

1

AN ALGERIAN *BILDUNGSROMAN* Pierre Bourdieu

In the lives of young people there are certain special, never-ending summers that shape and support them over their entire lives. One of these summers, that of 1958, is recorded by the French writer and Nobel Prize winner Annie Ernaux in her book *A Girl's Story*: 'It was a summer with no distinguishing meteorological features, the summer of de Gaulle's return, the new franc and the new Republic, of Pelé, soccer world champion, of Charly Gaul, winner of the Tour de France, and Dalida's "Histoire d'un amour".'[1] Ernaux relates her stay in a holiday camp and describes the girl she was at the time – her first sexual encounter, her freedom and desire, her powerlessness and shame, and, in the same breath, her perception of political events. She also weaves the Algerian War into her memories of 1958:

> That summer, too, thousands of servicemen left France to restore order in Algeria. Many had never been away from home before. In dozens of letters, they wrote about the heat, the djebel, the douars – tent villages – and the illiterate Arabs, who after one hundred years of occupation still did not speak French. They sent photos of themselves in shorts, grinning with friends in a dry and rocky landscape. They looked like Boy Scouts on an expedition, almost as if they were on holiday.[2]

Many French soldiers may indeed have felt that their stay in Algeria was like an exotic vacation in short trousers. For example, the former French President Jacques Chirac described his years as a second lieutenant in Algeria as 'the most exciting time of my life'.[3] This time was certainly exciting, but Chirac was spectacularly skirting the circumstances of his stay, in this 1978 statement. One of the bloodiest decolonial wars of the twentieth century took place in Algeria from 1954 to 1962. According to estimates, more than a million people died. For France, the North African country was more than a colony. With around a million European settlers, Algeria was an extension of the Republic on the other side of the Mediterranean. 'L'Algérie, c'est la France' ('Algeria is France') was the motto of the then Interior Minister François Mitterrand. The Algerian independence movement, led by the Front de libération nationale (FLN), thus needed to be suppressed by all possible means: forced relocations, torture, rape, and mass executions were the order of the day. In France, however, little was heard of the FLN's terrorist attacks and the French army's excesses of violence, due – among other things – to the state's euphemistic language, which described the deployment of the army as a 'public order measure'. Thus, even many years after its end, this armed conflict was remembered as a 'war without a name'. Between 1954 and 1962, more than two million young Frenchmen did their military service in Algeria. Half a million soldiers were mobilized, and tens of thousands of them died in battle.[4]

The young Pierre Bourdieu was one of these conscripts with experience of Algeria. When he was called up in 1955, he was twenty-five years old and had just finished his philosophy studies. His service in Algeria left a deep mark on him. What Bourdieu saw in the war-torn country shocked him so much that, after his military service, he decided to stay in the country. He wanted to understand what was going on; to find out what effects colonialism and war were having on Algerian society; to test out what it meant to get politically involved and to make oneself useful. Bourdieu was certainly also seeking self-development, in various ways. At the end of his five-year stay, the philosopher had become a sociologist who had ideas and material for a whole lifetime of research – and a political intellectual who from then on made it his task to bring the sociological knowledge he had acquired about the society in which he lived back into that society.

When Bourdieu, by now one of the world's most important sociologists, was asked in one of the last interviews before his death in 2002 what role his stay in Algeria had played in his personal and intellectual life, he replied that Algeria had enabled him to 'accept myself'.[5] These were astonishing words even for Bourdieu. Until then, he had never made a secret of his time in Algeria, and had by no means concealed his affinity for the country, but he had also never so clearly revealed the concrete personal extent of the influence Algeria had on him. He did so only in the last two years of his life, above all in his posthumously published *Sketch for a Self-Analysis*. What exactly did these words mean? Could they provide a key to understanding the sociologist's life and work, a key that would ultimately explain how his personal experiences of the Algerian War were connected to the development of his theories?

The soldier in the library

Actually, Bourdieu could have completely avoided the war. There were plenty of opportunities for him to do so. As a recent graduate of the renowned École normale supérieure (ENS) in Paris, he had the privilege of attending the reserve officer school. Military service, compulsory at the time and lasting a full two years, would have been comparatively tranquil: deployment to Algeria was not essential for ENS graduates with prospects of a classic university career. Bourdieu would even have had the opportunity to continue his doctoral thesis, which he had begun with the philosopher Georges Canguilhem, on the 'temporal structures of affective experience'. But he refused to attend officer school because he 'could not bear the idea of dissociating myself from the rank-and-file soldiers'.[6] Enjoying the privileged life of an academic with the other future officers while ordinary soldiers, often the sons of peasants and workers without higher education, were sent to Algeria – that seemed wrong to Bourdieu, who himself came from modest circumstances. This pronounced sensitivity for subtle social differences – a hallmark of his later scholarly work – was there right from the start. You can take the boy out of the Pyrenean farming village, but you can't take the Pyrenean farming village out of the boy.

But of course it wasn't just the 'muted guilt at sharing in the privileged idleness of a bourgeois adolescent'[7] that drove Bourdieu to Algeria, but above all his negative attitude towards the colonial war. At first, during his three-month basic training in Chartres, this rejection did indeed provoke displeasure among his superiors. However, the disciplinary measures were relatively mild: Bourdieu had to step out of rank every morning when his name was called, in order to be handed the *Express* in front of the assembled troops – this was a magazine that, at the time, stood for a progressive Algerian policy and to which Bourdieu had somewhat naively subscribed. He faced serious consequences only at his next posting, to the army's psychological unit in Versailles. There he had heated arguments with the high-ranking officers, all of whom wanted to convert him to the idea of French Algeria. But Bourdieu was resistant to the pressure. More than that: he doubted the legitimacy of the French presence in Algeria, insofar as this was possible for a military conscript. But this was enough for him to be despatched, as punishment, to Algeria – a bitter irony when you consider that an enemy of the war was being sent out to a 'war without a name'.

Did Bourdieu know what was in store for him when he boarded the military vessel to Algeria in October 1955? At least by the time of the crossing, it must have become clear to him what worldview he would be confronted with in Algeria: his own attitude would not get very far, at least among the soldiers. He did try to influence them politically, preaching to them that they should rebel against the absurd ongoing 'pacification', and trying to open their eyes to the situation. But all this talk was useless – his comrades were anything but open to his political views. They were also suspicious that this philosopher, unlike other academics on board, did not wear an officer's uniform. The recruits preferred to have their older comrades tell them stories from the last (and lost) war in Indochina, and detail the military mistakes that should not be made this time. The task of getting them in the mood for their mission also included swapping the common insults intended for the enemy. Before they even set foot on Algerian soil, the recruits had already absorbed the entire everyday vocabulary of racism.[8]

Bourdieu's first assignment was in the Chelif Valley, 150 kilometres west of Algiers, where he was assigned to the ground staff of an air force unit. His regiment was mainly tasked with guarding air bases and other strategic facilities such as explosives depots. The menial tasks of his rank and the night-long guard duty were so arduous that Bourdieu found his self-chosen fate difficult to bear, and asked for a transfer. After six months, in the spring of 1956, he was transferred to the General Government in Algiers, thanks to the goodwill of Colonel Docourneau, originally from Bourdieu's home region of Béarn. Bourdieu's parents had contacted the colonel through members of his family living in the neighbouring village. Docourneau headed the intelligence and documentation unit in the General Government, and Bourdieu was allowed to carry out secretarial duties: typing letters and writing reports.

Escaping military service by seeking civilian jobs in Algeria as a cook, chauffeur, teacher, or typist was a frequently chosen solution among the military-service intellectuals of Bourdieu's generation. Jacques Derrida, for example, could not avoid being drafted in his native country, but chose the lesser evil by taking a job as a teacher in a provincial school.[9] But the good fortune of not being directly involved in armed warfare or having to take responsibility for acts of violence spared these intellectuals neither a bad conscience nor the question of guilt. Although most of them were against the war, they still served in the army, and thus worked for the colonial regime in a military capacity. Bourdieu saw this situation, in which his own political convictions came into conflict with those of state and army discipline, as a moral dilemma, even as 'the original sin of the intellectual from the land of the colonial rulers'.[10] Such feelings were not unjustified, since after his transfer Bourdieu suddenly found himself at the centre of colonial state power. The General Government was a highly political place, a mixture of civilian colonial administration and military headquarters. The governor of Algiers was the highest representative of France in Algeria, appointed by decree from Paris with extensive powers, especially after the government of the socialist prime minister Guy Mollet prevented the Algerian parliament from meeting in December 1955. Following the declaration of martial law, the French military decided what happened in the General

Government, with the approval of the then governors Robert Lacoste and Jacques Soustelle. The latter was a particularly interesting case: originally a highly respected ethnologist known for his moderate attitude, Soustelle became a hard-line warmonger and open sympathizer of the French-Algerian fascists during the war. But, under him, the General Government was also a centre of intellectual life in Algeria. Top officials, scholars, and intellectuals were active in it, and it had one of the best-equipped libraries in the country, which says a lot about the importance of knowledge and education for colonial policy.

Here, in the library of the General Government, Bourdieu found his personal way out of this tricky situation, or at least a way of doing something 'useful' despite his entanglement in the 'colonial situation'.[11] His work in the intelligence and documentation section did not take up much of his time, so he spent most of the rest of his military service (from spring 1956 to autumn 1957) in the library. He was eager to understand Algerian society, and to do so he read mainly ethnological literature. What he found, however, was steeped in colonial and racist clichés. The works lacked any basis for a real understanding of a society and how it functions. The ambitious twenty-six-year-old philosopher with no sociological training was anxious to close this gap with a civic 'work of political pedagogy'.[12] He had in mind above all the many French people in the motherland who – regardless of whether they were on the left or the right, for or against the war – knew very little about Algeria, but still did not hesitate to make hasty judgements. Since many Algerians who had gone through the French school system also lacked any profound knowledge of the social structures of their country, Bourdieu felt that a small book of regional studies was needed that would present the history and society of Algeria and, above all, the people living there.

Bourdieu's *Sociologie de l'Algérie* (*Sociology of Algeria*) was published in 1958, shortly after the end of his military service (publication was out of the question while he was still a soldier). The book, Bourdieu's first monograph, was included by the Parisian Presses universitaires de France in its renowned encyclopaedic series 'Que sais-je?', produced by established scholars and aimed at a general audience. In keeping with its main purpose of explaining the country and its people to the French, the book is structured like a kaleidoscope of society:

the first three of its six chapters are devoted to traditional societies (Kabyles, Chaouia, Mozabites); the next deals with the Arabic-speaking population, another discusses the cultural and economic similarities of these four groups, while the last chapter deals with French-European colonial society.

The book was a provocation. Merely to include the different individual populations in a sociology of Algeria was a breach of taboo. Until then, anyone who had spoken sociologically of an Algerian society actually always meant the French-European settler population. The traditional societies and the Arab population were systematically excluded from the modern sociological understanding of society, as they were seen as 'underdeveloped' or 'foreign' groups. If they were studied at all, it was as the subject of ethnological or orientalist studies (in the sense of a disciplinary division of labour). By nonchalantly calling his regional studies a sociology of Algeria and including all population groups, Bourdieu thereby assumed, quite explicitly, that an Algerian society had a right to exist in which the colonizers and the colonized came together under one general term, and could also be examined together. In this short book, meant to educate ordinary citizens about the situation while refraining from any direct political judgements at the height of the war, Bourdieu was able to smuggle in several explosive sociological diagnoses of French colonial rule in Algeria, diagnoses that he spelled out only in later works. He stated, for example, that the original way of life of the Kabyles was being destroyed; that the capitalist colonial economy was undermining the economy of the indigenous population; that the colonial society functioned like a caste system based on origin and made the colonized subjects into foreigners who then became further alienated; and that the war was destroying an independent and valuable civilization.[13]

Bourdieu felt the effects of his taboo-breaking and his many pointed criticisms of the way colonialism worked. In particular, the clique of colonial ethnologists based in Algeria saw the publication of the book as an affront. In a letter to the historian André Nouschi, one of the few French scholars in Algeria who remained friends with him, Bourdieu wrote shortly after publication that he had 'never felt as isolated as just recently' and that the 'little book' – his 'opus minimum', as he liked to say – had something to do with it.[14] He was viewed in Algiers with a mixture of pity and hostility, with the latter predominating. Bourdieu had turned the colonial clique against him. It looked down upon the young ENS philosopher and anti-war activist as 'this metropolitan who barges in to say something about Algeria.'[15] Having probably hoped for more success in academic circles, Bourdieu expressed his disappointment in this letter, admitting that he had chosen the misguided strategy of an outsider with his little book – so much so that he could not help thinking that 'everything I've written is completely worthless and I'd have done better to keep silent.' Bourdieu himself recognized that the book also had scholarly weaknesses.[16] It was written almost exclusively on the basis of library reading and did not consistently adhere to the intended sociological mode of description.[17] 'I have the feeling, despite all the drivellers,' Bourdieu nonetheless assured Nouschi, 'of having done something useful.'[18]

An exalted *libido sciendi*

But there was still plenty of useful work for Bourdieu to do. What was initially intended as a small journalistic episode suddenly gained a whole new momentum. Instead of leaving Algeria for France as soon as he had finished his military service, as he had originally planned, and resuming his doctoral thesis in philosophy with the prospect of a university career, Bourdieu had decided, even before the publication of *Sociologie de l'Algérie*, to stay in the country and continue his ethnological and sociological studies. In the autumn of 1957 he had accepted a position as an assistant lecturer in philosophy and sociology at the University of Algiers. He was no longer an involuntary conscript in Algeria, but a university lecturer living and researching there of his own free will.

At that time, the University of Algiers was, with a few exceptions, a melting pot for reactionary and fascist movements, from students to professors.[19] In contrast to the universities in the mother country, it was more of a reflection of the local colonial system, with its own hierarchies and appointments system. The university was literally in the hands of a few family dynasties who divided power among themselves. This professorial colonial clique also consisted, appropriately enough, of Arabists and Orientalists. As experts on the region, they practised the regionally specific disciplines (ethnological, linguistic, cultural) as inherently colonial sciences, and deployed openly racist arguments. It is therefore hardly surprising that the opposition Bourdieu reported in his letters to André Nouschi on the occasion of the publication of his volume came primarily from the University of Algiers. Many of the scholars working there were patriotic French Algerians who did not tolerate dissent. During the war, quite a few of them even became supporters of the Organisation armée secrète (OAS), a paramilitary underground movement that, from 1958 onwards, rebelled against de Gaulle's Algerian policy, carrying out terrorist acts and fighting to maintain the colonial status quo.

With his new university position, Bourdieu had certainly not chosen a quiet place to work. A heated climate of intimidation and violence prevailed, especially on the part of the right-wing students. Almost all the politicians, organizations, and groups belonging to the nationalist right in France had set up camp in Algiers during the war and established close ties to the student milieu – including the later founder of the Front National, Jean-Marie Le Pen.[20] Anyone at the university who thought differently and openly expressed their views quickly became a target for the right-wing extremists. The historian André Mandouze was dismissed from the university for 'security reasons' after right-wing students tried to lynch him for supporting Algerian independence.[21] The case of the mathematician Maurice Audin spread the greatest ripples: the communist activist and FLN supporter was arrested by paratroopers during the 'Battle of Algiers' in 1957 and tortured to death.[22] Bourdieu was put under pressure in a different way at the university: he was often advised to deal with other topics, or simply to keep his mouth shut. He was also aware that he was a thorn in the side of the authorities and the right wing. Shortly after the military coup in May 1958, one of his students informed him that he was on the coup plotters' 'red list', the list of undesirables who were to be 'neutralized'.[23]

No less risky were the extensive trips that Bourdieu made during the university vacations to remote and sometimes contested areas of Algeria. These explorations were the main reason for his extended stay. He hoped to be able to underpin his previous work with more empirical first-hand data – to conduct more field research in the best sense of the word. It was appropriate that he was now also working for the Algerian branch of the French statistical office, the INSEE. The head of this partly independent research unit, the sociologist Alain Darbel, gave official approval to Bourdieu's research. The studies commissioned were primarily statistical surveys and analyses of the Algerian Muslim rural population. Together with a team of INSEE employees, Bourdieu travelled through the Algerian province, creating questionnaires and maps, collecting samples, checking birth rates, evaluating schools and social institutions, and conducting consumer surveys. The new insights were shocking: around a quarter of the Muslim rural population had been forcibly relocated to newly created villages and settlements as part of the French resettlement programmes. Bourdieu discovered an Algerian society that was uprooted, confined to camps, and impoverished.

As far as his work for the statistics office allowed, Bourdieu – who was, in a certain sense, already on site – simultaneously devoted himself to his ethnographic interests. He conducted interviews with Kabyle peasants and tribal leaders, secretly recorded market conversations, noted the characteristics of local languages and behavioural codes, documented rituals and family relationships, made sketches of typical houses and, above all, took a great number of photographs of landscapes, people, and objects. By the end of his stay he had taken around 3,000 pictures with his Zeiss camera, which he had bought in the GDR.[24]

Bourdieu threw himself into his work, sought to be 'in the field' as much as possible, and endeavoured to soak up all the events he witnessed, like a sponge. He did this with a passionate and restless devotion that sometimes bordered on the obsessive – his working days during field studies began at six in the morning and usually ended late at night.[25] Bourdieu described his state at the time as a 'somewhat

Above: Aïn Aghbel, Collo/Algeria, ca. 1960. Photograph by Pierre Bourdieu.
Below: Aïn Aghbel, Collo/Algeria, ca. 1960. Photograph by Pierre Bourdieu. The French military would habitually set fire to the roofs of houses to force the residents to leave their homes. The photo shows Bourdieu's assistant at the time, Abdelmalek Sayad, taking notes in the middle of the ruins.

Pierre Bourdieu (left in the picture) during the inquiry in Aïn Aghbel, Collo/Algeria, 1960.

exalted *libido sciendi*.'[26] This desire for knowledge was fed by two sources: the 'passion for everything about this country, its people and its landscapes', and the 'dull but constant sensation of guilt and revolt in the face of so much suffering and injustice'.[27] Love for, perhaps even identification with, the country and its people, coupled with feelings of guilt, indignation, and the awareness of having to justify his presence – this was the remarkable mixture of feelings that underlay his desire to find out more about Algeria.

For whatever reasons, he definitely started to undertake some kind of moral reflection at that time. There is hardly any other explanation for how, in 1959, Bourdieu came up with the idea of writing an existentialist-tinged text about Molière entitled 'Tartuffe ou le drame de la foi et de la mauvaise foi' ('Tartuffe or the drama of faith and bad faith'), in the midst of his Algerian field studies.[28] Bourdieu's very first article without any explicit reference to Algeria addresses human hypocrisy and the resulting questions of conscience, using one of the most famous figures in French literature, the hypocrite Tartuffe, as an example. It is a short exercise in moral philosophy. But given the place where it was written, the text can also be understood as an intimate examination of the moral costs of colonialism and war for an individual.

These questions of identification, guilt, and morality were indeed important circumstantial factors as well as driving forces for Bourdieu's scholarly zeal. However, an overemphasis on emotional structures easily runs the risk of obscuring other, less 'pathetic' conditions that can frame the production of scholarly knowledge. There were other reasons, other conditions of possibility, about which Bourdieu gave comparatively little information either at the time or later. The fact that his findings in the empirical social sciences actually developed from a personal, pleasurable, and somewhat feverish urge for knowledge in such a short time was only possible due to factors that had less to do with Bourdieu's own emotional balance than with the scholarly context and the colonial situation on site.

Like many other scholars before and after him, Bourdieu was part of a long tradition in the production of colonial knowledge. At an early stage, the colonies played an important role in the formation of disciplines such as ethnology and sociology, which in their early days as so-called colonial sciences often voluntarily placed their research at the service of the imperial colonial administrations. Even after both disciplines managed to free themselves from these state demands and increasingly gain scholarly autonomy, the colonial territories remained a preferred field of activity for social research. Between 1945 and 1960, around a third of French sociologists worked in and on the colonies. Algeria in particular, due to its proximity and its ambiguous status as a settler colony belonging to the French Republic, offered a kind of open laboratory for modern social research, whether in ethnological terms or as part of state-sponsored development and modernization projects drawn up and implemented in the country by French scientists and engineers.[29]

Bourdieu could rely on a number of colonial institutions in Algeria: the General Government, the university, and the statistical office.

As a Frenchman endowed with all kinds of social privileges, he found almost ideal working conditions and resources, and was able to quickly and relatively autonomously familiarize himself with the two highly demanding disciplines of ethnology and sociology. This is a factor that should not be underestimated. Having been trained only in philosophy, he had an acute need to catch up, but he was able to do so without much fuss and without additional studies back in Paris. Finally, it should not be forgotten that the scientific terrain that proved so fruitful for him and provided data for his intensive research – namely the phenomena of uprooting and resettlement that he observed and studied, as well as the 'foreign culture' of the indigenous population – had come into being precisely through imperial oppression. Even if Bourdieu vehemently rejected colonialism and criticized its devastating consequences, he, like many scholars before and after him, benefited from the existence of a scientific setting that would not have existed in this specific form without colonialism. His entanglement in colonial contexts was therefore not a purely political or moral matter, but also an epistemic one. In this phase his sociology was, and remained, a science under colonial auspices.

At the same time, it was also a science that arose in the difficult conditions of a war of liberation. In Algeria, it should be noted, there was not only a colonial situation but also a war of independence. Bourdieu certainly took risks, and his intense research activities attracted the attention of the military and security authorities, who ambushed him with minor persecutions, interrogations, and surveillance operations. In addition, on his excursions into abandoned villages set on fire by the French army he often encountered heavily armed Algerians. For example, in Tizi Ouzo, where he was determined at all costs to find out about the rituals of the Kabyle peasants, the skeletons of burnt-out cars stood on the streets, Algerian soldiers sat at the roadside, and the clatter of machine guns could be heard in the background.[30] When the fighting between the French army and members of the Algerian independence movement became too intense, Bourdieu and his team often sought refuge with the White Fathers, an apostolic missionary order based in Algeria since 1850 and valued or tolerated by the Algerians during the war because of its social spirit.[31] It is difficult to say which warring parties posed the greatest risk to him. In the end, however, it was the terrorist activities of the OAS that prompted his flight from Algeria. After his assistant Moulah Henine was shot dead by the OAS in front of Henine's house, and Bourdieu himself was informed by a high-ranking French officer that his life was also in danger, he decided to return to France. He left Algeria in May 1960 in a cloak-and-dagger operation. A military plane flew him safely out of Algiers.[32]

Return to the Béarn

Bourdieu's return to Paris was involuntary and abrupt, but he landed relatively softly on French soil. He was able to rely on a personal contact who opened doors for him in Paris: Raymond Aron, the doyen of French sociology and one of the country's most influential political intellectuals. The two had met in Algeria, of all places, when Aron was in the country in his capacity as Inspector General of the national education system (he was responsible for chairing the examination committees for the baccalaureate). In France, Aron secured assistant lectureships for Bourdieu, first at the Sorbonne, then in Lille. He also took over the supervision of Bourdieu's new dissertation in sociology – an arrangement with many far-reaching consequences. Leaving philosophy behind, Bourdieu finally embarked on a career as a sociologist, found a decisive supporter in Aron, and took over the management of the Centre de sociologie européenne from him a few years later.

Aron, in turn, contributed the foreword to the American edition of Bourdieu's *Sociologie de l'Algérie,* which was published under the title *The Algerians* and with the Algerian national flag on the cover, just in time for the country's independence in 1962. Aron, Sartre's eternal antipode, embodied the conservative French establishment, so he cannot have had all that much sympathy for anti-colonial liberation movements. On the Algerian question, however, he had been in favour of the colony's separation since at least 1957, mainly for economic reasons, as he stated in his book *La tragédie algérienne* ('The Algerian tragedy'). In the foreword to Bourdieu's book, Aron also wrote that the war had become too great a burden for France: 'For almost eight years the drama of Algeria weighed upon the French like an obsession, a guilt, and also like a duty. It precipitated the fall of a regime, split a nation asunder. It imperilled domestic peace and spread throughout the mother country a climate of passion and crime.'[33] One must finally admit, Aron continued, that the Algerian affair 'could no longer be considered a simple episode in a historically irresistible movement called "decolonization"; it became a tragic moment in the history of France'. Aron recommended Bourdieu's book to all 'those who care about the destiny of France and of the West [and who therefore] cannot remain indifferent to Algeria'.[34]

In 1960, Bourdieu returned to a crisis-ridden France that was increasingly threatening to slide into a quasi-civil war and seemed paralysed by the Algerian question. His expertise on Algeria provided him with a unique selling point among Parisian intellectuals. Many of them may have spoken out loudly as opponents of the war, or expressed solidarity with the FLN – but how many could claim not only to have served in Algeria but also to have been active in scholarly and political circles there? At secret meetings in Paris where Algerian and French intellectuals were already discussing the future of Algeria after independence, Bourdieu found an immediate audience.[35] In these circles he had considerable 'cultural capital', to use an expression from his own sociological theory. He was able to put this capital to active use, publishing his first articles on Algeria in renowned journals such as *Esprit* and *Les Temps modernes*.[36] This was followed by two major monographs, *Travail et travailleurs en Algérie* ('Labour and labourers in Algeria') and *Le Déracinement* ('On being uprooted'), written together with his colleagues. The focus of these texts was mainly on the working and living conditions of the Algerian population in times of colonialism and war.

Bourdieu was more than sceptical about the Parisian debates on Algeria, which were conducted from a relatively safe distance. He saw that many French people – as well as many Algerians living in France – knew very little about the country on the other side of the Mediterranean, and their political judgements were accordingly ill-founded. In Bourdieu's eyes, this applied even to the well-known spokesmen of the anti-colonial left, such as Jean-Paul Sartre and Frantz Fanon. Bourdieu, who had gained insight into the actual economic, social, and political conditions of the Algerian peasants and workers through his fieldwork, felt that Sartre's view of the Algerian peasantry as the only true revolutionary force in the country was a 'distortion of reality'[37] – he later even called Sartre's position 'completely idiotic'.[38] In Bourdieu's assessment, the Algerian peasants had certainly played an important role in the struggle, but they were not only protagonists, they were also the first victims of colonialism and war. They had undergone such exceptionally profound changes as a result of previous pillaging and expropriations and, more recently, due to war and displacement, that they were an explosive force; but they were also a desperate mass that could be deployed to achieve the most contradictory political goals. In other words, the Algerian peasants – even in the form of a proletariat that had migrated to the cities – were very far from being the revolutionaries that intellectuals and activists in Paris painted them as. To assume that they had a 'revolutionary consciousness' was, for Bourdieu, downright irresponsible in this specific context.

This analysis of the situation led Bourdieu to a cautious assessment of the Algerian leadership of the time and of its revolutionary goals. The 'Provisional Government of the Algerian Republic', operating in exile, saw a left-wing revolution at work in the fight for Algerian independence – an independent Algeria was to be transformed into a model socialist country. Its members welcomed the slogans of Sartre and Fanon. But Bourdieu's assessment was ultimately correct. As everyone knows, the desired revolution of peasants and proletarians did not occur in Algiers under the authoritarian FLN regime.[39]

These early interventions in political discussions can hardly be overestimated. They shaped Bourdieu's understanding of the role of research and his self-image as a political intellectual. But they were by no means the only field of activity in the, for him, highly productive early 1960s. An episode that casts Bourdieu's stay in Algeria and his intellectual career in a slightly different light occurred in exactly the same phase. The research he undertook in Algeria led him into a rather curious biographical and scholarly constellation: one of the first areas Bourdieu headed for after his successful reintegration into the French academic world was, of all places, Béarn, his home region in the Pyrenees. There, in the village of his parents and his childhood, he spent significant time carrying out research. After his first autodidactic steps in ethnology, he now wanted to try his hand at a sociology of rural areas.

The focus was on field research into peasant production methods and reproduction strategies in pre-industrial France. The aim was to understand why the eldest sons of peasant families remained unmarried, even though village society was known for its stubborn adherence to the right of primogeniture. But, from the outset, the entire project was directly linked to Bourdieu's parallel processing of data he had collected on the Kabyle peasants in Algeria. It had a deeply self-reflective character: Bourdieu had already drawn on his youthful everyday experiences among the Béarn peasants during his interviews with Kabyle informants in Algeria, and had repeatedly made connections between the two different, but in his eyes also sometimes very similar, groups. In Béarn, Bourdieu would continue his research and, to a certain extent, his practice in sociology, in order – in the spirit of scientific rigour – to objectify a subjective experience that had served him as a conscious or unconscious frame of reference in Algeria. He also tested his acquired knowledge of Kabyle society in Béarn, in an environment that was profoundly familiar to him.

In this case, unearthing the foreign aspects of one's own culture was not an ethnological cliché. For Bourdieu in his native Béarn, it meant examining processes of uprooting, kinship and gender relationships, and behavioural dispositions with the same intensity and dedication as he had in Algeria. On the one hand, this would enable him to classify what he had previously learned more consciously and without falling back into crude ethnocentrism or positivism. On the other hand, he could sharpen the ethnological view of local French conditions, of a rural community that existed far away from urban life and was, in Bourdieu's eyes, threatened with extinction as the country moved towards greater modernization and industrialization.

The groundbreaking masterpiece *Tristes Tropiques* by the French anthropologist Claude Lévi-Strauss served as a contrast. This book, published in 1955, became the manifesto of structuralism; in it, Lévi-Strauss demystified the West's excessively exotic and romanticized view of the culturally 'foreign'. His travelogue about the extinction of traditional cultures and societies in the Brazilian Amazon region also provided him with an opportunity to make universal cultural comparisons based on an ethnological view of the foreign, to ponder the role of Western civilizations, and to develop various theoretical reflections on the relationship between subjective experience and objective science. In Béarn, on the other hand, Bourdieu had nothing less in mind than to 'do a "*Tristes Tropiques* in reverse"'.[40] Instead of pursuing general theoretical reflections on the relationship between the ethnological observer and the object of his or her gaze, Bourdieu wanted to find out what it means to research something that one knows well but that is disappearing. He therefore devoted himself to the unhappy peasants of France – the inhabitants of France's own *tristes tropiques*, as it were.

Bourdieu was not alone in this project. He was assisted by his closest colleague, Abdelmalek Sayad, whom he knew from Algeria. Sayad, who came from a village in Kabylie, had studied with Bourdieu at the University of Algiers and was part of the permanent team of staff that accompanied him on his extensive ethnological field research in Algeria. Over the years, their initial acquaintance and collaboration developed into a close friendship. Both looked back on an eventful time: they had travelled to the most remote areas of Algeria, worked late into the night evaluating countless data, and had some rather adventurous encounters in remote villages. But they had also lost mutual friends to fascist terrorists.[41]

When Bourdieu invited his 'old brother', as he called Sayad in letters, to stay for a longer period at his parents' house to continue the research in Béarn together, he had in mind not only the personal bond but also a small-scale scholarly experiment.[42] The main idea behind it was as simple as it was unconventional: while in Kabylie Sayad had often acted as a local assistant and Bourdieu remained the foreign ethnologist from the country of the colonial rulers, in Béarn they swapped roles as and when – Sayad took on the role of the foreign ethnologist, while Bourdieu was the well-informed, but ultimately biased, local informant.

As part of the experiment, after his stay in south-west France Sayad undertook similar studies in his Kabyle home village of Aghbala. The exchange resulted in a kind of cross-field ethnography based on the two researchers' home villages, Lasseube and Aghbala. As can be seen from the correspondence between them, this dual mobilization of their own roots and their amalgamation was not intended to level out cultural differences. Rather, Bourdieu and Sayad wanted to bring out the differences between autochthonous primary experiences and ethnological foreign experiences, starting from the initially observed similarities. The letters they wrote to each other from France and Algeria make it clear how far this exchange of personal experiences extended into further scholarly and theoretical work, but also how it was thoroughly examined, framed, and monitored in each case.[43]

Bourdieu's return to the Pyrenees had a self-reflexive impact not only in a scholarly but doubtless also in a personal sense. It became a biographical event: Bourdieu now sought to apply the ethnological approach he had taken in Algeria to himself, to the people from his homeland, to his parents' house, and to the habitus of his father and mother. He wanted to re-appropriate all of this in a sober, scholarly way – not least because he had increasingly distanced himself from his original milieu when he moved to the faraway intellectual world of Paris. On this personal level, the studies had at least two meanings: they were intended to enable Bourdieu to achieve a kind of reconciliation with the things and people of his homeland, but at the same time to consolidate (or at least not endanger) his newly acquired role as a researcher, which above all meant that a scholarly attitude of distance and analysis needed to be adopted. Even as he turned back towards his parents' world, it became clear that his academic attitude had long since become an inescapable way of life – a layer of experience that could no longer be removed, and one that evoked a different view of his own life. To put it more vividly: not only can you not take the Pyrenean farming village out of the boy – you can't take the scientist out of him, either.

The attempt to regain a lost world, the shameful feeling of the change of social class he had experienced, the inner conflict of the uprooted intellectual, and ultimately his understanding of research as a redemptive, emancipatory, and therapeutic method – there is almost no trace of this in Bourdieu's individual studies on the decline of rural society published successively since 1962 and issued together in 2002 under the title *Le bal des célibataires* ('The bachelors' ball'). The texts pay homage to the sober scholarly style so typical of Bourdieu, filled with statistical analyses and devoid of explicit biographical references.

Only with the passage of time did Bourdieu speak more openly about the turbulent emotional atmosphere that surrounded his study of his native region at the time: first, relatively dryly, in a foreword written especially for *Le bal des célibataires*, then with particular emphasis in the aforementioned *Sketch for a Self-Analysis* – both texts were written shortly before Bourdieu's death and published only posthumously. In the last work in particular, Bourdieu speaks openly about a personal guilt and shame complex that dominated him at the time. His confessional report on the history of his research in the Béarn is permeated by a feeling of nostalgia, but at the same time supported by a self-understanding in which, despite 'the inner desolation of solitary grief', he has managed to forge a relationship with himself and his scholarly work.[44] The Béarn episode marks the narrative high point of the entire auto-sociobiographical text in the *Sketch for a Self-Analysis* after his experiences in Algeria. Not only the narrative text, but also the narrated life finds its purpose with the later return to the Béarn. The end of the intellectual *Bildungsroman* seemed to have been reached. Algeria in particular offered Bourdieu a variety of stages along the way: a theatre of war, an area of adventure, a field of scholarly experimentation, a place of projection and, almost continuously, the scene of a journey of self-discovery. But if Algeria really was what enabled Bourdieu to accept himself, as he emphasized in the interview mentioned above, then the Béarn would necessarily represent the always desired place of longing that he had to seek out and rediscover. Perhaps Bourdieu had actually returned to his homeland when he set off for Algeria.

The birth of the habitus

The almost five-year stay in Algeria may have found a meaningful and concluding moment in Bourdieu's own auto-sociobiography with his return home, but this homecoming was by no means the end of Bourdieu's Algerian story. Even after his stays on the other side of the Mediterranean and in Béarn, Algeria long remained a reference point in his academic work. What is less known, if known at all, is that in the decade after Algeria's independence, when the security risk posed by the fascists no longer played a role, Bourdieu regularly returned to Algeria for research purposes.[45] In theoretical-historical terms, it would therefore be a mistake to believe that the formative experiences and self-knowledge he acquired as a young intellectual of military age were sufficient. Quite the opposite: the observations and data Bourdieu gathered in Algeria were plentiful, and he had amassed an empirically dense pool of material from which he could draw extensively and to which he returned again and again. Above all, the ethnological field studies of Kabyle society subsequently demonstrated their social scholarly and theoretical potential. The comprehensive bibliography of his work shows how intensively Bourdieu constantly worked on and reworked his material and the texts that resulted from it in the 1960s, how he repeatedly rehashed the same texts well into the 1970s and 1980s and reused them in publications to the point of interchangeability, and how, over time, he expanded this extensive research into a correspondingly extensive theory.

The results of this work flowed directly into later major works, namely *Outline of a Theory of Practice* (1972), *The Logic of Practice* (1980), and *Masculine Domination* (1998).[46] If one realizes that the theoretical concepts relevant to his academic work, concepts such as 'habitus', 'practice', 'capital', 'field', and 'symbolic domination', were first fundamentally developed in these books, then it becomes clear that Bourdieu's social theory is hardly conceivable without reference to the way he drew on and utilized the Algerian context, or to his experiences and empirical studies in Algeria. This is not as self-evident as it may seem. In the international reception of Bourdieu, it was customary for a long time to decouple the content of the theory from the ethnological-Algerian context and to discuss it on a social science level that allowed it to be perceived with reference to Western societies. The ethnological material from which Bourdieu developed his theory, on the other hand, seemed less captivating and remained, in a narrower sense, the concern of anthropology. There were (and are) good reasons for this disciplinary division of labour, but from a theoretical-historical perspective it can be said that Algeria was undoubtedly also the laboratory for Bourdieu's theory of the social world.

The theoretical-historical significance of his stay in Algeria can be illustrated using the concept of habitus, by far the most famous term in the sociologist's theory box. The term itself has a rich philosophical and sociological tradition that can be traced back to antiquity. However, it was Bourdieu who gave the term its current and most effective use to date. The concept of 'habitus' is generally associated with the idea that people's practices and ideas are based on a system of permanent, embodied behavioural dispositions. A person's habitus is determined, for example, by the ways of thinking and seeing that are effective in a society, the patterns of perception, and the principles of judgement and evaluation. It is a way of acting that is profoundly socially conditioned and structured. On the other hand, due to its spontaneous and unconscious mode of practice, it also has a structuring effect: it produces and simultaneously reproduces social relationships. 'Habitus' describes – at least in its most common form – a person's lifestyle, clothing, taste, language, and attitude, while in today's use of the word the point is usually that these habitual characteristics are associated in the same breath with a certain social situation and origin. For Bourdieu, there is usually a coincidence between habitus and the social world, in which the structures of the habitus are always attuned to the objective structures of a social field. This connection between habitus and social structure also gives rise to the commonsense view that the social background in which the foundations of habitus are acquired plays a decisive role in the further course of a person's life – a groundbreaking thesis that Bourdieu underpinned in the 1960s with studies of the rigid French education system and its mechanisms for reproducing social inequality.[47]

So much for the basic features of the concept. Anyone who, on hearing the term 'habitus' (to give a small example from the famous social study *Distinction*), thinks of the class differences between well-off Parisian diplomats' sons with distinguished musical tastes and working-class children from the suburbs with less distinctive musical interests, is certainly correct. But there is a lesser-known Algerian history of the habitus concept. Bourdieu used it for the first time not in France, but in Algeria. But here the context was different – it was a matter of economic behavioural dispositions among Kabyle peasants. Before anyone spoke of a bourgeois, academic or proletarian habitus *à la française*, Bourdieu had explored a peasant habitus in Kabylie.

But first things first. How did Bourdieu come up with the idea of habitus? At the beginning it was in a classic ethnographic setting, with all the associated problematic terminology that comes with looking at foreign ways of life: during his ethnological field studies, Bourdieu had been able to observe how certain remote tribal societies in Kabylie had retained more or less intact traditions of a pre-capitalist economy to which the logic of the market was completely alien. For example, ordinary exchange processes among Kabyle peasants were regulated by strategies of honour that obeyed the logic of giving and receiving: milk and butter were not sold, but rather given to neighbours, with the expectation of benefiting from the principle of solidarity in the same way in another place and at another time. As a rule, trading was not carried out in public. Relationships that were reduced to their purely economic dimension were perceived as hostile and could only arise between strangers in a distant marketplace, while most exchange took place between relatives and neighbours in the village.[48] In this context, Bourdieu made another, momentous observation: large parts of the Kabyle population could not just unhesitatingly adopt the capitalist economic system promoted by the French; they had enormous difficulties in adapting to the changed economic and social conditions. Bourdieu found that these economic actors simply did not have 'the dispositions tacitly demanded by an economic order that for us is entirely familiar – in which, being an embodied and therefore naturalized social structure, they appear as self-evident, necessary and universal.'[49] He did not deny that these actors followed an economic logic and rationality, but in his eyes the latter were of a different nature, with the result that coexistence with the capitalist order did not seem to be a given. In Kabylie, at the end of the 1950s, a social experiment was underway that Bourdieu experienced at first hand: accelerated by war and resettlement, two very different economic systems with completely contradictory requirements – systems that had otherwise been separated by a period of several hundred years – collided with one another. It was, as Bourdieu wrote in 1959, a 'clash of civilizations' (a formulation reminiscent of Samuel P. Huntington's 1996 *Clash of Civilizations*, though it has precious little to do with the ideas of the American political scholar).[50]

Bourdieu derived two central insights from his observations of the so-called 'clash.' The first was of a general nature: the observed discrepancy between the attitudes formed in a pre-capitalist economy and the economic system often imposed by colonization led Bourdieu to conclude that 'access to elementary economic behaviour (wage labour, savings, credit, family planning, etc.) is by no means self-evident and that the economic actor called "rational" is the product of very specific historical circumstances'.[51] In this respect, every economic system, even the capitalist one with its modern understanding of rational action, has certain social prerequisites. Its functioning is tied to the existence of a given system of institutions, dispositions, and perceptions of the social world. This finding is really quite reminiscent of the work of the sociologist Max Weber, whose studies on modern economic thinking, especially *The Protestant Ethic and the Spirit of Capitalism*,[52] became an important source of inspiration for Bourdieu. Many of the terms used by Bourdieu for Kabylie, such as the categorical distinction between pre-capitalist and capitalist rationality, can be traced back to Weber. In Algeria, Bourdieu became an avowed Weberian, which later led to him being accused of unreflectively reproducing the dualism of traditional societies on the one hand and modern societies on the other, and thus also the dualism of Orient and Occident.[53]

Bourdieu related the second finding specifically to the situation of the Kabyle peasants. For them, the clash of economic worlds with their different rules of conduct had devastating consequences. According to Bourdieu, they found themselves in a destructive internal conflict between the social pressure to adapt their behaviour to capitalism and the impossibility of doing so profitably, since many of them had at the same time become representatives of a 'sub-proletariat' made up of the unemployed and small traders. Bourdieu by no means had in mind *all* Kabyle peasants (there were certainly social actors who had successfully adapted), but specifically those peasants who, dispossessed of their land, had to leave their villages, to move either to the larger cities or to the thousand or so urbanized resettlement camps scattered throughout the country, where they eked out a hopeless, dysfunctional existence. Among these uprooted people, he was particularly fascinated by the figure of the 'depeasantized peasant': no longer a peasant, but still far from becoming a city dweller, this 'man between two worlds' found himself in a pathological state of permanent transition without the happy ending of social integration

– condemned on the one hand to the realization that the world he had previously considered natural and unassailable was merely contingent, and on the other hand incapable of finding a stable halfway place for himself in society, or at least of navigating successfully between the two worlds.[54] The resettlement camps produced alienated subjects, or, as Bourdieu and Sayad put it in 1964, 'men of a new kind who self-destructively carry all contradictions within themselves and allow themselves to be defined only negatively by what they no longer and not yet are: depeasantized peasants.'[55] One must imagine Bourdieu's 'depeasantized peasants' as tragic figures.

Despite all the tragedy, one problem remained for Bourdieu: could the discrepancy between the economic dispositions of a certain individual and the world in which he is supposed to act also be expressed in 'positive' terms ('positive' in the sense of their explanatory force, and not in a negative or Marxist way as alienation)? That was the problem that Bourdieu tried to answer at the time. And it was precisely here, in this specific context of research, that talk of habitus first appeared. Bourdieu used the term primarily to define the social position and emotional state of the *paysan empaysanné* more precisely. One of the earliest uses of the term can be found in the essay 'Paysans déracinés' ('Uprooted peasants') that Bourdieu wrote together with Sayad in 1964. It states: 'The uprooted peasant, for whom the environment in which he was born is the only familiar environment and whose entire physical habitus is "adapted" to the space in which he usually moves, is deeply affected in his being, so deeply that he cannot even express his despair in words, let alone give reasons for it.'[56] This sentence gives a tangible shape to the dramatic way in which Bourdieu described the uprooted peasant (suffering, helpless, speechless). The habitus is particularly visible when it is not part of what is taken for granted, when it represents a pathology or a stigma, when it is out of place or is falling apart – in later years Bourdieu spoke of a 'cleft habitus' in this regard.[57] On the other hand, the sentence makes it clear that Bourdieu always understood habitus from the outset as an incorporated structure that mostly functions unconsciously and without language. For him, it is 'the language of the body, the way of carrying oneself, of holding one's head and walking, that expresses better than words the distraction and disorientation.'[58] It was important to study physical actions closely – for example to describe in detail how lost the Kabyle men seemed in the streets of the camp or in the urban cafés that were new to them, or how they could not cope with new forms of greeting such as the handshake because this was not set out in the code of honour of their old tribal societies. In this specific context of use, habitus had a relatively one-sided core meaning: it was 'history made flesh' – a socially determined and 'made' practice, but also one that seemed inert, automated, and unchangeable. The spontaneous, creative, and adaptable characteristics that also strongly characterize habitus and indicate its changeability ('habitus change') were not mentioned in Bourdieu's research at this time.[59]

In the early writings on Algeria from 1964 onwards, the concept of habitus remained theoretically underdetermined to a degree that is striking from today's perspective. In order to characterize permanent dispositions to action in a conceptual sense, Bourdieu, following Max Weber, spoke mostly of 'ethos'.[60] Not until 1967, under the influence of works by Norbert Elias and Marcel Mauss, did he use the term 'habitus' really systematically, in his translation and publication of a work by the art historian Erwin Panofsky and in his methodological manual *The Craft of Sociology*, published in 1968.[61] Another four years passed before Bourdieu theoretically formulated and developed the concept of habitus, in his *Outline of a Theory of Practice*, also based on the ethnological material on Kabyle society. In that work, Bourdieu himself points to this theoretical latency phase when he notes that the second theoretical part is based on notes from the years 1960 to 1965. In the first chapter of this second part, entitled 'Structures, habitus and practices', habitus is prominently presented as a new category that seeks to overcome the classic sociological opposition between structure and practice, accompanied by the often quoted definition that habitus forms are 'systems of durable, transposable *dispositions*, structured structures predisposed to function as structuring structures'.[62] The 1972 chapter on habitus was undoubtedly a milestone in Bourdieu's social theory. However, one should not forget that in the late 1970s and 1980s numerous differentiations and modifications of the concept took place. Many individual theoretical steps were required before the first observations on the uprooted Kabyle peasants in the Algerian resettlement camps could lead to a reliable theory of practice with the possibility of connecting to further research in the social sciences.

What does this theoretical history of the habitus concept show? First, the obvious point: in this case, Algeria was in fact the laboratory of the theory. In the war-torn French colony, Bourdieu first became aware of the bodily facets of behavioural dispositions. Here, in this specific local context, the question of the connection between habitus and social structure arose. Here, in this special space far from Paris, a theoretical concept was forged that was perhaps not yet complete, but which certainly displayed its first recognizable features and forms as well as its core meaning. Did the entire theory therefore also originate, emerge, or even come into being in Algeria? The later theory-building processes to which the concept was subjected show that the idea that Algeria was the founding scene in which the theory originated should be treated with caution. The narrative of the birth and origin of a theory in the history of ideas is often based on a teleological logic of origin that obscures rather than illuminates the historical development and contingency of the conception of ideas and their further development. The contingent nature of history also applies to the genesis and validity of theoretical structures of thought: many things could have turned out differently.

It is historically more appropriate to understand the history of the concept of habitus as a kind of transcultural interweaving and migration of theory. The concept of habitus is a traditional concept of European philosophy and sociology that was essentially given a new spin in Algeria through Bourdieu's ethnological application, and then became one of the most influential concepts in the modern humanities and social sciences in Europe in the 1970s and 1980s. A habitus can be related to any person or group of people, to Kabyle and Pyrenean peasants, to the French bourgeoisie and to the German working class – this is what makes the concept so enduringly strong. It should be remembered that it was nameless Kabyle peasants in Algerian resettlement camps who already had their habitus before it was 'discovered' as a theoretical concept. They have their own share in the theory.

JEAN-FRANÇOIS
LYOTARD

2

A HOPELESS CONTRADICTION
Jean-François Lyotard

Hardly any other name is as closely associated with postmodernism as that of Jean-François Lyotard. Born in Paris in 1924, the philosopher wrote *The Postmodern Condition* in 1979: it became the emblematic book of the theoretical movement that significantly influenced the intellectual debates of the 1980s and 1990s. It was originally intended as a simple commission for the University Council of the Government of Quebec in Canada: Lyotard was to write a report on 'the condition of knowledge in the most highly developed societies'. What he provided, however, was nothing less than the key word for the intellectual situation of the time, which led many supporters and critics to describe their present almost obsessively as 'postmodern'. It subsequently catapulted Lyotard to the forefront of the cultural struggles between the moderns and the postmoderns – a fate that was to make him a leading and eventually world-famous representative of French Theory – but it also for a long time became a millstone around his neck, as this one book overshadowed his other postmodern writings such as his main philosophical work *The Differend*. Last but not least, it made him the favourite punch bag for the critics of postmodernism who regularly popped up to voice their disagreement with him.

In addition to this postmodern side of Lyotard, there was also another, in the truest sense of the word, 'Algerian' side. Lyotard came onto the scene as a philosophical author relatively late. When his first major book, *Discourse, Figure*, was published in 1971, he was forty-six years old, and by the time he published his book on postmodernism, he was already in his mid-fifties. Before Lyotard became the figurehead of postmodernism, began to describe the end of grand narratives, and called for laughter, the thinking of intensities, and a patchwork quilt of minorities, he worked for decades as a high-school teacher and left-wing political activist. Algeria played a prominent role in both activities. Very early on, at the beginning of the 1950s, he was drawn to that country as a teacher. It was in Constantine (and not in Paris) that he discovered Marx for himself, became active in the trade unions, and was politically radicalized. Here, earlier than many others, he saw the colonial injustice that the Algerian population was suffering, and this led him to campaign for the cause of the oppressed. When the Algerian War broke out in 1954, Lyotard – now back in France – actively supported the Algerian independence movement (FLN) and published brilliant anonymous analyses of the political situation. He maintained his special affinity with Algeria even after the war and throughout his life – at least until the civil war in the 1990s, when the country threatened to slide into the terror of Islamism and military dictatorship.[1]

These little-known Algerian episodes from Lyotard's life are definitely worth relating and could stand on their own; but, when they are viewed over the span of his entire biography, the question arises whether the 'Algerian' Lyotard of the 1950s had anything to do with the 'postmodern' Lyotard and his works of the 1970s and 1980s. What traces did his time in Algeria leave in his philosophical work? Are there deeper connections between Lyotard's Algerian experiences and his philosophical theories?

Awakening in Constantine

The first trail leads to Constantine. Here, in the far east of Algeria, Lyotard took up a job as a teacher in October 1950 after completing his philosophy studies at the Sorbonne in Paris. For two years he taught philosophy to Constantine's youngsters at the Lycée d'Aumale (a boys' high school). Transferring ambitious Parisian university graduates to remote provincial schools was not unusual in the French educational system. Anyone who was preparing for a career in higher education and wanted their intellectual life to be financed by the French Republic had to make stopovers of this kind, whether they liked it or not. Lyotard had chosen faraway Algeria of his own free will, and he kept the decisive reasons for this to himself. Such a choice was not entirely unusual at the time. During the colonial period, Constantine was the capital of a French department of the same name. In 1848 the French had divided northern Algeria into the three departments of Algiers, Oran, and Constantine, thus making their main settlement area an integral part of the Republic, at least administratively.

So Lyotard was not really leaving France. Nevertheless, he arrived in a city that had occupied a particularly exotic place in the imagination of the French colonial empire since the conquest of Algeria in 1830. Constantine repeatedly attracted travellers from Europe, due to its antiquity and its spectacular location – the old town sits on a lofty, imposing rock formation surrounded by dizzying gorges up to 100 metres deep. Gustave Flaubert called Constantine 'the most beautiful thing' he saw on his trip to North Africa. Guy de Maupassant reported delightedly, in a typically Orientalist manner, on the 'magnificent beauty' of the women in the Jewish quarter, with their bared shoulders and arms. Alexandre Dumas, on the other hand, could only shake his head at the 'Arab alleys' in the old town. And for Albert Camus, who was born in Algeria, this city of rocks and ravines reminded him of Toledo in Spain. This is noteworthy because, here, a French Algerian who was quite familiar with the area sought to find a European equivalent.[2]

Lyotard was also enchanted by the beauty of Constantine. Like many others before and after him, he could not resist conjuring up an exotic world of images. Looking back later he wrote of how, when he thought of Constantine, the strange 'smells and looks' and 'the sharp light on the slopes and on the unmistakable rocks' immediately came to mind. Lyotard often emphasized that his affective relationship to the city was that of a 'lover' with his 'beloved' – and we can easily imagine who took which role in this love affair ...[3]

But Lyotard's passionate infatuation with Constantine did not mean that he closed his eyes to the colonial situation that surrounded him.

That would have been difficult, because things had been simmering in Algeria ever since the bloody events of 8 May 1945, when tens of thousands of people were killed by French troops and colonialists following demonstrations for greater self-determination in Sétif and other Algerian cities.[4] The Algerian War did not begin until November 1954, but the Sétif massacre was one of its harbingers. In Constantine, too, there were riots and bloody police actions. Lyotard witnessed these outbreaks of violence. He recognized early on that it made a fundamental difference whether one belonged to the 'European' or the 'Muslim' population (the terms commonly used at the time to distinguish the colonizers from the colonized), and that this distinction created subtle but existential nuances in everyday life in Algeria. Lyotard had to watch as special forces of the French police brutally pushed his Algerian comrades attending a trade union meeting against the wall and searched them, but left him, the head of the local teachers' union, alone.[5] It was experiences like this that made Lyotard aware of the 'immensity of injustice' with which the colonial regime treated the Algerian population, who were 'wronged, humiliated, denied their identity'.[6] He later summed up this policy of binary opposites as follows: 'Maghrebi society is a totalitarian society, where exploitation presupposes terror ... The cop who clubs or who tortures is European, the boss or the foreman is European, the officer is European, the professor is European: scorn is European and misery is "Arab".'[7]

The full extent of colonial injustice towards the Algerian population was revealed in school life, the centre of Lyotard's activity.[8] The state school – in France, in any case, a traditional place where the ideals of the Republic are transmitted and lived – was one of the most important state institutions in Algeria, where the colonial power manifested its presence and legitimacy. The occupation of Algeria,

View of Constantine in Algeria, ca. 1930s.

as well as French colonial expansion as a whole, were legitimized on a grand scale in terms of the *mission civilisatrice*: the French were only there to teach the 'indigenous' people French civilization and culture in the service of something higher and universal. In the name of the progressive republican ideals of liberty, equality, and fraternity, the uncultured subjects of the empire needed to be educated into becoming French subjects.

For Lyotard, the full ambiguity of this colonial ideology became apparent at school: 'The French Republic contrived to burden a few young Algerians with a borrowed culture while their own culture, that

of their people – its language, its space, its time – had been and continued to be devastated by a century of French occupation.'[9] In reality, the situation was even more serious: in Lyotard's philosophy class, as well as in the Lycée d'Aumale and other schools in colonial Algeria, the overwhelming majority of the students were of European origin. The presence of a sprinkling of Algerian students could not disguise the fact that the Algerian population did not benefit from the French educational mandate, despite the allegedly 'civilizing' mission; on the contrary, they were in fact systematically excluded. The illiteracy rate among the younger generation in Algeria was higher in the 1950s than in the period around 1830, when the French colonization of Algeria began. Anyone who spoke out against such facts – which shattered the intellectual comfort of the colonial establishment – and provided scholarly evidence for them drew the ire of the colonialists: one such example was the historian Marcel Emérit, who was hanged in effigy by far-right students.[10]

Jean-François Lyotard (first row, seated fourth from left) with his philosophy class at the Lycée d'Aumale, Constantine, Algeria, in the academic year 1950–51.

The central finding of Lyotard's postmodern theory is that the grand legitimizing narratives of modernity have lost their credibility. The universal discourses, the great promises and ideologies of progress, knowledge, history, and emancipation are at an end – like batteries that have gone flat. This finding also leads to Lyotard's minimal definition of postmodernism in *The Postmodern Condition*: it was an 'incredulity towards metanarratives', which Lyotard identified towards the end of the 1970s, especially in relation to the ideologies of progress in science or Marxism.[11] However, he had already encountered this problematic – the disturbing awareness of a time of decline in political ideologies and in universally binding values – in 1950s colonial Algeria, in the Constantine lycée. In this institution, where the universalizing promise of emancipation offered by French culture and the French Republic had quite obviously lost its long-recognized credibility and was now showing a completely different face, Lyotard had his very first personal experience of disillusionment with discourses of legitimacy. For the French civilizing mission was also a metanarrative of modernity which, in the spirit of the Enlightenment, relied on science on a grand scale and propagated the progress of all humanity with missionary zeal – until it lost its effectiveness in the course of decolonization. The confrontation with these double standards in schools and with the colonial racist ideology looming behind them laid the foundation for the philosopher's later postmodern scepticism.

'I simply owe my entire awakening to Constantine', Lyotard once wrote, looking back on his two years in Algeria. In the 1950s, 'Algeria did not name a "question" of revolutionary politics for me, it was also the name of a debt.'[12] As always, one must be cautious about retrospective self-depictions of this kind. All too often, one's own assessments of the experiences of one's younger years tend to be simplistic or idealized. They are also influenced by events that have happened between the time remembered and the moment of remembering. Lyotard is not an isolated case here: the motif of guilt, as well as the claim that his experience in a foreign country led to an awakening, can be found in many French intellectuals – be it Pierre Bourdieu's feelings of guilt in the face of colonial injustice, or Roland Barthes's erotically charged aesthetic awakening in Morocco. In Lyotard's case, it is relatively safe to say that his talk of awakening was not just a matter of looking at the past through rose-tinted spectacles: there was some justification for it. When Lyotard returned to France in 1952 with his wife and two daughters (partly out of fear that his family could become the target of reprisals due to his growing support for the Algerian liberation movement), he had become a different person. In Constantine, he had become politically radicalized and discovered the entire cosmos of left-wing revolutionary praxis (from a reading of Marx's theories to trade union work and anti-colonial commitment). He also took a fundamental philosophical insight back with him to France: an awareness of the fragility of the ideologies, narratives, and values of the French nation that seem so natural in everyday life, and the willingness to challenge and question the hegemonic thinking they involve. There was no literal mention of 'postmodernism' here. The main issue lay elsewhere: one of Lyotard's first endeavours on his return to France was to establish contact with the networks that supported the Algerian separatists.

Clandestino

The second trace that the Algerian years left in Lyotard's work takes us directly back to the time of the Algerian War. In comparison to many other French intellectuals, who expressed their views on the Algerian question in a variety of petitions and statements, Lyotard's involvement during the Algerian War was characterized by militant underground activism. As a passionate supporter of the Algerian independence movement since his time in Constantine, at the beginning of the war Lyotard joined a group of French people providing practical help to the FLN from France. As 'suitcase carriers' or the 'Jeanson network' (named after their leader Francis Jeanson), this group has gone down in the history books and acquired legendary status.[13] Suitcase carriers were people of every kind who smuggled suitcases full of money and propaganda across the border, arranged accommodation for FLN officials, forged passports, and sometimes even engaged in arms trafficking. Transporting money was the network's main activity. The FLN had levied a kind of revolutionary tax on Algerian immigrants in France for its fight against the French state. With an immigrant population of around 400,000, the collection quickly grew to a considerable sum. In order for the money to reach other countries (mainly Switzerland) safely, French people were needed since they could transport suitcases full of cash with less hindrance than the Algerians, who were under general suspicion at the time.

For French people opposed to the colonial regime, being a suitcase carrier was, next to taking up arms, the most subversive and riskiest practice. There was a considerable danger of being arrested by the secret service. Aiding the FLN was viewed as high treason, punishable by up to ten years in prison. Lyotard also took other risks. For example, he hid Algerians in his home, which sometimes led to bizarre situations. While playing hide-and-seek, Lyotard's daughters discovered an Algerian in the furthest corner of a walk-in wardrobe; their father had hidden him there after hearing an unexpected knock on the door.[14] In Lyotard's case, this underground activity is all the more remarkable because at the time – after his return from Algeria until 1959 – he was teaching at one of the most prestigious military schools in France. While supporting a hostile terrorist movement, he was simultaneously teaching philosophy to the country's future officer elite.[15]

Lyotard's political work on the journalistic front was also clandestine. Under the pseudonym 'François Laborde', he wrote a total of twelve long articles on the Algerian War in the magazine *Socialisme ou Barbarie*. In 1954, Lyotard and his wife Andrée joined the group of the same name, in which Claude Lefort and Cornelius Castoriadis were active. Founded in 1949, the organization was part of a left-wing radical tradition and was primarily concerned with a critique of Stalinism. With its unorthodox Marxism, it was also one of the political and intellectual forerunners of the 1968 student protest movement. In the group's view, the USSR was a state capitalist system that fostered exploitation and created a new ruling class: the bureaucracy. With the arrival of anti-colonialists like Lyotard, and the escalation of the Algerian conflict, the focus of Socialisme ou Barbarie shifted more to colonial issues. In 1955, Lyotard was commissioned by the group to write the 'Algeria' column for its magazine, and as a special reporter he devoted all of his articles to this new topic.

The articles are lengthy analyses characterized by the need to understand in depth the structures of the contemporary situation and to provide a theoretical understanding of the war. Lyotard bases his discussion on current events and debates, following the rhythm of current affairs, but he does not content himself with the kind of superficial moral and emotional statements often observed among the left at the time. He goes a step further, seeking to understand how the colonial system of exploitation and the tragedy of the Algerian people had come about, and why the achievement of national independence was such a painful process. To this end, he undertakes a meticulous deciphering of the various social actors (governments, the state, parties, revolutionaries, and counter-revolutionaries) and their interactions, strategies, and passions; he spares no one from criticism. The articles are not just about Algeria – he also discusses France, de Gaulle, the workers, and the hesitant attitude of the left. They are tours of a society in a state similar to civil war. Lyotard's analyses draw their theoretical tools from what today seem outdated (and partly contradictory) Marxist concepts taken from the world of dialectical materialism (one teeming with big capitalists, petty bourgeois, workers, and peasants), but they testify to a fresh, focused view of the French-Algerian situation.

Lyotard wrote his Algeria column for eight years. Fierce debates broke out among his comrades as to whether Socialisme ou Barbarie should support the Algerian revolution at all. The group rejected political and trade union organizations on principle, seeing them as an obstacle to the free development of popular uprisings and workers' councils. For this reason, they also had reservations about the Algerian national movement which, although it claimed to be revolutionary, had no real working-class character. On the contrary: in their eyes, the political organizational mode of the FLN had an openly bourgeois-bureaucratic character. Lyotard shared this assessment – as a 'suitcase carrier' he was already familiar with the military-hierarchical structures of the French branch of the FLN – and his analyses increasingly concentrated on bureaucracy. In his articles, the question of how the 'national bourgeoisie' of Algeria was dealing with the bureaucratic dimensions of the FLN became the decisive factor in the country's political future – a question that also preoccupied Frantz Fanon in *The Wretched of the Earth*, where he spent almost a hundred pages quietly anticipating the difficulties to be expected for the new African nation states and identifying their national bourgeois elites as the weak link. This analysis actually proved correct after Algeria's independence. In the immediate context of the war, however, the more pressing and basic question for the members of Socialisme ou Barbarie was whether or not they should support the FLN. During the war, Lyotard came to the conclusion that the only possible position on the matter was one characterized by a 'hopeless contradiction'.[16] First of all, he clearly saw that the Algerians had the right, even the duty, to achieve freedom and to be recognized as a free people on an equal footing with others. As he wrote in a 1956 article:

> We in France can therefore do nothing other than support this struggle in its extreme consequences. Contrary to the totality of the 'left,' our concern is in no way the preservation of the 'French presence in the Maghreb.' We are unconditionally opposed to all imperialism, French included. We are unconditionally hostile to the pursuits of terror.[17]

Nevertheless – and here the contradiction arises – this struggle offered no prospect of implementing any of the principles of workers' democracy; it would inevitably produce a new class society under the control of a bureaucratic military leadership:

> Under such conditions, the growth of conflicts seems inevitable, conflicts between privileged factions who will make themselves into the mirror image of imperialist greed and conflicts between the new masters and the exploited, on whose side all those dissatisfied with the dominant policy will stand.[18]

In other words, he felt considerable unease about the danger of helping the future exploiters to take power.

One is tempted to dismiss this unease as a side issue. The fate of the Algerians did not, of course, depend on the sensitivities of a left-wing splinter group. The contradiction, which was acrimoniously discussed and ultimately broke the group apart, took on an almost existential significance for its members. Basically, it was the classic question of the compatibility of theory and practice: how can one commit oneself to a practical cause ('Algerian liberation/freedom') that one should in fact reject and even fight against from a theoretical perspective (that of 'class struggle')? Lyotard embodied this apparent incompatibility like no other: he was partly a secret 'suitcase carrier,' and partly a sceptical analyst. But he lived with this ambiguity and did not consider it necessary to adapt his diagnosis to his practice. He increasingly came to the realization that Algerian liberation could no longer bring the hoped-for solution to social injustices and aporias. Rather, it was the displacement of these problems into other forms, and above all into the contradictions of the situation, that he experienced as a militant activist.[19]

The differend

Lyotard later returned again and again to this experience of hopeless contradiction. Interestingly, it appears not only in his autobiographical writings, but also in his texts on postmodernism. It is worth taking a closer look at where Lyotard positioned his key experience from the Algerian War, and for what end. In the *Instructions païennes* ('Pagan instructions') of 1977, for example, he draws on it to express his disillusionment with overly rigid Marxist universal narratives such as those of revolution, liberation, and history. This can also be safely construed as a retrospective justification of his own position:

> The fact that one could take the side of the FLN during the Algerian War and at the same time analyse and criticise the bureaucratic-military power structures that it had established after independence sounds inconsistent only as long as one believes in a universal narrative.[20]

The universal narrative here is that of revolution seen from a Marxist perspective. People were convinced that history would progress inexorably towards worldwide redemption, and that the Algerian revolution would fit this model. The point here is that Lyotard himself had still believed in this universal narrative during the war. He abandoned it fifteen years later, in view of the later history of Algeria and the failure of the Paris revolution of 1968. The year 1977 was the heyday of anti-Marxism in France; swansongs for Marx were increasingly to be heard. The grand narrative of the left-wing revolution had lost its persuasive power. Marxism itself came under suspicion of ideology and was held responsible for the crimes of totalitarian regimes. With the disappearance of the great Marxist alternative, postmodernism definitely took hold. But one should not forget that the postmodern enterprise was primarily a self-critical reckoning with the revolutionary promises and redemptive hopes of Marxism.

In Lyotard's 1981 'Rules and Paradoxes', this key experience then becomes an exemplary object of postmodern reflection on the relationship between truth and morality. Describing what he had experienced at the time, Lyotard makes the principle of contradiction a general rule in political matters:

> In other words, people were concretely experiencing the political, something we do every day: there are two families of phrases, one of which obeys the rule of truth and falsehood, another which has the just and the unjust as its rule. And these two families are independent; it is not possible to translate one into the other.[21]

In other words, in Lyotard's eyes, support for the FLN followed the rule of the just, while the critical analysis of the liberation struggle followed the system of truth. His activism during the Algerian War taught him that acting morally while simultaneously following the truth was impossible.

Finally, another reference to the hopeless contradiction between morality and analysis can be found in the text 'Le nom d'Algérie' ('The name of Algeria'). This is the preface to *La guerre des Algériens* ('The War of the Algerians'), a collection of Lyotard's political articles from the time of the Algerian War, published in 1989. The preface is full of interesting features – for example, the melancholy tone that Lyotard adopts in his recollection of the Algerian years, but also the embarrassment with which the postmodern thinker recalls his Marxist jargon from earlier days, while nevertheless endeavouring to remain faithful to his old left-wing radical positions. What is particularly striking in this context, however, is his attempt to insert a retrospective of his old political essays on the Algerian War into the structure of his own philosophical discourse, which had changed in the meantime. This attempt is not really a success. The ambiguity of Algeria is summarily declared to be an 'internal, insoluble differend.'[22]

When Lyotard speaks of a 'differend' in the specifically Algerian case, he is obviously trying to establish a theoretical continuity with later works, above all with his main work of the same name, *The Differend*. There it is less a matter of political struggles than of aporias between discourses, languages, and language games – in short, incommensurability. Strictly speaking,

> [a]s distinguished from a litigation, a differend [*différend*] would be a case of conflict, between (at least) two parties, that cannot be equitably

> resolved for lack of a rule of judgment applicable to both arguments. One side's legitimacy does not imply the other's lack of legitimacy. However, applying a single rule of judgment to both in order to settle their differend as though it were merely a litigation would wrong (at least) one of them (and both of them if neither side admits this rule).[23]

As interesting as these considerations are in themselves, the significance of these sentences and of the entire work can be understood only against the background of the initial postmodern problematic, in which recourse to grand narratives is excluded. For if the great framework of legitimation and judgement is missing (i.e. if there are no common rules), then cases of conflict between group interests and languages can no longer be settled within the framework of an overarching meta-discourse. It is pointless to try to find truth or justice in a universal discourse. The question that Lyotard poses in *The Differend* is therefore one that achieves its explosive effect only in the wake of his postmodern diagnosis of the times. That question is: how can one still pass any judgement on questions of truth and justice when everything in our postmodern world is relative? How are justice and ethics still possible when the singular prevails?

Lyotard's philosophical project is an attempt to find an answer to these questions. It is a serious endeavour to prevent the slide into postmodern arbitrariness, to search for new idioms, and to translate the positions blocked by the differend into new forms of argumentation and understanding. For Lyotard, however, this is possible only in a patchwork of language games, in the telling of small stories, or as an analysis of individual cases, as a way of deciding on a case-by-case basis. *The Differend* is essentially a collection of case studies: Lyotard examines countless moments of contradiction and looks for the disparate types of discourse that cause these cases to arise.

To return to the Algerian context, Lyotard had encountered precisely this basic problem of conflict during the Algerian War:

> Two different genres of discourse (the speculative idea of freedom and the materialist dialectic of class struggle) were linked to the same event, without it being possible to make a clear decision and say either: 'We will not become your accomplices' or: 'You are the salt of the earth.'[24]

Lyotard's ambition here is obvious: the ambiguity no longer leads to hopelessness and confusion as it had during the Algerian War. Lyotard now uses this ambiguity to show that his analysis at the time was open to different systems of argumentation and language games and that, by addressing both topics, he allowed both positions to be maintained.[25] Even if he suggests in his retrospective that he had been aware of his contradictory attitude towards the national bourgeoisie of Algeria in his earlier essays, the philosophical interpretation of this former tension as a 'differend' remains, on closer inspection, an exaggeration, since the positions are not necessarily mutually exclusive. Lyotard's idea of incorporating, by hook or by crook, the old Marxist and anti-colonial positions into his postmodern philosophy of conflict is, in the last analysis, flimsy. There may have been something ambiguous in his key experience, but strictly speaking it was not a postmodern mode of incommensurability.

Perhaps this terminological discrepancy does not have to be interpreted so strictly, and Lyotard's attempt to straighten things out should not be taken as his last word. If one ignores these self-depictions of his own life's work, and if one also leaves the narrow framework of the text, then the interpretation of the Algerian War period in the mode of conflict turns out to be a rather interesting opportunity. One just has to understand the term 'differend' more as a figure of thought, and broaden the scope of observation to include the whole of French-Algerian colonial history. Then, new perspectives on old stories open up: think above all of the permanent contradiction and hypocrisy that the French colonial power created through its presence, its ways of speaking, and its actions – for example when it came up with 'L'Algérie, c'est la France' ('Algeria is France') as a slogan; when it waged a bloody war without ever directly naming it as such; when it spoke loudly of its mission to civilize the Algerian population but actually did the opposite, turning the indigenous population into uneducated and nameless foreigners; and when it declared all its citizens to be French, but at the same time, as in the 1875 Code de l'indigénat, distinguished between 'French citizens of European origin' (*citoyens*) and 'French natives in the colonies' (*sujets*). It would be a mistake to believe that such contortions of French colonialism remained mere linguistic manoeuvres. They were real. They affected the legal, social, and economic criteria by which colonial reality was defined. Perhaps the whole Franco-Algerian conflict was an out-of-control differend – one which from that moment on proved to be insoluble and then had to end in bloodshed when the pitiful failure of the colonial promise of emancipation became apparent.[26]

In 1954, Lyotard wrote that the highest task of philosophy was 'the elucidation of history'.[27] Could he have already guessed that the Algerian War, which began at the same time as the collapse of the French colonies, would form the contemporary terrain on which this philosophical understanding of history would grow and develop? His early Marxist as well as his later postmodern theories are in any case unambiguous attempts to understand this 'colonial history' and to conceptually grasp both the personal experiences associated with it and the social developments happening around him. In this historical line, Lyotard's postmodern philosophy is also part of the colonial legacy.

At first glance, Lyotard's postmodern reflections therefore seem to belong unmistakably to a definite past. They extend by and large from the late 1970s to the early 1990s and – at least as far as the key historical experiences are concerned – even reach back to the time of colonialism and the Algerian War. Even the main targets of postmodern critique (the progressive ideologies of the Enlightenment, Marxism, and science) were mainly part of the twentieth-century mindset. Finally, we must not forget that a large part of postmodern critique was fuelled by frustration over the unfulfilled Marxist promises of revolution, and the collapse of the political aspirations of the 1968 generation.

On closer inspection, however, this past is not as distant from us as it seems. The basic idea of Lyotard's *The Differend* – the question of how to deal with the incommensurability of group discourses when the singular prevails – is more relevant than ever. In today's society, which is preoccupied with constant irreconcilable disagreements and debates, and which capitalizes on the expression of opinions and resentments in unprecedentedly widespread social media, Lyotard's philosophical project seems like an unexpectedly welcome summons from back in the 1980s. Not necessarily because Lyotard prophetically anticipated our current issues and could help us to see and understand them more clearly, but rather because he takes into account the discursive (and thus reality-producing) structures of disagreements, and in doing so seeks an ethically reflected approach to the paradoxes and ambiguities of postmodern societies.

It is precisely in this question of the 'right' approach that there is a potential in Lyotard's work that has been either overlooked or forgotten until now. What we can learn from it is that we cannot resolve social and discursive contradictions in the name of a higher cause or truth (for that would be modern), nor can we just leave incompatible positions as natural dichotomies (for that would be a declaration of moral bankruptcy, since these incompatibilities are usually linked to the production of injustice). The path to enlightenment lies rather in making these paradoxes and ambiguities visible and reflecting on them, ultimately in what Lyotard calls 'legitimation through paralogy'. But it would be a mistake to believe that Lyotard is thereby adhering to a postmodern morality according to which justice is impossible in a world of incompatibilities. For him, every single case of a differend can sharpen our sense of general, recurring problems; but in an ideal case it can also reveal concrete solutions, the implementation of which would take place outside of supposedly overarching norms.[28]

Finally, a second lesson can be drawn from Lyotard's moral, political, and theoretical contradictions during the Algerian War. This lesson can initially be put in a very abstract way: one can stand up for a cause, but at the same time criticize its theoretical or political premises. In other words, one does not have to completely and absolutely accept all of its side effects. This idea can be left as a general notion, and interpreted simply and unpretentiously. But, starting from this idea, one can also formulate new demands for an appropriate approach to questions of moral, political, and theoretical integrity, and glean a new morality of political judgements. And this is particularly appropriate today, at a time of new forms and practices of political moralism.

ROLAND
BARTHES

3

A MOROCCAN EPIPHANY
Roland Barthes

One of the most fascinating oddities of the cultural history of France is that many of its intellectual greats experienced their decisive moments of awakening in the so-called Orient. One of the best-known examples is the writer Gustave Flaubert, who came up with the idea for the novel *Madame Bovary* during his trip to Egypt in 1850. His travelling companion at the time, Maxime Du Camp, recorded the pivotal scene as follows:

> On the confines of Lower Nubia, when we stood on the summit of Djebel-Aboukir, which overlooks the Second Cataract, while we watched the Nile dashing against the serried black granite rocks, he [Flaubert] uttered a cry: 'I have found it! Eureka! Eureka! I will call her "Emma Bovary". He repeated the name of Bovary several times as if with a kind of enjoyment, and pronounced the letter *o* in it quite short.[1]

Flaubert's biographers are largely in agreement about the meaning of this anecdote. Prior to this trip to the Orient, Flaubert had written fifty minor literary works but not published a single one of them. And right after this trip he began writing *Madame Bovary*. Despite the fact that the only things he wrote in Egypt were his travel notes and letters, it was here that he found his unmistakable style – so suddenly that one has the impression of an instantaneous literary conversion.[2]

The semiotician and philosopher Roland Barthes experienced a similar moment in his life abroad, one that seemed to change everything. In Barthes's case it was a Moroccan epiphany, and it can be dated exactly, to 15 April 1978. Barthes was spending his holidays with his friend Alain Benchaya in Casablanca. Shortly before, he had completed his first semester as a newly appointed professor at the renowned Collège de France in Paris. Barthes describes the initially unremarkable Saturday as follows:

> The sluggishness of the afternoon. The sky clouds over, there's a slight chill in the air. A group of us go in two cars to the Waterfall (a pretty little valley on the way to Rabat). *The same, uninterrupted* sadness, a kind of listlessness that (since a recent bereavement) bears upon everything I do, everything I think (lack of investment).[3]

He has been dominated by this state of mind since his mother died the year before: it has deprived him of his zest for life.

Even when he returns to the empty apartment in Casablanca, sadness reigns. Barthes tries his luck with a 'marinade' – that is, what he calls the practice of intensive reflection, which he has copied from none other than Flaubert. Whenever the lowest point of his work was reached, the latter would throw himself onto the green velvet sofa next to his desk and stew in his own juices, waiting for the time he would be able to start producing again.[4] Barthes has barely started his marinade in bed when an idea suddenly appears, which he describes as 'something like a "literary" conversion ... to enter into literature, into writing; *to write,* as if I'd never written before: to do only that.'[5]

It is the vision of a literary existence that is here making its appearance – the flash of an epiphany about his wish to write, and the longing to enter a world in which writing is the only authentic and desirable form of life. In the case of Barthes, this had a certain irony, as the theorist had already written a large number of books of a thoroughly literary nature, books that had elevated their author to the rank of a man of letters. But writing as if he had never done so before, and doing nothing else, meant, for Barthes, in this particular moment of epiphany, taking a decisive step further. From now on, he would no longer be concerned with writing books about literature, but would produce literature himself; no longer shamefully expose himself to the accusation of being a frustrated writer, but fully claim for himself the writer's life that he had constantly observed and coveted in others. Last but not least, it also meant leaving behind what he felt was the arduous everyday working life of a professor – his first thought after this idea came to him was of 'resigning from the Collège [de France] in order to settle into a life of writing (for the lecture course often comes into conflict with writing).'[6]

Barthes's desire for change did not come out of the blue. It had arisen at a fragile stage in his life. The break was due to the awareness that, 'having reached a certain age, "our days are numbered"', and that 'there comes a time when what you've done, written (past labors and practices) looks like repeated material, doomed to repetition, to the lassitude of repetition.'[7] The feeling of irreversibility and the awareness of one's own mortality, coupled with academic frustration about what he had done so far – the prospect of continuing in such a state filled him with dread: 'What? From now on until I die I'll be writing articles, preparing my teaching, giving lectures – or, at best, writing books – *on* subjects, which are all that'll vary (and so little!)?'[8] Such is the horror show of an exhausted professor suffering a midlife crisis.

At least the epiphany shows the way out of the 'motionless state of being stuck in the quicksands' of academic writing. A new way of writing is needed, one that converts one's own existence into writing, into 'life writing,' and thus also creates a new form of being. Anyone who wants to change their life must also write differently. So what could be more natural for a literary critic who has been washed clean by all the waters of theory than to write a novel that deals precisely with this change, this conversion of life into writing? Barthes gives his planned new novel the title *Vita Nova*, alluding to Dante, and hopes that 'each moment of my life' will henceforth be 'integrated into the Grand Project.'[9]

The experiences in Casablanca – from the attack of melancholia during the excursion to the moment of literary conversion to the project of an autobiographical novel – were described by Barthes himself. He speaks of them as 'a little personal anecdote' in the first session of his lectures in the winter semester of 1978–79 at the Collège de France, published posthumously under the title *The Preparation of the Novel.*[10] Barthes thus reacts to the longing for a new life and for writing in his own way, not by leaving the Collège de France, as he had planned, but by combining work on the planned novel with his lectures, seeing them as part of the same undertaking. Instead of writing the novel of his life straight away, he lectured over the course of two academic years on what it means to write a novel. The lectures then became more of a general anatomy of creative writing in which Barthes meticulously examined the conditions under which writing situations and literary works came into being, with a constant eye on Flaubert, Proust, Gide, and Kafka. He combined this type of research with reflections on his own writing, but the whole endeavour left it completely open, over time, as to whether a real novel was actually being written in parallel or whether the desire for a new life was not already fulfilled by this compromise. In any case, we will never know what would have become of *Vita Nova*: two days after finishing his lectures, Barthes was hit by a van while crossing the Rue des Écoles, directly in front of the Collège de France. He died in March 1980 as a result of this accident.

The Preparation of the Novel has captivated numerous readers since its publication. The story of a person who wants to write: that is bound to arouse interest. The 15 April 1978 lecture especially has been received with particular fascination by Barthes aficionados. Barthes's eureka moment is illuminated down to the smallest detail, and developed into a blueprint for scenarios of writing.[11] Morocco, however, as the real setting of this gleaming epiphany, is a surprisingly faint presence. (This is also surprising because Barthes's philology violates a central rule of his anatomy of creative writing, namely that all things which belong to a scenario of writing, including the location, must be included.) So is Casablanca just a beautiful setting for a holiday? Just a promising name? As in the eponymous film, is it the stage for a story that could just as well have taken place somewhere else? The fact that Barthes experienced his literary conversion in Casablanca of all places is either not worth mentioning at all, or it is treated as if it were a given – as if the city in North Africa were the natural habitat of Parisian intellectuals, in line with the motto 'Recently, in Casablanca ...' In both cases, a certain ignorance is expressed. Thus, whether intentionally or not, we ultimately get a distorted picture of Barthes, just as can be seen in the stories and representations of other protagonists of French Theory: thinking is relocated to a context-free, ahistorical space. The only really tangible context is actually the place where the experience is reflected upon, written down, presented, published, and finally celebrated: Paris.

However, if we want to demystify this enigmatic literary conversion a little, we need to be much more aware of the immense and diverse role that Morocco played for Barthes. The scene of 15 April 1978 marked just the climax of a long series of experiences and events that linked him to the North African country. Barthes travelled to Morocco two or three times a year from the early 1960s until his death. In most cases these were short and purely pleasure-oriented trips, during which summertime relaxation, lavish parties, and sexual encounters with Moroccan men were the focus – for example, on the trip to Marrakesh and Tangiers that he took with Michel Foucault in 1963, during which they fell out over a boy they both coveted.[12] Some of the stays also had a more professional aspect (in the best case, personal and professional interests were combined): Barthes regularly gave seminars and lectures at Moroccan universities, and maintained long-standing friendships with authors such as Abdelkebir Khatibi and Zaghloul Morsy.[13] In Morocco, he completed two of his most famous works, the study of Balzac, *S/Z*, and the evocation of Japan in *Empire of Signs*. So Morocco was many things for Barthes: a place of relaxation, pleasure, and erotic adventures, but also a place of retreat, inspiration, and concentrated work. It is no coincidence that Barthes fantasized about his literary conversion in Morocco of all places.

Pleasure in Tangiers, frustration in Rabat

The significance of Morocco for Barthes can best be captured by looking at one of his longer stays in the country. In September 1969, Barthes was transferred to the University of Rabat as a professor of French literature, at his own request. He had often taken advantage of such stays abroad organized for university lecturers by the French Ministry of Education. In 1949, he ended up in Alexandria in Egypt, where he taught at a French school for a year. His many trips to Japan in the 1960s, from which *Empire of Signs* emerged, also belong in this context of French cultural and foreign policy. Barthes loved to travel, and the French state was happy to help him with this academic tourism.

However, there was a special reason for his transfer to Rabat. It wasn't that Barthes was especially eager for something new, as he was already very familiar with the country from his previous trips. This time, the trigger was the immediate urge to leave Paris and forget the frustration that had built up in him during the May riots of 1968. His initial sympathy with the protests had long since evaporated – especially when his classes at the École pratique des hautes études were affected and he was obliged to take a long break because of the student strikes. While the students in Paris were rehearsing the uprising[14] and grabbing the world's attention, Barthes just wanted to make a quick getaway. As another trip to Japan was not possible, in July 1968 he chose Morocco as his place of refuge. By the end of that year he had stayed there four times, mainly in Tangiers, which he reached by car and ferry. During one of these stays he decided to live and work in Morocco for a longer period. The official Moroccan invitation required for this came at the instigation of the writer Zaghloul Morsy, whom Barthes knew from previous trips. His plan was to spend three years at the University of Rabat.[15]

Three years turned out to be a bridge too far. In contrast to the carefree life of the tourist Barthes – who was able to act without too many responsibilities or obligations – teaching at the University of Rabat did not at all meet the expectations raised by his previous experiences. His plan for a peaceful retreat was more than thwarted. When he finally left Paris for Morocco in September 1969, he found a country that was no less troubled than France. Here, too, there was great political unrest, with student revolts that brought university operations to a standstill and prevented Barthes from teaching. With their strikes and slogans, the Moroccan students were not only rebelling against the current government under the rule of King Hassan II. They were also denouncing the French presence at the university, which in their eyes represented the culture of the former colonial power. Barthes too became a target of their critique. By choosing a relatively canonical French programme – he gave lectures on Marcel Proust and Jules Verne – he offended all those in Morocco who wanted to free the study of the French language from its bourgeois and colonial baggage. Barthes considered their demands to be 'reactionary' – a remark that won him no friends.[16] The politicized Moroccan students, with an authoritarian regime in their sights (and also breathing down their necks), could not do much with Barthes's paean to literature as a means of liberation from the subject. For them, such aesthetic arguments were an expression of French cultural imperialism, and Barthes was its representative. In February 1970 – just five months after taking up the post – an exasperated Barthes informed the dean of the faculty that he would not be fulfilling his three-year contract. He would be leaving at the end of the 1969–70 academic year.

There are many stories surrounding the reasons for this withdrawal.[17] Barthes himself spoke about the disappointment of his stay in Morocco in 'One always fails in speaking of what one loves', his very last text. The focus of this article is actually Stendhal and his fractured love affair with Italy. But Barthes also – quite explicitly – projects himself into the relationship between exoticism and appropriation (and its failure) observed in Stendhal. In the middle of his analysis of Stendhal, we read:

> Italy is the country where Stendhal, being neither entirely a traveler (a tourist) nor entirely a native, is voluptuously delivered from the responsibility of the citizen; if Stendhal were an Italian citizen, he would die 'poisoned by melancholy': whereas, a Milanese by affection rather than civil status, he need merely harvest the brilliant effects of a civilization for which he is not responsible. I have been able to experience the convenience of this devious dialectic myself: I used to love Morocco, I often visited the country as a tourist, even spending rather long vacations there; therefore, it occurred to me to spend a year there as a professor: the magic vanished; confronted by administrative and professional problems, I plunged into the ungrateful world of causes and allegiances, I surrendered Festivity for Duty.[18]

However, these sentences give only part of the story, deliberately selected for the public. Barthes's diaries and posthumously published autobiographical texts cast a different and more multifaceted light on his time in Morocco. They show that he filled the time made available by leaving his academic post by writing books, travelling extensively, and looking for sexual partners. And they suggest that even as a professor in Rabat, he never really left the 'festival' he spoke of. Nor did he leave behind the 'comfort of this complicated dialectic' that he believed he and Stendhal enjoyed when it came to 'harvesting the brilliant effects of a civilization' for which they were not responsible, free of any civic accountability. If we are to believe his own testimony, then a large part of his efforts and undertakings in Morocco were primarily of an erotic nature: the 'hunting for prey' that Barthes undertook in Morocco, according to his biographer Tiphaine Samoyault, was part of this irresponsible tourist 'harvest'.[19] Morocco was the place where Barthes felt he could live out and pursue his desires without hindrance.

This was already evident on the first day of his arrival in the country. His diary entry recorded the evening in Tangiers, where he apparently preferred to stay rather than Rabat:

> Saturday 27 September 1969: Arrived around 12.30 p.m. Sunshine, warm wind. Hotel, slept, read the paper at the Petit Socco. Relaxed. Renewed zest for this city, a chosen city. It turns cloudy, the wind becomes stormy, it's overcast. I get bored here: absolute solitude, with no relief. Café on the Place de France. Passages. Bought a few things (I can't resist buying things here). Walked back to the hotel. Slept. Terrace bar at the top of the hotel: attractive thematically. Went to M's, dazzling (five!). Called in at the Petit Socco (nothing), a light dinner at the Café de Paris. Isba, found Kiki and the eternal Abdulah. Blow up. Kiki, drunk or crazy, bugs me and hassles me; he wants to be my 'slave'. At the festival, first with Abdulah, then picked up by a certain Ahmed from Oudja. Came back upstairs at 2, read a bit more Jules Verne.[20]

The literary scholar Samoyault, who deserves credit for having written the first comprehensive biography of Barthes, strangely uses this passage as an opportunity to portray Barthes as a homosexual traveller who alternates between euphoria and despondency, but is somehow always desperate, struggling with his sexuality and sensing the pressure of death.[21] But this diary entry actually shows something completely different and more banal, namely that Barthes was cruising

– mainly wandering around looking for gay sex partners. In Morocco, where these partners were readily available (mostly for money), Barthes fell into a real frenzy, in which he indulged without restraint. This does not exclude the possibility that the melancholy and inevitably dissatisfied feelings conjured up by Samoyault also arose. But the basic tenor of Barthes's experience – especially in the context of gay sexuality and self-empowerment at the end of the 1960s – remained one of sexual liberation and sensual exuberance, something which he did not experience in France.

Of all the Moroccan cities at that time, Tangiers offered the greatest freedom. The 'white city' on the Strait of Gibraltar still benefited from its former status as an international zone. After Morocco was declared a French protectorate in 1912, Tangiers remained a neutral territory that was to be jointly administered by the major European powers – something that the city also owed to its exceptional and geopolitically important location on the edge of the Mediterranean, between the continents of Africa and Europe. Appreciated by diplomats, artists, and drug addicts, Tangiers quickly gained a reputation as a cosmopolitan place of freedom and decadence. Hashish was smoked on the streets, and hard drugs were available in pharmacies without a prescription. The police were often reluctant to intervene, at least with Europeans. Brothels for every taste operated with total impunity. It is therefore no wonder that visitors from the West found life here more alluring. From the 1940s and well into the period after Morocco's independence (1956), the exotic aura of Tangiers attracted American writers in particular, above all the stars of the Beat Generation: Jack Kerouac, William Burroughs, Allen Ginsberg, Tennessee Williams, Truman Capote, and Paul and Jane Bowles. They all visited the city for inspiration and relaxation, which was mostly facilitated by drugs and visits to brothels. When Barthes travelled to Tangiers at the end of the 1960s, the Beatniks' big party was already over. A different type of Western tourist now dominated: hippies were arriving in the port city in droves (Barthes even dedicated a short essay to the hippies, who had a greater impact on the cityscape than the Beatniks).[22] Morocco was one of the most popular travel destinations for all the young freedom seekers who wanted a change from the classic hippy path to India, and Tangiers became their first port of call.

Barthes was particularly fascinated by the city's colourful population. For him, this included not only the Moroccan inhabitants and the hippies, but also the French who remained in the country – Barthes called one of them 'a derelict of the Protectorate.'[23] All of these figures found their way into *Incidents*, a diary-like notebook that Barthes wrote during his stay in 1969–70. *Incidents*, which was initially destined for publication in the magazine *Tel Quel* but appeared only posthumously, is at first glance just a loose collection of Barthes's personal Moroccan impressions and encounters. At the same time, it also represents a specific writing project, an effort to capture in prose something directly experienced or seen. Barthes here intertwines the practices of life and writing, and attempts to find a narrative mode derived from the diary. It is therefore no coincidence that he viewed *Incidents* as important preliminary work for his planned novel *Vita Nova* – especially after his supposed Moroccan epiphany on 15 April 1978 – and wanted to integrate his notes into that novel.

A look at the slim volume provides an idea of why it must have been difficult for Barthes to publish the text without further context during his lifetime. Many of the notes tell of his apparently countless erotic encounters with young Moroccan men, often presented in short scenes. Here are a few samples:

> Mustafa is in love with his cap. He won't take it off to make love.

> Amidou, second-year student, future gym teacher, encountered one Sunday morning in the dust of the flea market, poor and good-natured, his raincoat too short, his big shoes coming apart, his fine Moroccan eyes, his kinky hair, has to 'reflect' for tomorrow on 'Molière's notion of comedy' ... I enjoy Amidou's vocabulary: *dream* and *burst* for *get an erection* and *have an orgasm*. *Burst* is vegetal, scattering, disseminating, not moralistic, narcissistic, closed off.

> The little Marrakesh schoolteacher: 'I'll do whatever you want,' he says, effusively, his eyes filled with kindness and complicity. And this means: *I'll fuck you*, and that's all.[24]

Barthes's explicit descriptions (and certainly the sheer extent of his homosexual adventures) created quite a stir when the book was published in 1987 in France, Morocco, and elsewhere – and the reactions were sometimes negative.[25] Since then, the clearest criticism has been expressed primarily in the field of postcolonialism.[26] Essentially, three accusations are voiced. Firstly, despite all the sexual liberation involved, it is claimed that Barthes's activities were a form of neo-colonial exploitation, since the easy availability of male bodies in Morocco functioned in a historically developed colonial context and Barthes evidently had no moral qualms about exploiting his financial superiority in the context of the rampant prostitution of the poor, and transforming it into erotic pleasure. Even where his encounters were not sexual services in the strict sense, the neo-colonial asymmetry remained at work. Secondly, Barthes's fragments display a condescending mode of expression that embodies sexism and chauvinism and also shows a lack of recognition and representation of the other. In other words: Barthes fails to give other voices a hearing. This is true insofar as the Moroccan characters, as objects of desire, may be given first names but are either portrayed as stupid and naive or remain indistinct, passive figures. Both criticisms culminate in a third accusation, the suspicion of Orientalism: in *Incidents*, Barthes prolongs a Western discourse about the Orient based on stereotypes of available Arabs and other exotic fantasies, and does not establish any recognizable links to the history and society of the country. He also failed to acknowledge Arab culture and, above all, its language.[27] In this reading, Barthes's sexual Orientalism is a reactivated form of colonial blindness and ignorance.[28]

Neo-colonial exploitation, prostitution, sexism, chauvinism, 'othering', Orientalism – there is no doubt about the validity of these criticisms. They enable a long-overdue problematization of Barthes's stay in Morocco and his corresponding writings. In this context, people often used to speak euphemistically of 'travel reports' or 'adventures' – postcolonial criticism has now made this way of speaking more difficult. However, some voices in Barthes research see such criticisms as a reflection of the new dogma of political correctness, which is increasingly spilling over from the Anglo-Saxon universities, where postcolonial studies were now entrenched, not only to France but also to Morocco.[29] Their objection: the postcolonial view sometimes runs the risk of taking Barthes too literally and thus ignoring the textual, aesthetic, and fictional dimensions of *Incidents.* According to literary scholar and Barthes editor Éric Marty, in *Incidents* Barthes speaks neither about nor for Morocco, nor even about himself, but rather 'quotes' the country without the usual 'hysterical appropriation.'[30] This position could be described as taking into account the interweaving of self-representational and fictionalizing elements in Barthes's writings, which attempt to decentre the author's position: only in this way, and not as a quasi-authentic biographical fragment, should one read Barthes, the author of 'The Death of the Author.'[31]

It is true: in the late 1960s, in the light of structuralism and discourse analysis, Barthes and others had not only rejected the idea of a unity of the subject, but also denied that it was possible to paint a true picture of oneself in autobiographical speaking and writing.[32] Even in Barthes's experimental autobiographical writing there are elements of both his own distancing from himself and his neutrality towards the things and people narrated. The question, however, would still be how well he ultimately succeeded in implementing this literary theoretical programme in *Incidents.*

How can overly simplistic moral, political, and aesthetic judgements be avoided here? One possibility would be to retain the postcolonial perspective, but to look more closely, in a more differentiated way. One could take into account, for example, that Barthes was certainly aware of the dangerous temptation of overly Orientalist fantasies and patterns, that he reflected on them and incorporated them into his aesthetic treatment by making them the subject of his own discussions – many of his writings and interviews on the cultural economy of exoticism testify to this.[33] Barthes also knew that with his stays in Morocco he would be continuing a long tradition of travelling to the Orient and was likely to end up in a compromising role. The naive innocence and condescension that previous travellers to the Orient had shown (Flaubert, Loti, and Gide, among others) had become impossible for Barthes, both morally and linguistically – and lumping him together with them would also mean ignoring the historical difference between a colonial and a postcolonial situation. It would therefore not do Barthes justice to reduce him to the role of the lustful, ignorant intellectual from the country of the former colonial masters. The fact that he primarily visited young men in Morocco and indulged in exotic and sexual fantasies does not mean that he did not have a significant problem with colonialism and French rule in North Africa. The opposite was the case. To show this, we need to leave the Moroccan setting and take a step back to Paris in the 1950s, when Barthes revealed a slightly different side during the fall of the French colonial empire.

Myths of colonialism

Barthes had already dealt extensively and critically with the colonial question in the 1950s: first as an eyewitness in Alexandria, where he had to contend with the French colonial clique based there; then as a contemporary of the great decolonizations in Indochina and the Maghreb; but above all as a brilliant enlightener and commentator on a colonial ideology deeply rooted in French society. His criticism of colonialism is particularly impactful in *Mythologies*, by far Barthes's most famous work. This book, which was published in 1957 and quickly became a cult classic, is a collection of fifty-four short articles that Barthes wrote monthly between 1954 and 1956 and published in the magazine *Les Lettres nouvelles*. Each of these essays contains reflections on selected myths of everyday French life, based on some current event. They all follow the large-scale attempt to criticize the ideology and language of so-called mass culture as it began to spread in the everyday lives of the French during the years of reconstruction and the *Trente Glorieuses* (the years of affluence between 1945 and 1975).

The myths were hidden in the most diverse phenomena, be it the promise of happiness in detergent advertisements, the potential of French fries to arouse longing, the world of wrestling, or the divine qualities of the Citroën DS. In this piece of sarcastic social analysis, Barthes did not aim so much to disparage the taste and the values of the French lower middle class as expressed in these phenomena, but rather to 'account *in detail* for the mystification which transforms petit bourgeois culture into a universal nature.'[34] What precisely this means becomes clear in the foreword, which still seems relevant today:

> The starting point of these reflections was usually a feeling of impatience with the 'naturalness' which common sense, the press, and the arts continually invoke to dress up a reality which, though the one we live in, is nonetheless quite historical: in a word, I resented seeing Nature and History repeatedly confused in the description of our reality, and I wanted to expose in the decorative display of what-goes-without-saying the ideological abuse I believed was hidden there.[35]

When the myths of everyday life are discussed, the most relevant national shrines and stereotypes of French culture are easily found – *haute cuisine*, the Tour de France, the beefsteak. What is really surprising when we look at the complete French edition of *Mythologies*, however, is the high proportion of texts in which Barthes deals with the contemporary mystifications of French colonialism. Topics covered include racist clichés about Africa in tabloids and the colourful exoticism of a documentary film about Indonesia, as well as the colonial dimensions of wine-growing or the double standards of the French colonial army when recruiting. This tangible presence of the colonial may astonish some readers who come to Barthes through translated editions, due to various publishing decisions. For example, in the German editions, which until a few years ago were always abridged, many of the articles on colonialism were not presented in full.[36] As a result, the colonial references in them were overlooked for decades, which had a decisive effect on the German-speaking reception of Barthes.

On closer inspection, however, it becomes quite obvious that the book has many thematic references to colonialism. This is due, first of all, to a historical coincidence. Written between 1954 and 1956, the articles fell directly into the most turbulent period of French decolonization. In November 1954, France lost the decisive battle of Dien Bien Phu and with it Indochina (nowadays Vietnam, Laos, and Cambodia). In 1956, the protectorates of Morocco and Tunisia gained their independence. And the conflict in Algeria that began in 1954 developed into a real war in precisely those two years, although it was never publicly called a war – a cover-up tactic that Barthes also mentioned in his *Mythologies*. The highly controversial colonial question of the 1950s was thus an easy target for Barthes's demystification: colonialism united precisely those collective convictions and opinions that were unquestioningly accepted as normal and self-evident by French society. It seemed only logical to decipher the mass-market language, culture, and ideology present in everyday life in the context of colonial discourses.

A clear example of this is the article 'African grammar', which deals with 'the official vocabulary of African policy'.[37] In it, Barthes uses key words to examine how French policy linguistically determines France's relationship with Africa and the colonies and protectorates there. His sources are statements made by French officials and dignitaries in the press. The quotations are primarily taken from the context of French–Moroccan relations, which is why the article was called 'Grammaire marocaine' in its original magazine version from 1955, before it was expanded to include the African continent for the French book edition.[38] 'African grammar' did not appear in the early German book versions, but it is an important text in *Mythologies*. Barthes devotes more space to this article than practically any other. As a semiotician he is particularly interested in how and why Africa is discussed in political discourse. According to him, the vocabulary used has no informational value, but aims rather at intimidating the reader. It is a 'cosmetic way of writing' that seeks to secure a cynical reality with a noble morality and that aims at 'covering the facts with a sound of language'.[39]

In order to uncover this process of concealing a deeply colonial reality, Barthes decodes the ideology hidden behind the sentences, highlighting the rhetorical nature of certain terms such as 'war', 'population', 'mission', and 'destiny'. In the case of 'war', for example, the aim is to deny the reality either by mentioning it as rarely as possible or by speaking of its opposite, 'pacification'. 'Population', on the other hand, is a favourite word in bourgeois vocabulary, and serves as an antidote to the overly politicized concept of 'class'. The term is generally emphasized by its plural: 'the *Muslim populations*, which does not fail to suggest a difference in maturity between the Metropolitan unity and the pluralism of the colonized, France *gathering* beneath her what is by nature diverse and numerous'.[40] For Barthes, there is a reason that nouns dominate in political language. The codification of the official language and its substantivization go hand in hand. The myth, says Barthes, 'is fundamentally nominal, insofar as nomination is the first procedure of distraction'. He describes these nouns in the grammatical sense as an example of *l'assiette notoire* ('notorious plate') – a term in French grammar by which the definite article is used to imply that the substance of the noun is always already presumed to be known.

> We are here at the very heart of the myth's formation: it is because France's *mission*, the *laceration* of the Moroccan people, or Algeria's *destiny* is given grammatically as a postulate (a quality generally conferred upon each by the use of the definite article) that we cannot contest them discursively. Notoriety is the first form of naturalization.[41]

In the 'Wine and milk' article, Barthes also takes a critical approach to the apparently self-evident, lacing his analysis with a heavy dose of sarcasm. He first describes the extent to which drinking wine, as a specific property of the French nation, is an aspect of the raison d'état: as part of folklore, it involves a collective duty of belonging and adorns even the smallest ceremonies of everyday life. Towards the end of the article, he reminds his readers even more emphatically that wine, as a 'lovable myth', is nevertheless not 'innocent'. It is a product of capitalist exploitation and, above all, colonial expropriation. In the 1950s, a large proportion of French *vin ordinaire* came from Algeria. Anyone who drank table wine in France was usually consuming an Algerian product. The large-scale wine-growing carried out by the French (wine accounted for four-fifths of Algerian exports) was based on massive expropriations of land from the Algerian rural population, who had grown grain on these fields for the local market. So it was not just land that was stolen: by planting vines here, the French deprived the Algerian population of one of their main food resources. And worse, they produced a drink that was rarely consumed by the Algerians themselves. The viticulture of the 'big Algerian settlers', according to Barthes, 'imposes on the Muslims, on the very land of which they have been dispossessed, a crop for which they have no use, while they actually lack bread'.[42] The reality and mythology of French wine thus contained a good deal of colonial history – and Barthes revealed this colonial context, so often concealed in everyday life, in just a few sentences.

Colonialism is omnipresent in *Mythologies*. Many of its articles contain explicit anti-colonial statements. They denounce the repressive ideology of colonial discourses, dismantle the hypocritical rhetoric of French politics, and criticize the colonial formatting of existing social conditions. Even in the theoretical section 'Myth Today', which Barthes added to his fifty-four studies as a separate part of the book, and in which he presents a comprehensive programme of semiotic theory, one can find discussions of the colonial world of images and myths of the 1950s. In a passage dealing specifically with the 'right-wing myth', Barthes describes the fundamental role that exoticism plays as an ideological tool in the construction of, and identification with, national myths. Exoticism is a key phenomenon in Barthes's analysis of myths. Its social function consists in compensating for the French Empire's experience of loss, concealing colonial and racist oppression, denying any historical context, and ultimately robbing non-French people of their history. 'The petit bourgeois is a man unable to imagine the Other', Barthes says unequivocally. In exoticism, he continues, 'the Other becomes a pure object, a spectacle, a clown' and is 'relegated to the confines of humanity'.[43]

Barthes's most impressive reflection on France's relationship to its colonial empire is also found in this theoretical section. It is the famous structuralist analysis of an image on the cover of the French magazine *Paris Match*, which shows a young Black man in soldier's uniform, saluting. In analysing this image, Barthes illustrates not only his theories on myth as a semiological system, but also his special approach as a mythologist of everyday life. He is very careful to first emphasize the everyday casualness of the scene, informing us that the issue of *Paris Match* was handed to him in a barber's shop. He then describes the ideological content of the image as follows:

> But, whether naïvely or not, I see very well what it signifies to me: that France is a great Empire, that all her sons, without any color discrimination, faithfully serve under her flag, and that there is no better answer to the detractors of an alleged colonialism than the zeal shown by this Negro in serving his so-called oppressors.[44]

In the image of the young Black man saluting the French flag, the myth thus exists once France as an empire appears 'natural'. At the same time, this loose description of the image is already an important part of the initial demystification; as Samoyault emphasizes: 'if [the image] was recognized or laid bare as an alibi of colonialism, it would destroy itself. The method was extremely effective, presenting the two discourses at the same time, giving the reader the feeling that he was playing a part in the process of elucidation.'[45] This playful enlightenment also contains the political core of the entire mythology project. Barthes is concerned with raising awareness, with revealing hidden meanings, and with the breaking of signs, or 'semioclasm.' Colonialism may have been difficult to defeat, and it was far from being a myth, but it was definitely a huge myth-making machine that had to be torn apart.

In the last pages of his book, however, Barthes also writes about the limits of mythological work and says 'a few words about the mythologist himself.' In this passage, Barthes is very concerned to portray the mythologist as a figure outside of society who is 'condemned to metalanguage.' At the same time, he makes it clear that this eccentric position has its limits. The mythologist is constantly in danger of 'either always speaking *excessively* about reality' or 'causing to disappear the reality which he purports to protect': 'wine is objectively good, and *at the same time*, the goodness of wine is a myth: here is the aporia.' The mythologist tries 'as best he can' to get out of the aporia, but ultimately he too remains a prisoner of the society and mythical world that surrounds him. He will inevitably continue catching himself enjoying a glass of 'objectively good' wine, reading the tabloid magazine at the hairdresser's, or dreaming of his next vacation in a faraway land.[46]

In 1956, when Barthes wrote these lines, Morocco was still a relatively unknown country for him. It was not until the early 1960s that he discovered it for himself and learned to love it. It became a place of relaxation and pleasure, and ultimately the best possible setting for fantasizing about being a novelist. But was not Morocco also an exotic and almost mythical place where, for Barthes, the other, and others, sometimes became a 'pure object, a spectacle, a curiosity'? Did Barthes's affective relationship to the country really differ so much from that of the lower middle classes and their attested inability to imagine the other? Whether Barthes's anti-colonialist analysis of mythology actually enables him to shake off the accusation of exoticism that he incurred in Morocco remains to be seen. There is still a certain dissonance between his critical comments in the 1950s and his visits to and writings about Morocco in the 1960s and 1970s – a dissonance that cannot be completely resolved by invoking the different historical contexts or the all-too-human contradictions in the life and work of an intellectual. But it is also important to note that, judging by his preparatory work and fragmentary texts such as *Incidents*, Barthes's planned autobiographical novel *Vita Nova* would, among other things, most likely have narrated these Moroccan episodes with all their inherent contradictions. But it remained at the stage of an epiphany.

MICHEL FOUCAULT

4

ENJOYMENT AND SILENCE Michel Foucault

A few kilometres north of Tunis there is a coastal village with the pleasant-sounding name of Sidi Bou Said. It sits on the Rock of Carthage, which rises at the north-western tip of the Gulf of Tunis and offers a sweeping view of the Mediterranean. The place consists of a few winding streets, most of which lead steeply down to the beach and the harbour. Sidi Bou Said is known for its white Cubist-style villas with blue windows and doors. This sight makes you think you are in Andalusia or the Cyclades, and there's a reason for this: in 1912, a British-French baron settled here and had the village restored in a mix of Andalusian and Greek styles. Originally a pilgrim village from the Ottoman era, Sidi Bou Said became an artists' colony for painters such as Paul Klee and August Macke, and later also a popular residence for the French colonial elite who stayed in the country during the protectorate (1881–1956). Even after Tunisia's independence in 1956, it retained its exclusive character – the French expatriates who continued to live in the country particularly enjoyed their times there. Today, Sidi Bou Said is a fashionable seaside resort for summer vacationers and day trippers from Tunis and elsewhere. Anyone walking through its streets easily gets the impression that the old haunt of colonial rulers has now been taken over by rich Tunisians and Western tourists.

The philosopher Michel Foucault lived in Sidi Bou Said for two years from 1966 to 1968. He resided successively in three different blue and white villas, which offered a panorama out onto the sea – he wrote to Paris that he was looking for 'a direct, absolute relationship to the sea, free from civilization'.[1] These were not insignificant years in Foucault's life: in 1966 his book *The Order of Things* was published, making him instantly famous and elevating him to the Olympus of Parisian star intellectuals. In Tunisia, he was able to enjoy the media hype surrounding him from a distance. He had taken a position as a philosophy professor, for the first time in his career, at the University of Tunis (before that, he had been employed in a psychology department). It was in Sidi Bou Said that Foucault began and finished work on *The Archaeology of Knowledge*. From here, eventually, he followed the events in Paris in May 1968.

Sidi Bou Said also provided Foucault with the backdrop for numerous more or less extravagant occupations. His partner Daniel Defert remembers that Foucault developed a new lifestyle here: 'He emulated Nietzsche and resolved to become a little more Greek, more athletic, more suntanned, more ascetic every day'.[2] This new lifestyle included daily walks on the beach and naked sunbathing, as well as the ritual of shaving his head every morning. The famous Foucault look, which has since become familiar from so many photographs, was created here. Foucault explained his decision by saying that this ritual freed him from worrying about hair loss.[3] If David Macey's biography is to be believed, Foucault had a wide range of pleasures at his disposal in Sidi Bou Said, from local cannabis, kif, which was easy to obtain and of good quality, to high-proof alcohol, which Foucault consumed more moderately than usual, as well as easily arranged sexual encounters with young Tunisian men. For Foucault, says Macey, pleasure was no longer a question of frivolity or potential self-destruction. It became part of a disciplined aesthetic of existence.[4] In other words, pleasure without regret.

So should we see Foucault in Tunisia as, like Camus's Sisyphus, happy? That at least is what the numerous companions and biographers of the French philosopher suggest. Almost all of them report that he was mentally unstable and at odds with himself for a long time, but that, after spending many years in the chillier lands of the European north (Warsaw, Uppsala, Hamburg) and in the depths of the French provinces (Clermont-Ferrand), he finally discovered the delights of the south and of life.

View of the Dar Zarrouk palace, Sidi Bou Said/Tunisia.

Perhaps the most striking description of Foucault's state of mind during his years in Sidi Bou Said comes from Jean Daniel, the founder of the French weekly *Le Nouvel Observateur*, who met Foucault there:

> In this village, where he was happy, everyone knew him for his habit of starting work early in the morning, in front of the windows of his villa overlooking the bay, and for his obsession with loving and living in the sunlight. He was homosexual in the most discreet way. Without the rumours of the little good-for-nothings in the village, no one would have suspected it. In any case, it would not have made any difference for anyone in this free society. On each of my trips I would pick him up for a walk: he loved to step out for long, fast, restless excursions. He invited me into a room that was carefully kept cool and dark; in the background he had a kind of large raised slab on which he placed the mat that served as his bed, rolling it up during the day, like the Arabs and the Japanese. His monk's skull, that famous Mandarin-like laugh that literally cut through his face, his withering look even when he wanted to be tender, his demeanour, as attentive as it was ceremonial – all this indicated to me at the time an inner struggle between a violent temptation to lust

> and the obvious will to contain this temptation and transform it into a method of asceticism, or a conceptual exercise. Later, I was one of those who were not surprised by his desire to write a philosophy of the various histories of sexuality.[5]

Foucault himself gave considerable impetus to this image of a sun-hungry hedonist who became political as if by the way when, in an interview with the Tunisian daily newspaper *La Presse de Tunisie* in April 1967, he gave the only public information about the reasons for his stay in the country. Asked what he thought of Tunisia, he replied: 'I came because of the mythical image that all Europeans have of Tunisia: sun, sea, the great dryness of Africa – in short, I was looking for an oasis of peace without asceticism.' This statement must surely also be seen as a self-ironizing play on exoticism. Whether he had really found his own personal Thebes was a question he left open – he ended his reply with the dry remark that he had, surprisingly, found 'Tunisian students with a serious passion and an insatiable thirst for knowledge', which sounded a bit trite, but was perhaps also a polite way of drawing attention to the situation of the student revolts in Tunis.[6]

The Tunisian interviewer, on the other hand, hoped that the philosopher would talk about the very latest novelty from Paris, structuralism. Shortly before Foucault's departure, there had been a public spat with Jean-Paul Sartre, who had called Foucault the 'last barricade of the bourgeoisie' and thus hoisted him to the forefront of the discussions about structuralism.[7] Foucault now made every effort to downplay his role in the dispute. When the interviewer suggested he was the 'high priest of structuralism', Foucault replied that he was 'at most the choirboy': 'Let's say I rang the bell, the believers kneeled down, the unbelievers started yelling. But the mass began a long time ago. I did not perform the true mystery. I'm just an innocent observer in a white surplice, that's how I see things.'[8] Foucault's modest demeanour probably only partially convinced the journalist. In the lead story, he was described as someone who, in a well-tailored beige suit and with a black briefcase, looked 'like a young civil servant with a brilliant future ahead of him.'[9]

Foucault's interview with *La Presse de Tunisie* remained his only public statement on Tunisia during his entire stay. This low yield is astonishing when you consider that he lived there for two years and during that time was not above giving numerous interviews on all sorts of topics. Even later (with one small exception, to which I will return later), he would not comment further on Tunisia, nor on the neo-colonial living conditions during his stay, let alone the bloody history of French colonial rule in North Africa. The topic of colonialism as well as neo-colonialism remains a glaring gap in Foucault's work.

And that is where the real problem lies: in this silence. It is not surprising that the two hints Foucault gave in this interview – his exotic image of Tunisia and his enthusiasm for the Tunisian students – appear so prominently in biographies and anecdotes and are exploited in the absence of any other evidence. What is more problematic is that the silence itself is adopted without question; that historical debate about the neo-colonial circumstances of Foucault's stay is so radically absent; that the implications for his thinking are not drawn out. Why have the many Foucault aficionados failed to address his silence and thus the sensitive question of colonialism? Was it due to their own colonial clichés and fantasies, in which Tunisia appears like an extension of southern France? Was it due to the general colonial blind spot in French society, which, among other things, ensures that the continuing power asymmetries between the old colonial state and the newly independent state are not seen? Or did the figure of the neo-colonial dandy simply not fit the image of the star philosopher? Admittedly, it is difficult to talk about a silence. But to avoid it is, in this case, more than just negligence.

There are actually plenty of points from which Foucault's living and working conditions in Tunisia can be viewed in a slightly less whitewashed and much less biased way. We can begin with the circumstances of his decision to go to Tunis. His wish to go abroad again arose only because the long-desired position at the Sorbonne in Paris did not materialize – Foucault's letters from Tunisia show that he spent a lot of time there tinkering over his stalled career in Paris.[10] And he would actually have far preferred to go to the Congo. He had asked his contact in the Foreign Ministry, Jean Sirinelli, to get him a position at the University of Kinshasa. Sirinelli, a friend from old times at the École normale supérieure and head of the French ministerial department for education overseas, strongly advised Foucault against it. The reason was, on the one hand, security concerns (Mobutu had recently seized power in a very bloody coup), and on the other hand, the worry that Foucault would be somewhat out of place there, since the university was still in the hands of Belgian professors from the recent colonial period.[11] Only after the Kinshasa plan had been finally abandoned did Foucault decide to apply for the vacant philosophy position at the University of Tunis, which had been recommended to him by two French philosophers who had previously worked there.[12] Foucault knew the country and North Africa from previous visits and vacations with Daniel Defert and Roland Barthes.[13] Tunisia also seemed to be a pragmatic solution: relatively close to France and yet sufficiently far away.

Kinshasa or Tunis – it didn't matter, so long as it was in Africa! Life in Sidi Bou Said cannot have been all that exotic for Foucault. An expatriate community of French people had formed in the coastal village, leading a bohemian life at a distance from Tunis. They kept to themselves and they stayed like that. It is fitting that almost all of the notable acquaintances Foucault made in Sidi Bou Said were either French scholars working at the University of Tunis or Parisian intellectuals on their travels. Jean Daniel describes this milieu as a 'free society' in which no one cared about the consumer habits or sexual orientation of others – though it must be added that this freedom was limited to Europeans.[14] Foucault was able to develop his new lifestyle, which included not only the controlled intake of figs and mint tea, but also the free availability of sex and drugs, thanks to this privilege and perhaps only in this special milieu.

The new lifestyle sometimes seemed like a caricature of a bad French colonial film – for example when Foucault bought himself a white convertible, a Peugeot 404, so that he could quickly drive to Tunis; or when the sociologist Jean Duvignaud found Foucault at home at Easter 1968, reading Feuerbach in peace in the midst of a horde of Tunisian children; or when the journalist Catherine von Bülow, while walking on the beach, noticed Foucault presenting 'the astonishing figure of a European dressed entirely in white'; or when 'Islam' was discussed at one of the regular dinners in Foucault's French circle of acquaintances and he remained silent – in fact, when asked about the evening, he could not think of anything to say but mused on the 'archaeology of dinner', by which he meant more the domestic interior of his hosts than the stereotypical ideas of the company at table.[15]

Foucault in Tunisia

At the University of Tunis, Foucault also moved within a French bubble. He was part of the French teaching staff, all of whose members had been sent out by the government in Paris, received double salaries, and worked within the framework of an educational agreement between Tunisia and France. Foucault taught mainly philosophy and art history, including courses on Descartes, Nietzsche, Husserl, and the history of the Renaissance art. He also gave public lectures, for example on 'Man in modern Western thought', 'Madness and society' and 'The painting of Manet', some of which took place in the Tahar Hadad Club, a cultural centre whose audience consisted of students and the educated French-speaking elite of Tunisia. The individual titles of these lectures, which were well attended, already indicate that Foucault was delivering a classic repertoire of Western thought in Tunis. Over time, many students considered Foucault to be 'too western to understand the Tunisians'.[16]

If one had to apply standards of intercultural competence here, Foucault would probably fail. From everything that can be reconstructed, one must assume that he had little interest in the country or its people. He neither learned the Arabic language nor made any significant contacts with Tunisians – apart from his nameless sexual partners and also Jalila Hafsia, the head of the Tahar Hadad Club, who, as she later confessed, fell hopelessly in love with him.[17] The only things Foucault could find to say about Tunisia included, of all things, a European reference: it was 'a country blessed by history and, because it gave birth to Hannibal and Saint Augustine, deserving of eternal life', he remarked to Hafsia when visiting the ruins of Carthage, the famous archaeological site in the Bay of Tunis.[18] Foucault did travel extensively, however. This made him a highly suspect figure, at least by Gustave Flaubert's tenets. Flaubert, himself a passionate traveller to the Orient, had a mocking but apt definition of an orientalist in his dictionary of commonplaces: 'Someone who has travelled a lot.'[19]

The theorist of the Club Med

Intensive self-absorption in an exclusive environment, coupled with a lack of interest in Tunisian culture and history – these are two factors that initially give little reason to suspect that Foucault's stay in this country left any traces in his work. Was his thinking influenced at all by the Tunisian environment? What can be said with certainty is that Sidi Bou Said offered comfortable working conditions, and an impressive backdrop for key intellectual experiences. This at least is how we can understand the exuberant news that Foucault sent on 16 December 1966 to Defert in Paris: 'I found yesterday, this morning, just now, the definition of discourse that I've needed for years.'[20] Just like Barthes's Moroccan epiphany of 1978, the scene fits perfectly into a potential collection of anecdotes titled 'European Intellectuals and Their Eureka Moments in the Orient.' But beyond this scene, which in Foucault's case is not very revealing, are there any passages in his work where some kind of Tunisian experience is reflected in theory?

In *The Archaeology of Knowledge*, which Foucault wrote in Sidi Bou Said, there are certainly no explicit references to Tunisia. But to expect the book to deal with the place where it was written would be asking too much. *The Archaeology of Knowledge* is a book about methods, in which fundamental questions such as 'What is a discourse?' and 'What is a statement?' are discussed. Remarks about Tunisia were out of place here. The text reads more like a large-scale attempt to gain methodological clarity about his previous work – which up to that point consisted mainly of *The History of Madness*, *The Birth of the Clinic*, and *The Order of Things* – and at the same time to provide his growing readership and perhaps also himself with a more systematic grounding. Here Foucault develops his understanding of concepts such as discourse analysis, archaeology, and the history of knowledge, which would go on to have a remarkable career in the humanities and social sciences.

You cannot tell that this book, of such importance for the Western academic world, was written in North Africa. However, if one knows about Foucault's lifestyle in Sidi Bou Said, then the contrast between the strict, colourless sentences of *The Archaeology of Knowledge* and the lush, colourful surroundings – which is how Foucault experienced them – is striking. In terms of desire, there is a rigorous division of labour: the pleasure in the body and the pleasures of life that Foucault discovered in Sidi Bou Said do not seem to have sparked a new pleasure in the text. His work on this text shows much greater ascetic rigour than in the previous books. While in the texts of Nietzsche, Foucault's favourite author at the time, one can literally smell and see the Engadin, everything sensual and spatial in *The Archaeology of Knowledge* is virtually banished: at best it lives on in the form of spatial metaphors, with which the book teems. The same principle of banishment also applies to many ideological forms of the subjective, personal side of authorship, which Foucault attacks with a programme critical of the subject. At the end of the introduction, for example, he expresses his attitude of refusal with the following famous words: 'Do not ask who I am and do not ask me to remain the same: leave it to our bureaucrats and our police to see that our papers are in order. At least spare us their morality when we write.'[21]

Foucault's famous lecture on 'Heterotopias', which clearly reflects the place where it was written, also falls within the period of his stay in Tunisia. Significantly, it is an examination of spaces in which his personal experience of the Tunisian environment and its reflection in theory become most visible. He first gave the lecture in December 1966, for the radio station France Culture, and then a second time in a slightly modified form to Parisian architects in March 1967.[22] Foucault understands 'heterotopias' as 'counter-sites' or 'other spaces' in which all the real places that can be found in culture are simultaneously represented, questioned, and turned into their opposites.[23] Examples of such counter-sites are gardens, cemeteries, cinemas, motels, mental institutions, prisons, and ships, as well as 'Scandinavian saunas' and 'the hammam [*sic*] of the Muslims.'[24] Their actual function is to question all other spaces. Either they create an illusion that exposes the rest of reality as an illusion (Foucault's reference point here is the brothel), or they create another real space that creates a perfect order in contrast to the confusing disorder of our space (the reference point here is most European colonies).[25]

Tunisia plays a part in this lecture when Foucault includes the holiday villages of the Club Méditerranée in the list of counter-sites. The Club Med is the epitome of the exclusive clubs that emerged in the 1950s and 1960s, in which the idea of the perfect holiday is uncannily combined with the fantasies and set pieces of the colonial era. One of the first of these holiday villages was established in Djerba, Tunisia. Foucault knew the complex in Djerba from his previous trips to the south of the country, when Defert was doing the civilian version of national service in Sfax. In his lecture Foucault mentions the 'straw huts of Djerba' – not, as one would expect today, as places of neo-colonial imagination, but as an example of 'temporary heterotopias' in which 'time in the mode of the festival' is celebrated: 'Quite recently, a new kind of temporal heterotopia has been invented: vacation villages, such as those Polynesian villages that offer a compact three weeks of primitive and eternal nudity to the inhabitants of the cities.' His interpretation of these Polynesian villages is brief and ironic, but also contains a spark of fascination: 'It is about erasing time in order to return to the nakedness and innocence of the Fall.'[26]

Was not Sidi Bou Said also a temporary heterotopia for Foucault, in which he celebrated a festival with time and the body – not for three weeks, but for two whole years? A lived heterotopia in which the bright cheerfulness of the village offered an alternative to the hustle and bustle of the metropolis?[27] An artificial paradise in which, for a while, utopian fantasies of having a perfect body seemed to be realized? There is much to suggest this. The topic of a second radio lecture that Foucault gave two weeks later for France Culture also testifies to it. Its subject is the 'utopian body' – and when Foucault talks of being able to lie 'on the beach and melt in the sun', it does not take much imagination to recognize the impact of his times on the beach in Sidi Bou Said.[28]

But we do not need to overstretch the terminology or content of the two radio lectures to recognize that, in Tunisia, Foucault

Beach and holiday resort of the Club Méditerranée in the 'Polynesian straw-hut style', Djerba, Tunisia, late 1950s.

was on a grand quest for unusual or 'civilization-free' spaces.[29] The surroundings offered plenty of opportunities for this: at Christmas 1966 he undertook a trip to the Tassili n'Ajjer, a mountain plateau in the southern Algerian Sahara, where he spent days camping in the company of donkeys and camels.[30] In the emptiness, silence, and endless expanse of this landscape he came up with the idea that the desert was the only place in the world that was not culturally shaped – a rather contentious view, but nevertheless one that brought with it a lifelong fascination with deserts.[31] In 1975, Foucault was able to repeat this experience of limit places when he made a short trip to Death Valley in California at the invitation of two American students – this time, however, with a dose of LSD in his luggage. His drug-fuelled sojourns in California are now well documented, often accompanied by the sensationalist suggestion that they had a great influence on his thinking.[32] In the same breath, it is also often emphasized how Foucault and his associates transformed the intellectual life of the United States under the label of French Theory.[33]

In the case of Tunisia, things are a little different: if one were to describe the intellectual commerce between France and Tunisia reflected in Foucault's work as a kind of an import–export transaction, then the balance for Tunisia would be negative. This can be clearly seen in the lectures: in Tunis, Foucault lectured exclusively on classic themes of Western culture, which the Tunisians found of little interest; but in Paris, on national cultural radio, and in front of enthusiastic architects, he gave lectures on spaces and bodies, lectures that were strongly inspired by Tunisia. Rather like a late descendant of the colonial civilizing mission, Foucault exported French culture to North Africa, and imported experiences of 'other' spaces to Western Europe. That may be more or less acceptable. But what is astonishing and almost scandalous is that, since then, the Tunisian sources of his inspiration have not been taken into account. All traces of Foucault's stay there were erased from the written version of the 1967 radio lecture, which Foucault prepared and released for publication, at the request of Berlin architects, only in 1984, shortly before his death.[34] We no longer get to read about the straw huts in Djerba and the Club Med. In the passages mentioned, Foucault speaks solely of our 'Western culture.'[35] Since its publication, the text – with the new title 'Of other spaces' – has delighted theory-savvy architects and designers all over the world, but Tunisia, the cultural-historical site of the authorship, hardly gets a look-in. The neo-colonial dimensions of Foucault's analysis of space thus remain in the dark. One should beware of these problematic little cases in the history of ideas when intellectual traces are erased and intellectual property is centralized. They are also part of the larger debates about the epistemic violence of colonialism, the recognition of the colonial heritage, and the importance of intangible cultural assets. The history of ideas is littered with these cases of epistemic injustice.

The lecture on other spaces remains the only document in which the Tunisian experience also plays a philosophical role and is processed directly in theory. Apart from that, there is a great void in this regard in Foucault's academic work. Neither in the later monographs nor in the four-volume collected works are there any indications that suggest further engagement with Tunisia. The intellectual yield is therefore limited. Compared to countries such as the United States, Japan, and Iran, where Foucault stayed for shorter periods of time and where he was not afraid to give his diagnosis of the times and present his cultural analyses, this is small beer.[36] He was not very forthcoming about questions of colonialism and neo-colonialism, and in some ways his Tunisian experiences had little direct impact on his thinking.

Tunisian spring

Perhaps the scanty philosophical yield of Foucault's stay in Tunisia is also a reason why his biographers and interpreters have striven to find some kind of balance on the political side, portraying him as a model political activist for the Tunisian cause. For Didier Eribon and David Macey, Tunisia simply becomes the accidental scene of a comprehensive political transformation. The narrative of this 'political baptism of fire' goes as follows.[37] Until 1966, Foucault was an apolitical academic, extremely reticent about making public statements. In Tunisia, he encountered an unbearable political situation, stood up for his students, and slipped into the role of the committed intellectual (a role that was already waiting for him). When he returned to Paris in the autumn of 1968, Foucault was a transformed man: he signed petitions, demonstrated, shouted into megaphones, and became an activist. His new iconic look also fits this story: shaved head and white turtleneck sweater. It's almost too good to be true.

Foucault did indeed find himself in a heated political climate at the University of Tunis. Almost his entire time there was marked by student protests and unrest, which from June 1967 to June 1968 were directed primarily against the regime of President Habib Bourguiba, the first president of the republic founded in 1957, known for his authoritarian leadership style. Bourguiba violently suppressed the student strikes and unrest. The police regularly entered the university, beat up students, injured several of them, and threw them in prison with long sentences.[38] Foucault was not unaffected by this. Together with other French members of the teaching staff, he protested against the arrests and torture. However, there were clear limits to his commitment. Like all the other French teachers, Foucault was subject to the obligation of non-interference abroad, as stipulated in their contracts. When, in June 1967, the question arose as to how far solidarity with the students should go, the majority of the teaching staff invoked this non-interference clause – and Foucault adhered to the majority decision, even if he disagreed and appealed in vain for more support.[39] Moreover, his sympathy with the students was not unlimited. This was shown by the outbreak of violence during the Arab–Israeli Six-Day War in June 1967, when pro-Arab demonstrations turned into antisemitic riots, with synagogues being desecrated. Foucault was shocked by the 'pogrom atmosphere', by the 'nationalism and racism' that the students supported out of 'left-wing radicalism', and he openly expressed his disgust.[40]

These two examples show that one should not oversimplify things and mythify Foucault's politicization. Political baptisms of fire look different. In Foucault's case, things were more ambiguous than one might think. He did not come to Tunisia specifically to gain political experience. Rather, little by little, in the course of the worldwide upheavals towards the end of the 1960s, he slipped into a historical situation that he was able to observe carefully from his comparatively safe position as a French professor, and give support with a series of controlled actions on secure ground. Foucault's politicization in the spring of 1967 had less to do with Tunisia than with himself, his political past, his role in the intellectual field of France, and in general with French conditions. In Sidi Bou Said he frequently dealt with the accusation previously levelled against him that his work was too structuralist and too unpolitical. Here, he had enough distance and time to examine the political dimensions of his thinking in a new light. This fresh start also included him filling gaps in his knowledge by reading the writings of Rosa Luxemburg, Leon Trotsky, and the Black Panthers. Of great importance were the friendships he made in Sidi Bou Said with Jean Daniel and Catherine von Bülow, who were to offer him a forum in the *Nouvel Observateur* in the 1970s. In short, as so often, it was a whole series of factors that fuelled politicization.

A central role in Foucault's exploration of the political was played by his partner Daniel Defert, who knew Tunisia well and regularly visited Foucault in Sidi Bou Said. Defert was a political activist who had been anti-colonial 'with all his heart' since the colonial wars in Indochina and Algeria.[41] Born in 1937, this philosopher and sociologist was a typical representative of the 'Algerian War generation' that became politically radicalized in the student milieu and in the wake of violent anti-war demonstrations towards the end of the 1950s. Initially heavily involved in the communist student union, Defert turned his back on the Communist Party in 1960 due to its ambivalent stance on the Algerian question, and joined groups on the New Left. He was also in close contact with Algerian students and activists from the independence movement, but never directly supported the FLN.[42] He retained his anti-colonial attitude and a certain solidarity with the fate of the French colonies even after the war – as demonstrated by his decision to do his national service in a civilian capacity after completing his studies in 1964, teaching philosophy in a school in Sfax in southern Tunisia.

The influence of a left-wing anti-colonial activist like Defert also prevented Foucault from displaying political attitudes in Tunisia similar to those he had adopted during the Algerian War. If we can believe the memories of old friends from the 1950s, such as Maurice Pinguet, the Algerian War did not really affect Foucault.[43] He reacted to it with indifference – and with a medical certificate that exempted him from military service.[44] But it would be wrong to see in this a general apolitical position, or to justify it by pointing out that Foucault spent most of the war abroad as a cultural ambassador and did not see much of what was happening. The truth is that he *did* have clear political views on the war – they just did not really fit into the left-wing intellectual milieu of its die-hard opponents. Foucault was not averse to Gaullism at the time, and often associated with high-ranking figures very close to Charles de Gaulle who were preparing his seizure of power in 1958. Like Barthes, Foucault himself was convinced that de Gaulle's seizure of power was by no means a fascist coup that would maintain the French presence in Algeria, which was the prevailing opinion among leftists at the time. He believed that it represented a historic opportunity for France and also for Algeria (an opinion that Barthes did not share).[45] Even if Foucault was not entirely wrong in retrospect (as is well known, de Gaulle did not cling on to Algeria, and negotiated in secret), we are almost obliged to say that, given his later fame as a radical intellectual, it was fortunate that almost no one knew his name at the time, and no one demanded a clear commitment from him. Foucault never expressed his views on the Algerian War publicly. The cultural diplomatic arena in which he worked in Warsaw,

Rue de Vaugirard, Paris. Daniel Defert and Michel Foucault in Foucault's apartment, mid-1970s.

Uppsala, and Hamburg required a certain amount of restraint and thus protected him from overly extreme and controversial positions.

In Tunisia, too, Foucault was obliged to observe a kind of neutrality, but this time he clearly pushed the limits of his contractually agreed non-interference – especially after the student protests and state repression reached a bloody climax in March 1968. He took a stance on several occasions, protecting his students, protesting against their arbitrary arrest, giving them shelter, hiding the copying machine used to produce leaflets, driving underground activists around in the back seat of his Peugeot, and supporting students such as Ahmad Othmani by testifying in court and intervening with ministers.[46]

The impact of these activities should not be overestimated. Foucault's interventions were mostly unsuccessful. But they were enough to attract the attention of the authorities – to the point that Foucault believed he was being monitored by the police and was an unwelcome guest in the country. This became a certainty when, early one morning, he was driving home a young Tunisian student who had spent the night with him. His car was stopped at a traffic checkpoint, which turned out to be an ambush: a group of men in plain clothes brutally beat Foucault up. To this day, opinions differ as to whether the beating was a warning against further political interference, or a reaction to Foucault's homosexual activities.[47] What is clear is that the incident caused him to end his stay in the country prematurely. He gave up his plan to buy a house in Sidi Bou Said and, in the autumn of 1968, took a ship to Marseilles. The two years in Tunisia ended abruptly.

When Foucault returned to France, the student protests that had plunged the country into a serious political crisis were already over. He had followed the May '68 events in Paris with enthusiasm and sympathy, but apart from a short trip he had not been there and had not been involved in any major political actions. In the aftermath of May he plunged deeper into the political fray. When he accepted the position of professor of philosophy at the newly founded, somewhat experimental, left-wing university of Vincennes in December 1968, he was right at the centre of the fierce conflicts between the students on one hand and the government and the police on the other. To the surprise of many of his Parisian acquaintances, Foucault enthusiastically took on the role of militant professor that he had already tried out in Tunis. He criticized the state monopoly on knowledge, denounced police violence, protested alongside the students, and was ultimately arrested himself. The difference between this and Tunis was that, in Vincennes, these defiant actions posed no real risk for him, but only brought him more into the public spotlight. The image of Foucault as a radical intellectual, which has fascinated so many since then, is closely linked to Vincennes (and less so to Tunis).

Nevertheless, Foucault never really escaped the accusation that he had missed a decisive moment in history. Great and small ideologists of the revolution such as Herbert Marcuse and Maurice Blanchot liked to ask, in a reproachful tone, what Foucault had actually been doing during the Paris barricades of May '68. In 1978, in a major interview with Duccio Trombadori, Foucault responded to such attacks with a certain asperity: 'Well, I was in Tunisia. And I must add that it was an important experience.' Up to that point, Foucault had not once spoken publicly about his experiences in Tunisia. Only now, looking back on May '68 ten years later, did the Tunisian student revolt of

March '68 take on its full significance as 'a real political experience' for him. In the interview, Foucault says he was 'deeply impressed by the young men and women who put themselves at great risk when they wrote leaflets, distributed them, and called for a strike.' In Tunisia, he felt compelled 'to help the students, and to get to know something completely different from the humdrum noise of the institutions and political discourses of Europe.' He acknowledges that the Tunisian youth revolt was an existential act full of moral energy and authenticity that overwhelmed him: 'So, Tunisia, for me, represented in some ways the chance to reinsert myself in the political debate. It wasn't May of '68 in France that changed me; it was March of '68, in a third-world country.'[48]

Once he got going in this interview, Foucault drew an unprompted and revealing comparison:

> When I returned to France in November–December 1968, I was quite surprised and amazed – and rather disappointed – when I compared the situation to what I had seen in Tunisia. The struggles, though marked by violence and intense involvement, had never brought with them the same price, the same sacrifices. There's no comparison between the barricades of the Latin Quarter and the risk of doing fifteen years in prison, as was the case in Tunisia.[49]

It was undoubtedly true that Tunisian students risked more than their French counterparts. But Foucault's statements also contain a touch of self-justification and self-fashioning. Answering the question about his non-participation in the Paris events of May '68 by referring to the Tunisian events of March '68 is one thing, but dressing up one's own absence in Paris by invoking a supposedly more dangerous stay in a 'third world' country is another.

Postcolonial parricide

Classic thinkers are often said to have the ability to continually address and shed light on the present. In this respect, Michel Foucault more than lives up to his reputation. The philosopher, who died in 1984 from the effects of AIDS, provided the relevant key words for many global contexts in recent years. In addition to issues such as neoliberalism and migration, this was particularly evident at the beginning of the Covid-19 pandemic, when, faced with state measures to contain and combat the virus, some people turned to Foucault, the 'thinker of infection', consulting his studies in the hope of better understanding the situation.[50]

However, Foucault is less useful on another major topic of recent years: the global debates about the legacy of colonialism. His work offers little in this regard, and the famous toolbox remains unopened. The fact that Foucault is less visible in this area can be blamed on him only by those who have too high expectations of the prophetic abilities and moral integrity of intellectuals, and who perceive philosophy simply as a particularly demanding form of moral commitment. However, the accusation has been raised seriously for a long time, especially in the field of postcolonial studies – where, in fact, Foucault played an important role as a provider of theory. Here, the absence of any examination of colonialism or race in his work was resented from an early stage.[51] As a result, other facets of Foucault were scrutinized: his Eurocentrism, his privileged status as a white male intellectual, and his alleged turning a blind eye to major anti-racist movements and the apartheid regime in South Africa.[52] It should be noted that this criticism came, and still comes, from authors who had previously based their postcolonial theories squarely on Foucault's thinking. Often, what is well known and valued highly is also what is most eagerly and sharply subjected to criticism.

Foucault and postcolonial studies – this is also the story of an intimate, theory-led reception that culminated in an intellectual parricide committed for political and moral reasons. The best example of this is the case of Edward Said. In his 1978 book *Orientalism*, the American-Palestinian literary scholar cleverly used Foucault's concept of discourse to show how the traditional Western ways of speaking and perceiving the Orient are permeated with European fantasies of superiority and various forms of racism, sexism, imperialism, and chauvinism. *Orientalism* became the founding book of postcolonial studies and made its author instantly famous.

Said also got to know Foucault personally a little later, when he was invited to Paris in January 1979 by Jean-Paul Sartre and Simone de Beauvoir for a meeting on 'peace in the Middle East', and the meeting was abruptly moved to Foucault's apartment – 'for security reasons', allegedly.[53] To the great disappointment of Said, an advocate of the Palestinian cause in the Middle East conflict, his French theoretical idol made it unmistakably clear that he was simply agreeing to make his own premises available and did not want to contribute anything of substance to the discussion. Foucault made no secret of his unconditional pro-Israel stance, and soon disappeared to put in his daily stint at the Bibliothèque nationale.

The scene is reported by Said, who recorded his memory of this meeting in the *London Review of Books* in 2000. His report reads like the retrospective reckoning of a man disappointed with his intellectual idols of the past. Everything revolves around a single set of problems: whether the meagre support for the Palestinians on the part of Sartre, Beauvoir, and Foucault was not due to a 'fundamental lack of sympathy for the Arab cause' that was 'culturally or perhaps religiously influenced' and also affected other issues in the Middle East. Said's account is peppered with comical and sometimes malicious descriptions of French intellectuals and their oriental fantasies – including a conceited Simone de Beauvoir in a turban, who can hardly wait for her forthcoming trip to Iran to demonstrate against the chador. Or Foucault, who, still impressed by his recent trip to Iran, described how he had walked through Tehran disguised in a wig and found the Islamic Revolution 'very exciting, very strange, crazy'. Said makes all sorts of other claims – for example that Foucault was thrown out of Tunisia not because of his political stance, but because of his 'homosexual activities with students'.[54] Said's article always follows the same pattern of argumentation: intellectuals such as Beauvoir and Foucault are portrayed as intellectually stimulating but morally and politically disappointing figures who fall under the suspicion of Orientalism. This makes them appear as worthy successors to those French writers such as Gérard de Nerval and Gustave Flaubert, whom Said scrutinized, along with others, in *Orientalism*.

Can the suspicion of Orientalism also be applied to Foucault's stay in Tunisia? In criticizing Foucault we do not have to go as far as Said and other representatives of postcolonialism did, but we can acknowledge that the Tunisian episode also contains elements of an Orientalist disposition. Otherwise, the mixture of hedonism and ignorance, kitsch and appropriation, liberation and exploitation that Foucault revealed in that country can hardly be understood – unless one deems the story of the white man who travels to an exotic country and finds his sexual and aesthetic fantasies fulfilled there to be entirely unproblematic. In Tunisia, Foucault exactly embodies the classic type of male European intellectual who finds himself in a recognizably neo-colonial context, enjoys the situation to the full, profits from it, and sees no reason to enjoy it other than in silence.

Where is the stumbling block here? It is not so much the stay in Tunisia itself, nor Foucault's desires, motives, experiences, and actions. What is problematic is Foucault's astonishing ability to ignore the neo-colonial dimensions of his situation: his ability not to see (or not to find disturbing) his involvement in a context characterized by clear power asymmetries from colonial times; his privilege of travelling around Tunisia relatively unchallenged, constantly making his mark by talking about 'other spaces', for example – only to end up in the Club Med. All of this seems all the more problematic the more one realizes how staunchly Foucault campaigned in his writings and political positions for the excluded, oppressed, and marginalized in society (such as prisoners, the insane, and the sick). In their 1972 conversation 'Intellectuals and Power', he and Gilles Deleuze highlighted perhaps the most important political contribution of poststructuralist theory: that intellectuals must try to reveal and recognize the discourse of the Other in society. The wretched of the earth, the colonized or recently decolonized subjects of the 'global South', were not who they had in mind: these groups seem not to have met Foucault's criteria for their conditions to be recognized, and were consigned to silence.[55]

Foucault's own silence can be interpreted as a neo-colonial privilege. But can anything be gained from it? Might silence not also be interpreted as a conscientious form of behaviour? This possibility should at least be considered. Without falling too deeply into biographical speculation, one can assume that Foucault – like Barthes – was well aware of some of the pitfalls of Western Orientalism. In *The History of Madness* he had already addressed the fateful historical demarcation between the 'Orient' and the 'Occident' and thus provided building blocks for a theory of Orientalism in Said's sense: 'The Orient is for the Occident everything that it is not, while remaining the place in which its primitive truth must be sought.'[56] Foucault also knew that in Tunisia he was joining a long tradition of Europeans who travelled primarily to North Africa to take advantage of the free availability of Arab men; and even then it could not have escaped him that sexual, overly gushing statements made by Europeans about a foreign country only further cemented the stereotypical images of the Orient. There were therefore enough good reasons for Foucault to refrain from further entanglements during his stay in Tunisia and beyond, and above all not to comment on them publicly. Compromising himself in the manner of French travellers to the Orient – such as André Gide, Julien Gracq, and even Roland Barthes – by recording for posterity his sexual adventures, intellectual limit experiences, and political views on North Africa never seemed to have been an option for Foucault (even if he did read Gide and Gracq in Sidi Bou Said, on Barthes's recommendation). In this light, Foucault's silence appears perhaps more a virtue than a vice.

This reticence should not, however, be confused with a practice of resistance. Compared to other philosophers' handling of their own postcolonial situations, Foucault does not exactly cover himself in glory. We should remember: Pierre Bourdieu, who maintained his ties with Algeria and its people even after the war, and incorporated his experiences and the observations he made there into his scholarly and political work; Étienne Balibar, who set off for Algiers after Algerian independence to take part in the country's revolutionary and academic reconstruction; and finally and above all Roland Barthes, who, like Foucault, primarily sought pleasure and inspiration in North Africa, but did not lack anti-colonial commitment and offered an articulate set of reflections on his own position. Despite all the similarities between the two friends, this is the biggest difference in their respective Orientalist settings: Barthes did not remain silent or stick to enjoying himself in secret. In fairness, however, it must also be said that the boundaries between anti-colonial commitments and colonial entanglements are never clearly marked in Bourdieu, Balibar, or Barthes – just as it is usually only nuances that decide whether a position is morally justifiable. In this forcefield, a proper place must also be reserved for Foucault's Tunisian episode.

The Frankfurt School headed by Theodor W. Adorno and Max Horkheimer is sometimes said to have taken up residence in the 'Grand Hotel Abyss' – an acerbic remark made by the Marxist philosopher György Lukács, who accused the Frankfurters of having settled too comfortably into the upper-bourgeois world of yesterday in making their critical observations of social conditions and catastrophes, instead of leading an activist life.[57] You can think what you want of the accusation, but the image of them viewing the abyss from a safe distance is an apt way of describing the fundamental tension intellectuals face between the insights of theory and the realities of life, between the privilege of distanced thinking and the oppressed humanity on whose behalf they think. A similar image could be chosen to represent Foucault and many others among the French intelligentsia with their colonial dilemmas between insight and reality. If Adorno and Horkheimer lived in the 'Grand Hotel Abyss', Foucault and Barthes resided, along with their fellow holidaymakers, in the Club Méditerranée.

JACQUES
DERRIDA

5

IDENTITY AND ITS DISCONTENTS
Jacques Derrida

Anyone who goes in search of colonial traces in Jacques Derrida's life and work will quickly find several. The philosopher, born in 1930 in El Biar, a suburb of Algiers, laid out these traces himself towards the end of his life – initially with some hesitation, and hidden in a few texts, then explicitly and all the more forcefully in the documentary *Derrida's Elsewhere* (1999).[1] The Egyptian filmmaker Safaa Fathy accompanies Derrida to a wide variety of places, including Algeria (though the sites are not always clearly identified). Immediately after the opening scene, which shows Derrida in the middle of a dry savannah landscape, we see him climbing the slope of an imposing cliff, holding his sun-tanned face up to the camera and then looking out over the open sea. As we watch the seagulls flying over the water, Derrida talks about his writing: 'I once said in a very specific context that my writing was the search for an identity. But I was actually more interested in what makes an identity impossible, that is, the loss, the lack of an identity.'[2]

What this identity could mean, among other things, becomes clear in the following sequence, where Derrida strolls through the elegant rooms of the Palais de la Porte Dorée in Paris. In the middle of this former French colonial museum, as he walks past African sculptures, he feels that this is a reminder that he himself is something of a colonial product: 'No matter what I say or what happens to me, I am part of a certain history of the French colonies. In a certain way, everything I do, write and try to think has a certain affinity with postcolonialism.'[3]

These sentences seem like a great invitation to delve into the philosopher's work and explore the alleged affinity of his thinking with colonial and postcolonial conditions. But at the same time they are also very surprising. Before these films were shot, Derrida had hardly ever spoken in public about his Algerian origins or the colonial background of his upbringing, let alone of his thinking. The most astonishing thing is that not a single one of his many books from the main phase of his work between 1966 and 1989, including the major works *Of Grammatology, Writing and Difference* and *Speech and Phenomena,* contains even the slightest allusion to Algeria or colonialism. Even when Derrida later spoke about these connections, he was still proud to claim that one could never recognize from any of his past works that he was French-Algerian.[4] When it came to revealing personal details, resistance from Derrida was to be expected. (For a long time he stuck to the line of his favourite philosopher, Heidegger, who in a lecture on Aristotle restricted his remarks about the latter's life to the fact that Aristotle was born, lived, and died.) His own biography and his Algerian origins were a self-imposed taboo.

It was only towards the end of the 1980s that Derrida began to make individual fragments of his own life story public. The biographical turn produced two of his best-known and most beautiful texts: 'Circumfession' and *Monolingualism of the Other*. The first text is a quasi-autobiography written between January 1989 and April 1990 and divided into fifty-nine short sections (corresponding to the years of his life), which Derrida wrote as a kind of written wake for his dying mother. At the same time, it is an attempt, inspired by Augustine, to deal with his own circumcision in the style of a confession, and in doing so to evoke memories of early childhood in Algeria. In *Monolingualism of the Other,* against the background of his experiences as a member of the Jewish-French-Maghreb minority in Algeria, Derrida poses the question of native language identity in all its radicalness: his discussion is so virtuosic that debates such as those about multiculturalism, national identity, citizenship, and Francophonie are deconstructed too. This very personal text – first given as a lecture in the United States in 1992, and published in 1996

– is a mixture of memoir, dialogue, stories, theories, and political statements. 'Circumfession' and *Monolingualism of the Other* are certainly not autobiographies in the classic sense. But they nonetheless marked a phase that lasted until Derrida's death, in which the philosopher often, readily, and sometimes somewhat obsessively spoke and wrote about himself.

Since the publication of these two books, numerous Derrida interpreters have been hard at work explaining the biographical turn that appears in the texts and reconciling it with the common image of the subject-critical philosopher. Derrida is, after all, considered a thinker of a larger French theoretical current that thought very little of such biographical writing and, in a gesture of theoretical anti-humanism, proclaimed the death of the author or of the subject. Hadn't Derrida, the inventor of deconstruction, just set out to destroy all those categories and logics associated with a sovereign subject, such as identity, meaning, language, reason, descendance, and origin? Why did Derrida suddenly speak so freely and extensively about himself in the first person, about his origins and life story as a Jewish French-Algerian man, about his early impressions and traumas in colonial Algeria? To answer this, various reasons have been put forward, as varied as they are plausible: they all refer to the historical context of the early 1990s. In addition to the suggestion, or rather assumption, that the death of Derrida's mother triggered autobiographical reflexes and emotional upwellings of memory in the now almost sixty-year-old man, there are larger historical explanations: Derrida's involvement with Algeria occurred at a time when – for the first time in France and about thirty years after the war itself – a gradual public remembrance and reappraisal of the Algerian War, the atrocities committed there, and the colonial past as a whole got underway, albeit only hesitantly and in a rudimentary form. At the same time, Algeria was sinking into a bloody civil war that gave rise to Islamist terror and repressive state countermeasures. This conflict, which was closely followed in France, also triggered emotional reactions in Derrida. Algeria would not be a peaceful place of return for him in the near future.

Finally, a theoretical background must be mentioned, which is more related to Derrida's role as a globally celebrated star intellectual and the rise of postcolonial theory in the universities of the English-speaking world. In the ranks of the French poststructuralists, Derrida, with his philosophy of deconstruction, stood like no other for the fundamental questioning of the metaphysical certainties of a Western, hegemonic reason. In this way, Derrida not only represented the core concerns of the entire French theoretical movement, but was also considered a key inspiration for work in the field of postcolonial theory, which, in the spirit of deconstruction, scrutinized the canonical texts of European cultural and scientific history for moments of epistemic violence and for implicit hierarchies. But it was precisely on the side of postcolonialism that voices were more frequently raised in the 1990s, asking Derrida exactly how he stood on the controversial questions of coloniality and postcoloniality. The fact that Derrida now explicitly placed his own life's work in close relation to postcoloniality, and in doing so illuminated his origins in colonial Algeria, must therefore also be interpreted as a belated attempt to provide an answer to the pressing questions of postcolonialism, or to satisfy its critical faction.

One particular aspect is completely overlooked in these attempts at explanation: Derrida's decades-long silence. Why did he say nothing for so long? What had prevented him from speaking and writing about 'his' Algeria? These questions are more difficult to answer because, in discussing them, we are groping in the darkness of the unsaid and running the risk of psychologizing the silence. In order to understand this silence, we need to take a closer look at the early biographical material from the 1940s to the early 1960s; with a few exceptions, this has been criminally neglected so far: in Derrida research, the focus is on the period after 1966.[5] Here, with Derrida's experiences of racism, antisemitism, and colonialism, as well as his experiences during the Algerian War, there are plenty of clues that shed light on the reasons for his silence and also on the roots of his thinking.

The earthquake

The issue of identity, as so often, arises with the proper name. Derrida's real name was not Jacques. The philosopher adopted this perhaps most classic of all French first names only in the early 1960s in Paris, when, at the age of thirty, he was about to give his first publications an author's name. Derrida was born Jackie, named after the American child star Jackie Coogan from the Charlie Chaplin film *The Kid*, which his film-loving parents had seen in one of the many cinemas in Algiers. When he was circumcised, he was also given the Jewish first name Élie, which was never officially registered and was dropped when he finally changed his name in 1962. This short history of the name alone allows us to identify two major themes in Derrida's life: the adaptation of a young man born in Algeria to a bourgeois French national culture and, associated with this, the fading and often the concealment of his Jewish-Algerian identity.[6]

Derrida's ancestors were Sephardic Jews from Spain who had emigrated to North Africa during the Inquisition, i.e. long before the French colonization of Algeria in 1830. Derrida grew up in an assimilated Jewish family in which Ladino, Hebrew, and Arabic were no longer spoken as in previous generations, but only French. In *Monolingualism of the Other* he later wrote: 'I only have one language; it is not mine.'[7] Religion also no longer played a central role in the Derridas' everyday lives. This had a lot to do with the Crémieux Decree of 1870: this law suddenly turned the approximately 35,000 Algerian Jews of the time into French citizens and ensured their comparatively rapid transformation and assimilation into French culture. Citizenship gave the Algerian Jews legal equality with the European settler population, freeing them from the discriminatory status of 'indigenous' that continued to apply to the Algerian Muslim population. Despite their integration into the Republic, however, the Algerian Jews had only half secured their place in Algeria's colonial society. The situation remained complicated: they continued to be confronted, sometimes more than ever, with the antisemitism of the French Algerians. In Algeria, especially after the Dreyfus affair of 1897, there were violent antisemitic pogroms. Added to this was the mistrust they met with from the disadvantaged Arab-Muslim population. The Jews of Algeria belonged neither entirely to the French colonial class nor to the group of oppressed colonized subjects, and thus did not fit into the prevailing two-part social grid of colonizers and colonized. Anyone who grew up as a Jew in Algerian society in the 1930s, like Derrida, found themselves in an extremely explosive social position: not only hemmed in by two forms of group-based hatred, but also constantly in danger of being caught between the opposing forces in an explosive colonial situation for which they themselves were not responsible.[8]

The decisive experience in Derrida's youth, which caused what he himself described as a 'disorder of identity [trouble d'identité]' and left a deep wound that never really healed, was the 'earthquake' of 1940.[9] This was how Derrida described the sudden revocation of French citizenship for the Jews of Algeria by the fascist Vichy regime. The perfidious thing about the revocation of the Crémieux Decree – after only sixty years – was that the Pétain state, which collaborated with the Nazis during the Second World War, decided on this measure without any prompting from the Germans, but rather at the instigation of antisemitic French-Algerian inhabitants. In contrast to the French motherland, Algeria was never occupied by the Germans and did not see a single German soldier during the war. For young Jackie, the withdrawal of citizenship meant exclusion as a Frenchman and statelessness for around two years. In addition, state-supported antisemitism spread in the classrooms of Algeria, making slogans such as 'French culture is not made for little Jews' socially acceptable.[10] Due to a strict quota for Jewish students, Derrida was expelled from the Lycée Ben Aknoun on the first day of school in 1942 and sent home – a shocking moment in his life.

But that was by no means the end of the 'earthquake': Derrida could not really come to terms with the Jewish replacement school set up by the Jewish teachers who had already been removed from their public positions in 1940. He experienced the sudden throwback to Jewishness – to a collective, homogeneous Jewish identity and community which he had not previously known in this form or with this intensity – as a reflexive 'herd identification', as he expressed it in retrospect.[11] This fits with Derrida's memory that he first heard the word 'Jew' in the French school in the early 1940s, initially as an insult from French schoolmates, and later also as a self-designation. In any case, he found the atmosphere at the Jewish school difficult to endure and secretly played truant for a whole year. The twelve-year-old skipped school, but in doing so he also in some ways skipped being Jewish.[12]

Derrida was thus confronted with a double identity problem: on the one hand, the loss of French identity and exclusion from its cultural community, and on the other, the reluctance to accept an alternative constructed identity imposed from outside. He experienced both the traumatic wound of antisemitism and the fundamental aversion of a wounded person to collective identities and affiliations. The two are not the same thing; but both experiences taken together resulted in a deep-rooted dissatisfaction, a discontent that made Derrida unsuited to the experience of community for his entire life. From then on, he remained unable to enjoy any form of belonging: 'Whenever a belonging hems me in, ... someone or something shouts "Be careful, a trap, you're caught! Run! Free yourself!"'[13]

In the course of his life Derrida referred several times to the 'earthquake' of his youth and his resulting allergic sensitivity to belonging – above all in the autobiographical texts we have already mentioned, 'Circumfession' and *Monolingualism of the Other*. The experiences of the early 1940s mark the breaking points of a damaged life. But for Derrida they seem to have been more than just an early biographical experience: they also point to his later and immensely productive philosophical preoccupation with the major category of 'identity', or rather with the question of how, in the face of the loss and impossibility of identity, certain elements of the self and the I can still be thought of, or thought of differently. Thus, one of the central turning points in Derrida's philosophical work is his attempt to think something like heterogeneity or an 'other' at the heart of the self and the subject, i.e. difference in identity. In view of this, it is advisable to take a closer look at this philosophical project and ask what broader lines should be drawn between a person's biographical experience and their philosophical work.

For some observers and interpreters of Derrida's oeuvre, his experiences at the French and Jewish schools represent the 'primal scene' of his entire philosophical thinking of deconstruction.[14] This is the direction taken, for example, by Geoffrey Bennington, who interprets the 1942 causality in his portrait of the philosopher – written together with Derrida – in the following way: 'I think that J.D.'s entire work is afflicted by this discontent with belonging, one could almost say with identification – and the deconstruction of the authentic seems to me to be the thinking of this discontent itself, a thinking discontent.'[15] One must be cautious with such interpretations, which suggest a causality between biography and theory without further explanation – especially if Derrida, who is the subject here, is directly involved in the interpretation of his life and work, and one has only to nod in agreement. The matter becomes even more complicated when we realize that the talk of the primal scene is a rhetorical figure of origin that Derrida actually took great pains to dismantle in his work. In this respect, the principles established by Derrida himself are being stretched to the limit.

Nevertheless, Bennington makes an important point that cannot be dismissed out of hand, but does require an explanation. This might run as follows: Derrida's discontent with belonging expresses an attitude that is initially presented as a philosophical maxim of life, but at its core already bears the hallmarks of deconstruction. Nothing in the world is self-evident and stable, not even the self, and certainly not group and language affiliations. It is therefore better to question these categories before one is constantly and fatally 'described' by them, as happened in the case of Derrida.

From here, however, it is actually not a big step to the great and admittedly always somewhat nebulous project of deconstruction, which in the narrower philosophical sense is nothing other than a practice of thinking and reading that incessantly questions the apparently self-evident, the supposedly natural, the self and the other.[16] In a broader sense, deconstruction also represents a process that primarily works on canonical texts and ultimately attempts to undermine language itself. If we ignore this for now and stay on the philosophical level, it becomes clear that Derrida, with the deconstruction of self and other, is also questioning other binary juxtapositions of Western metaphysics: the opposition of truth and myth, of centre and periphery, of majority and minority, of life and death. He subjects all these hegemonic, meaning- and identity-creating orders of Western culture to the principle of difference. Derrida is a thinker of differences.

In this reading, deconstruction becomes a form of cultural and intellectual decolonization of philosophy. It opens up other spaces for thought, redefines relationships, and reflects the conditions of one's own meditations. This perhaps also explains why Bennington, in line with Derrida, uses the figure of the primal scene, despite Derrida's claim to be taking tradition apart. In this sense, straining one's own principles is an elementary component of the deconstructive procedure, which in this case aims to proceed with and against the idea of origin in such a way that, at the provisional – but never conclusive – end of the thought process, the 'prostheses of origin' at least will become visible. Significantly, the full title of Derrida's book is *Monolingualism of the Other; or, the Prosthesis of Origin.*

What can we draw from this Jewish-Algerian genealogy of Derrida's deconstruction? Perhaps we do not have to go so far as to claim that, before becoming the inventor of deconstruction and a thinker of differences, Derrida was himself 'deconstructed' in the 1940s; that 'he lived *différance* long before the concept'; or that his early experiences were indispensable for the delayed development of an entire theoretical edifice.[17] Who knows whether or not deconstruction would have come about even without the 'earthquake' of 1940? The Algerian genealogy does not explain everything. But it does make it clear how strongly Derrida's life and work were influenced by this reference to an 'other', by the name of Algeria, and that the personal experience of the demand for identity and the philosophical production of difference are by no means mutually exclusive, but rather overlap. In the best case, this genealogy brings human experience so close to the theoretical domain that one can better understand both.

Fault lines

The Jewish-French fault line was not the only ordeal in Derrida's Algerian youth. After he returned to the Algiers lycée in 1943 (in the meantime the Allies had landed in Algeria with Charles de Gaulle in tow), other, completely different fault lines became apparent, which were to become no less important for him. In *Monolingualism of the Other*, Derrida named two further divisions that determined the 'community' of the French Algerians and thus explicitly also his own identity formation – almost always 'disintegrating', 'dissociative', or 'neurotic' divisions, as Derrida never tired of emphasizing, in the vocabulary of psychology.[18] One dividing line ran between French Algerians and Algerians, the other between the French Algerians of the colony and the French of the mainland. Both lines were not simply given, but were ethnically and culturally codified. In Derrida's world, they were experienced primarily as a 'school matter' – not a measure or a decision, but rather a pedagogical arrangement that was conveyed in and through language.[19]

The first experience concerned the almost complete absence of Algerian students. While there were still a moderate number of Algerians in primary school, very few of them went on to the lycée. In a certain way, the slogan from the Vichy years quoted above, 'French culture is not made for little Jews', could also be extended to the context of Algerian children: French culture was clearly not 'made for little Arabs' either. This form of discrimination was reflected in the status of Arabic, which was treated like a foreign language in school – not to mention Berber. Given that there were around seven million Arabic-speaking people in Algeria at the time, this was tantamount to a cultural ban.

The situation in schools was only an apparent contrast to everyday life. For Derrida as a child, Arabic was not a distant foreign language; it was more of a 'neighbours' language', because he and his family lived on the edge of an Arab neighbourhood and probably heard it spoken often enough in everyday life.[20] But even this geographical proximity did not mean much. There were subtle and less subtle boundaries that separated Derrida from the Arab neighbours' children and their language. For example, the father's job – he was a wine merchant – probably did not bring the Derridas into much contact with Muslim families. And at night, the borders between the European and Arab quarters, which were perfectly passable during the day, became almost insurmountable thresholds of segregation.

Frantz Fanon vividly described the socio-geographical and urban shape of the colonial world in the first pages of *The Wretched of the Earth*. For him, it was a world divided into compartments, into two parts consisting of separate zones for colonial rulers and the colonized: on the one side, the new European housing developments made of stone and iron, with asphalted and illuminated streets; on the other, the medinas and kasbahs with a bad reputation, the starving slums into which, according to Fanon, one was born 'somehow' and in which one ultimately dies of 'something'.[21] The dividing line was often marked by barracks and police stations. The young Derrida was one of those who experienced this border at first hand. But at least he was able to do so from the more comfortable side of the border.

The marginalization of the non-French languages spoken in Algeria – the process by which Arabic and Berber became weakened, suppressed, and thus the most foreign languages of all – went hand in hand with a revaluation of French. Colonial policy aimed at a French Algeria in which the Algerian population was cut off from its own languages and cultures. Derrida found clear words for this policy, which exercised colonial power without the use of physical force:

> All culture is originally colonial ... Every culture institutes itself through the unilateral imposition of some 'politics' of language. Mastery begins, as we know, through the power of naming, of imposing and legitimating appellations ... [T]he monolingualism of the other would be that sovereignty, that law originating from elsewhere, certainly, but also primarily the very language of the Law. And the Law as Language ... The monolingualism imposed by the other operates by relying upon that foundation, here, through a sovereignty whose essence is always colonial, which tends, repressibly and irrepressibly, to reduce language to the One, that is, to the hegemony of the homogeneous.[22]

The hegemonic law of a homogeneous French culture and language coming from 'somewhere else' also applied to the French Algerians – the fault line between settler colony and metropolis. Compared to the fate of the colonized Algerian population, this fault line had a clearly graduated impact, but one must not forget that the French Algerians also found themselves in a special situation in relation to the 'mother country' on the other side of the Mediterranean. Despite official declarations of mutual affiliation, the so-called *pieds-noirs* were in a socially and culturally asymmetrical relationship. For the French Algerians, too, France represented a centralized and hegemonic reference system that they had to orient themselves by, imposed on them from outside. For Derrida, this fault line was nowhere more clearly evident than at school, where, for example, the history and geography of France were taught in great detail and with great ideological zeal, while 'not a word was said about Algeria, not a single word about its history and geography'. Derrida's description of how he and his schoolmates 'could draw the coastline of Brittany and the mouth of the Garonne with their eyes closed', without ever having seen these regions, is particularly impressive; they had to know, and indeed recite by heart, the capitals of all the French departments, the smallest tributaries of the Seine, the Rhône, the Loire, and the Garonne from their source to their estuary, while the cities and rivers of Algeria remained literally white spots on the map. France (the metropolis, the motherland, the Hexagon, the European mainland, etc.) was the main point of reference and yet at the same time remained a fabulous 'elsewhere' in which one had to immerse oneself – a place that was very far and very close, not really foreign (because one knew so much about it), but rather strange, fantastic, phantom-like, and ghostly. Derrida wondered, indeed, whether one of his 'first and most imposing figures of spectrality, of spectrality itself, was not France; I mean everything that bore that name'.[23]

Immersion in this elsewhere inevitably began with language. In French classes, where pure French was taught and the distinctive Algerian accent was suppressed and drilled out of the students – where, according to Derrida, one could truly enter French literature only by losing one's accent – the whole dissociative process of enculturation was, in a particular way, a burning issue: 'For everyone, French was supposedly a mother tongue, whose source, norms, rules, and laws were located elsewhere.'[24] The only language that young Jackie possessed – or rather, that possessed him – was not his own, but the language of the colonizers.

But French was precisely the language in which he was immersed and that he very quickly learned to love. In an interview Derrida conducted with Jean Birnbaum shortly before his death in 2004, he once again summed up his intimate relationship with the French language, which he had outlined in *Monolingualism of the Other*: 'If I love this language as I love my life – and sometimes even more than this or that native Frenchman loves it – then it is probably because I love it like a foreigner who has been welcomed and who has appropriated this language as the only one possible for him.'[25] In the same interview, it also becomes clear what far-reaching consequences this specific experience of linguistic appropriation had for Derrida's philosophical and literary approach to language and writing:

> And just as I love life – and my life – I also love what has made me who I am and whose element is precisely language, this French language, which is the only language that I was taught to cultivate, and also the only one for which I can consider myself more or less responsible. That is why in my writing there is a – I would not exactly say perverse, but somewhat violent – way of dealing with this language. Out of love. Love in general is about the love of language, which is neither nationalistic nor conservative, but requires proofs (*preuves*). And tests (*épreuves*). You can't do anything you want with language, it exists before us, it survives us ... Leaving traces in the history of the French language, that is what interests me.[26]

Algiers–Paris, and back again

Derrida left Algeria in 1949 in the hope of leaving his unloved life behind. By now he was an enthusiast for philosophy and had come up with the idea of seeking his fortune in Paris – of all places in the elite training ground of the École normale supérieure (ENS), which he had happened to hear about in a broadcast on Radio Alger. It mentioned a training programme that accepted the best philosophy students in the country and promised to prepare them for rapid promotion in a career in higher education.[27] The unwritten – and perhaps all the more powerful – law of the French intellectual world, which has been in force for centuries and summons people from the provinces to the metropolis, also applied to the young Derrida. However, in this case there was a – one might say 'colonial' – peculiarity, because between the Algerian province and the French capital lay the Mediterranean Sea, for Derrida 'symbolically an infinite space for all the students of the French school in Algeria.' On his way to boarding school in Paris, Derrida crossed this 'abyss' for the first time at the age of nineteen, sailing on the ship the *Ville d'Alger*. The crossing from Algiers to Marseilles took a whole day. It is an irony of history that Derrida – the sensitive future theorist of border crossings – suffered from seasickness and vomiting for twenty-four hours on his first trip to the so-called motherland, in 'the first translation of my life.'[28]

In Paris, he attended the philosophy preparatory classes at the Lycée Louis-le-Grand for three years, and after three attempts was finally, in

1952, admitted to the ENS (an institution that would host him, with a few interruptions, for a total of thirty years, first as a student and then as a teacher). For Derrida this was an extremely stimulating time intellectually, with personal mentors such as Louis Althusser and Michel Foucault, but also a difficult phase of depression and breakdown.[29] However, his malaise contained a good deal of deconstructive spirit early on, as can be seen in a letter he wrote to an old school friend: 'I am good for nothing but taking the world apart and putting it back together again (but I am less and less successful at the latter).'[30] If you are less and less successful at putting it back together, you have to fall back on taking it apart.

During his studies, Derrida preferred to largely ignore Algeria. He returned there only for the long summer holidays to pay the obligatory visits to his family. He usually made the arduous journey to Algeria by ship, but sometimes also by small transport plane, in which he had to sit uncomfortably on a bench between vegetable crates as a half-stowaway passenger.[31] During his visits, Derrida became more and more convinced that the Algerian environment prevented him from working, despite or precisely because of its beauty. In this respect, he evidently agreed with his French-Algerian contemporary Camus and his *bon mot* about Algeria in *Nuptials*: 'In one sense, but only in one sense, life here is too good for anyone to think of reading, perhaps even too good for anyone to think.'[32]

Algerian reality quickly caught up with him again when the War of Independence broke out in 1954 and the Algerian question became a daily political issue in Paris too. The vast majority of students at the ENS were ardent supporters of the French Communist Party and, as such, were fundamentally anti-colonial. Derrida was also against the French state's policy of colonial oppression, but he wanted nothing to do with the dogmatism of the would-be Stalinists at the ENS – another reluctance to belong. Instead, together with his closest friends Lucien Bianco and Pierre Bourdieu, he founded a section of the 'Action Committee of Intellectuals for the Defence of Civil Rights' at the ENS, which brought together undogmatic leftists.[33] Overall, however, Derrida did not display excessive political zeal during the Algerian War. Compared to other fellow students who, endowed with an uncanny sense of mission, believed they were on the right side of

Algiers, early 1959. From left to right: Marie-Louise and Lucien Bianco (with their daughter Sylvie), Marguerite Derrida, Pierre Bourdieu, and Jacques Derrida.

history, Derrida's personal hunger for power and desire to make a name for himself were limited. He explained to his friend Bianco: 'If fate gave me the opportunity to play the role of Lenin, I might well refuse.'[34]

Fate had another role in store for Derrida. After finishing his studies in 1957, he was drafted into military service and, at the height of the war, had to go to ... Algeria. Being posted to Algeria was not unusual at the time (Bianco, who was the same age, also did his military service there), but in Derrida's case it had a special twist, because here was someone being forced to return to his homeland. This meant, among other things, that he now had to worry about possibly having to turn his weapon on his former neighbours. After basic training, however, thanks to family connections, Derrida got a job teaching soldiers' children in Koléa, a small town not far from Algiers. His position as a simple soldier in civilian clothes was a lifesaver in the circumstances. It also allowed him to meet regularly with Bourdieu in Algiers, where the latter had taken a job at the university after his military service. It was nevertheless a time of privation for Derrida and his wife Marguerite. At night, the war could not be ignored, and at other times, too, they could hardly close their eyes to the violence and horror. One evening they both witnessed how French soldiers, after executing a leader of the FLN, tied a rope around his neck, dragged him to the Kasbah in a jeep and then left the body in front of a mosque because they thought that this would intimidate the Algerians.[35] The Derridas lived in isolation for two years in a military milieu that, with its hatred of the rebellious Algerians, became increasingly open to the ultra-right and fascist tendencies rampant in the army. In the barracks of Koléa, the Derridas experienced at first hand the coup of 13 May 1958, carried out by French military forces in Algiers: it plunged the whole of France into a serious crisis, enabled the return of de Gaulle, and resulted in the end of the Fourth Republic. For Derrida as a soldier it was practically impossible to express himself openly and critically. Only in secret could he utter his favourite slogan at the time, 'Fascism will not win.'[36]

The breaking point: 1961–62

Where Derrida stood on the Algerian question was clearly shown in his argument with Pierre Nora, his former classmate at the Lycée Louis-le-Grand, who would later become one of France's most important historians and publishers. The reason for the dispute was Nora's book *Les Français d'Algérie* (*The French of Algeria*) published in March 1961. In it, Nora, who had previously worked for two years as a lycée teacher in Oran, Algeria, sharply criticized the French Algerians, holding them to be largely to blame for the bloody war. The target of his polemic was less the French-Algerian ultras than the voices he denigrated as liberal, such as the ethnologist Germaine Tillion and the recently deceased Albert Camus, both of whom had advocated a French-Muslim coexistence among equals. In Nora's eyes, however, their plea for reconciliation supported the continuation of colonial rule. For his part, Nora advocated an immediate decoupling of Algeria without regard for the European settler population, for whom he did not have much affection. For example, he denied the French Algerians any French affiliation, and made fun of their accent. Derrida thereupon wrote his former classmate a nineteen-page letter. Although he agreed with Nora that independence was now inevitable, he found Nora's condescending tone towards the French Algerians out of place. Derrida felt that he was being attacked as one of them and reacted aggressively. He saw Nora's accusations as absolving the real 'masters' of Algeria of any responsibility – that is, 'all governments and the whole army (in other words the whole French people in whose name they act).'[37] He was particularly outraged by Nora's distorted image of the 'liberal' French Algerians, among whom he certainly included himself without saying so explicitly. Derrida was against both the colonialist partisans of a French Algeria and the terror and future autocracy of the FLN. Instead, he sympathized – here agreeing with the conciliatory positions of Tillion and Camus, which he vehemently defended in the letter – with a third way that would give greater consideration to all the different ethnic groups in the population. Derrida, like Camus, wanted a 'French-Muslim Algeria,' although nowhere in the letter to Nora is it clear what this Algeria independent of France would look like.[38] Should the French Algerians give up any of their privileges? What might a compromise have looked like? What could the Algerians have hoped to gain from such a solution? There was not a word about this, or about the concerns of the Algerians in general, in Derrida's long letter.

Nora, who as a political journalist was already very keen to spark debates, suggested to Derrida that the discussion that arose from the correspondence should be published. But Derrida politely declined: 'there is no question – for reasons too many to mention – of writing an article.'[39] One of these reasons was certainly concern for his relatives in Algeria. Derrida knew what happened to people in the public eye who refused to completely dissociate themselves from Algeria. The fate of Camus in 1957 was still fresh in his memory. In contrast to most other left-wing intellectuals in France, who supported the Algerian struggle for independence, Camus had increasingly avoided taking a clear side during the war. As we have seen, Camus's silence, and his later claim that he would defend his own mother rather than side with terrorism, aroused considerable resentment.[40] Derrida therefore knew exactly what he stood to lose if he publicly expressed his position on the Algerian question. The most he could have agreed to was publishing the long letter anonymously (signed 'a friend from Algiers'), but nothing came of this idea.[41] In another letter to his old school friend, which Derrida sent a few weeks later in August 1961 from El-Biar, where he spent his last Algerian summer, he again referred to his difficult relationship with Algeria:

> I'm having a strange holiday here: between a bit of work ... and the pleasures of the sea, the day is taken up, in the midst of this strange society, brooding over unthinkable problems. And I realize that I love this country more and more, love it madly, which does not contradict the aversion I have long stated for it.[42]

These sentences express a movement that was as existential as it is dramatic: where the loss of an initially rejected homeland loomed, an intense affection for it rose up. A bittersweet realization.

Derrida's private statements on the Algerian question came to light only in the early 2010s, when Pierre Nora included Derrida's letter in a new edition of his book on the French Algerians, and Benoît Peeters dealt in detail with the subsequent correspondence between the two in his biography of Derrida. The posthumous publication of the letters revealed a previously unknown image of Derrida, one which disappointed many of his postcolonial admirers and surprised his no less numerous conservative critics. A Derrida who had an affection for French Algeria did not quite fit the usual image of the postmodern deconstructionist with a sympathy for postcolonialism. From today's perspective, one can view the matter more dispassionately, thanks in part to having a better overview of his entire oeuvre. There are certainly lines of continuity between Derrida's experiences during the Algerian War and the later political-philosophical writings of the 1990s in which he formulated the moral sensibility of his political thought: the attention to nuances; the refusal to choose sides; the philosophy of the in-between; the occasional utopianism. These are all characteristics and attitudes that Derrida displayed in his discussion of the Israel–Palestine question as well as in dealing with the past of the apartheid regime in South Africa. Wherever he showed a concern with developing a policy of forgiveness, the Algerian trauma continued to have an impact.[43]

Derrida's worries were by no means unfounded. During his stay in Algeria in the summer of 1961, he had an inkling of what might be in store for his family. Long before Algeria gained independence in July 1962, there was already a palpable tension among the French Algerians. Unaffected by the official statements of the French government, which spoke right up to the end of its unconditional commitment to Algeria while secretly conducting negotiations on independence with the FLN, the pressure on the Derrida family, as on many others, to leave the country while there was still time increased. When major riots and acts of violence against the French-Algerian population broke out in the spring of 1962 (during those bloody weeks, one of Derrida's neighbours had his throat cut in the street), Derrida's family decided to give up their house in El-Biar, leave their homeland, and flee to France.

In many ways, 1962 marked a profound turning point in Derrida's intellectual biography. After his experiences of racism and antisemitism during his school days, this time it was more the 'Algerian' wounds that would shape him. With the end of the Algerian War and the country's subsequent independence, the Algeria of Derrida's childhood and youth ceased to exist. The country seemed lost to him – he returned to his country of birth only twice after that. From then on, he associated 1962 with the end of a phase of his life, not without a sense of pathos: 'My adolescence lasted until I was 32.'[44] At the same time, 1962 represented a new beginning: it was the year his academic career took off, and the year he published his first book, a long commentary on Husserl's *Origin of Geometry*. The fact that the manuscript was finished in July 1961 on paper from the University of Algiers with the letterhead 'Faculté des Lettres, histoire de la colonisation' is a plot twist that no novelist could have thought up.[45] His beginnings as a philosophical author went hand in hand with his change of name to Jacques. Last but not least, it was during this time that Derrida's personal 'independence from Algeria' began, which he later called *nostalgérie* – a brilliantly enigmatic expression that would enable him to dream longingly of the lost country without having to explicitly address it (even though it would repeatedly haunt him).[46] Algeria thus acquired a hidden place in his memory, one that could be equated neither with nostalgia nor with an actual desire to return. For Derrida, *nostalgérie* even fulfilled an opposite need: not to speak under any circumstances about his Algerian origins, his personal experiences there, or other political matters connected with Algeria. All of this disappeared under a cloak of silence, for decades.

Much later, in the early 1990s, this freedom to speak became possible. There are at least as many stories to tell about how Derrida overcame his Algerian obstacle as there are about his silence. But sometimes a single scene is enough to illustrate this regained ease of speaking. It comes from the film *Derrida's Elsewhere*, mentioned at the beginning of this chapter. Here you can watch Derrida driving his car through the university district of Paris and sharing memories and remarks about the various places he had worked. In one scene he turns into the Rue d'Ulm, where the École normale supérieure is located. Meanwhile, from the radio cassette in his car, we can hear Lili Labassi, an Algerian singer and violinist with Jewish roots who was a kind of mid-twentieth-century Algerian Django Reinhardt and whose music showed a mix of Arab-Andalusian influences. Derrida reacts to the scene with just one lapidary sentence: 'The Rue d'Ulm with a soundtrack by Lili Labassi isn't bad, is it?!' It's a sentence that seeks to emphasize the connection between two cultural codes that at first glance do not immediately fit together: on the one hand, the venerable centre of French academic high culture, on the other, the Arabic sounds of a Jewish musician. But this sentence also seems to express Derrida's own life path: he has made it to the top in the intellectual field and, at the same time, is returning to his Algerian origins, to music, and to what fills him with a productive nostalgia. This interpretation, like so much in the film and in Derrida, can be seen as the convenient self-fashioning of an established intellectual, as a playful staging of the harmony of Algerian authenticity and European philosophy. But then, if only as a counter-move, it is permissible to ask which other French intellectuals could have played this game at all? It is important to remember Derrida as an Algerian thinker.

HÉLÈNE CIXOUS

6

INFERNAL PARADISE
Hélène Cixous

When it comes to the life and work of the writer and philosopher Hélène Cixous, superlatives are readily available: Grande Dame of poststructuralism, icon of feminism, initiator of feminine writing, glamorous intellectual, and 'last survivor' of the great generation of theorists from France.[1] Born in Algeria in 1937, Cixous has produced such a comprehensive and diverse body of work that it is difficult to describe it with just one label. She is considered one of the leading theoreticians of feminism and deconstruction; she is the in-house dramaturge at Ariane Mnouchkine's Théâtre du Soleil; and she co-founded the legendary University of Vincennes, where she was a professor for more than thirty years. An English specialist by training, she played a key role in the triumph of French Theory at American universities, where she also held visiting professorships. Then there is her literary and essayistic work: after her debut in 1967, around seventy books followed, many of which have won awards and been translated into several languages. In the last twenty years alone, thirty-six books have been published by her French publisher Galilée – an average of almost two books per year.

Cixous rose to worldwide fame in 1975 with her feminist manifesto 'The Laugh of the Medusa.' This key work of feminist theory is still by far her most famous text: a forty-page performance overflowing with vigour and irony, a polemic against patriarchy and at the same time an unprecedented call for female writing of a form for which

Cixous invented the term *écriture féminine*. Its first lines have already achieved legendary status: 'It is essential that women write themselves: that women write from the perspective of women and make women write, creating a writing from which they have been kept away by force, just as they were kept away from their bodies.' On the same page: 'I write this as a woman to women. When I say "the woman," I am talking about women in their inevitable struggle with the classic man; and of a woman who is a universal subject and who should help women to find their meaning and their history.' And then one page later, the ultimate empowerment: 'Write! Writing is for you, you are for you, your body is yours, take it ... Write, no one should stop you, nothing should stop you.'[2]

When it was published, 'The Laugh of the Medusa' shook up the French feminist scene. For some, the call to anchor female self-confidence in writing seemed like the next avant-garde step within the women's movement; for others, this very connection between femininity and literature seemed like a step back into a time from which they needed to emerge. As a contribution to the feminist debate, the text was undoubtedly a provocation, even in 1975.[3] Many critics saw in Cixous's manifesto an idealization and romanticization of the female body, which led to an essentialism of the feminine. Her unconventional, meandering writing was also a bone of contention: all the wordplay meant there was a lack of any concrete political perspective or advice on how to improve women's living conditions. Even today, 'The Laugh of the Medusa' provokes mixed reactions – a sign that the text has lost none of its appeal, despite its historical distance from us. Medusa's call to pursue writing seems to have a timeless validity, even if feminist discourse has since changed in a variety of ways.

In Germany, Cixous is not well known outside of feminist and poststructuralist circles.[4] For a long time, 'The Laugh of the Medusa' could be read only in French and English, perhaps due to translation difficulties; but it is still surprising when you consider that, in the same period, most of the other central and equally difficult texts of French Theory were translated into German relatively quickly. More recently, Cixous's work has been slowly discovered in German-speaking countries, thanks to the Vienna-based Passagen Verlag. She is revealed as an author who has developed her own unmistakable style, mixing autobiography, literature, and theory – a style that she describes as 'autobiografiction': half autobiography, half fiction, and always underpinned by a mix of psychoanalysis, feminism, deconstruction, and poststructuralism. She succeeds in making the transitions between genres so instinctively that sometimes you are not sure whether the result is a poetry of philosophy or a philosophy of poetry – it's probably both.

Algeria plays a prominent role in Cixous's work, and especially in her 'autobiografiction' project. In it, Cixous ceaselessly recounts her childhood in Oran, her family history and Jewish origins, her traumatic experiences of antisemitism and colonial violence, and finally her departure from the country in the 1950s. In order to give her ambivalent relationship with Algeria a language of its own, Cixous has even created a new word: *Algériance,* a portmanteau of the two words *Algérie* and *allégeance* (meaning loyalty or faithfulness). For Cixous, *Algériance,* like Derrida's *nostalgérie,* refers less to a concrete place called 'Algeria' than to an emotional relationship of loyalty and belonging that emerges only in the mode of an ongoing process of memory:

> What I have called 'my Algériance' refers to the electrified high-voltage region caught in a network of contradictions in which I found myself every time I turned to Algeria, standing at the door, neither inside nor outside, and which served me as a stage on which I could preserve the treasures of my childhood.[5]

Unlike with Barthes, Foucault, or Lyotard, one does not have to look far for the colonial roots of Cixous's thinking. Cixous herself has made her Algerian origins a crucial theme in her work. Indeed, origin and identity are the starting point for her endeavour to put her own life into writing. She emphasizes that everything that moves her and preoccupies her, including her writing, can be traced back 'to the gates of Oran.'[6] Her attempt to emphasize her Algerian influence is strongly reminiscent of Derrida: they were bound by their Algerian-Jewish background and their deep friendship. However, there is an important difference: Cixous dealt with her Algerian past earlier, more intensively, and in her own way. It is all the more important, then, to trace her life story and her memories, paying attention both to the connection between biography and theory and to the specific circumstances of her early involvement with Algeria.

The two worlds

It all began in Oran, Cixous's birthplace. The second largest city in Algeria is located on the west coast of the country, close to the Moroccan border. Its individual districts line up along the Mediterranean coast like pearls on a string and are bordered by steep cliffs at both ends. From one of these cliffs, the imposing statue of the Virgin Mary looks down on the city. This landmark, together with the Santa Cruz Cathedral, was built by the French after the end of the devastating cholera epidemic of 1849 – the event that inspired the Algerian writer Albert Camus to write his world-famous novel *The Plague*. In it, Oran is the scene of an epidemic that begins with rats and then strikes the city's inhabitants. Eventually, the city is quarantined, with all the social consequences that this entails – including the courageous acts and grim deeds of which humans are capable. Camus's 1947 classic attracted renewed attention during the Covid-19 pandemic, when it offered readers a way of making sense of events, and perhaps even of finding a footing in literature, and it quickly sold out.[7] If one had to bet which city readers, the majority of whom were locked up within their own four walls during the pandemic, were most likely to get to know or to rediscover, then Oran would come out top.

The city itself comes off rather poorly in the novel – as one might suspect from the subject matter. Camus also had little real-life interest in Oran, where he lived at the beginning of the Second World War and where the first ideas for the novel came to him. The action was originally to have taken place in 1941, but was then dated by Camus to '194X'. He had already painted a brief but bitter portrait of the city in his 1939 essay 'Minotaur'. In half-fascinated, half-repelled tones he describes it thus: 'The streets of Oran are doomed to dust, pebbles, and heat. If it rains, there is a deluge and a sea of mud. But rain or shine, the shops have the same extravagant and absurd look. All the bad taste of Europe and the Orient has managed to converge in them.'[8]

According to Greek legend, the Minotaur was a hybrid creature: half human, half bull, trapped in the Labyrinth. Anyone who reads Camus's text against this background might think that he was intent on describing the contradictions of the city he portrayed. As usual, Camus hardly mentions the Arab population in this multicultural city. He approaches the smaller-scale, everyday variety of life there with biting irony. For example, in the shops of Oran 'one finds, helter-skelter, marble greyhounds, ballerinas with swans, versions of Diana the Huntress in green galalith, discus-throwers and reapers, everything that is used for birthday and wedding gifts, the whole race of painful figurines constantly called forth by a commercial and playful genie on our mantelpieces.'[9]

At the time Camus wrote these lines, there was a shop on the corner of the Place d'Armes, the city's central square, that could also have come straight out of his descriptions. In addition to tobacco products and postcards, it also sold hats and military decorations. This shop belonged to none other than Hélène Cixous's grandfather, Samuel Cixous, and was called 'Les Deux Mondes.' Cixous never found out why her grandfather chose to call it 'The Two Worlds,' but this name has had an enormous fascination for her since childhood, as she has confirmed in numerous texts and interviews.[10] The name evokes many things for Cixous. It triggers speculation about the backstory of her grandfather's decision ('Could the "two worlds" have been Africa and Europe?'), becomes a symbol for her own childhood experiences in Algeria ('In my childhood there were a lot of "two worlds"'), and offers the opportunity to link her own memories with a personal piece of biographical insight: 'All I know is that the world is more than one world. Since I could walk, I have known that the world consists of two worlds. There were two worlds plus two worlds plus two worlds.'[11] Cixous makes

The 'Les Deux Mondes' shop run by Cixous's grandfather on the Place d'Armes in Oran, Algeria.

this idea sound like a little piece of wisdom from Oran, an encomium to diversity, but it contains her entire philosophy of difference – or rather of differences in the plural, as the point here is not the affirmation of a binary world, but the multiplication and displacement of differences, be they of a gendered, ethnic, colonial, linguistic, or religious nature.

In the context of her childhood in Algeria, Cixous's talk of the two worlds is initially based on diverging family histories. She once described the geography of her family memory as follows:

> I stand at the edge of North Africa. On its beach. To my left, that is, to the West, my paternal family – which followed the classic trajectory of the Jews chased from Spain to Morocco. My father's grandparents are from Tetuán or Tangier. They travelled on donkey-back. No doubt following the French army – as peddlers and interpreters – they arrive at the western edge of Algeria: Oran. My native city. A very Spanish city. In my father's family, French and Spanish are spoken.[12]

Cixous also tells a story of assimilation that is typical for the Sephardic Jews of Algeria: from 1870 onwards they had French citizenship; the grandfather admired France and thought that the future of his family and of the Jews as a whole was in good hands there because it offered them the possibility of social advancement. His son Georges, Hélène's father, was the best example: he was not a practising Jew, but an atheist, studying medicine first in Algiers and then in Paris (degrees were awarded only in the capital), in order to return to Algeria and, so he hoped, start a career as a doctor.

In the family geography, Cixous sees not only the 'West' but also a 'North.'[13] It is a different world: the Ashkenazi family on her mother's side comes from Central and Eastern Europe and is scattered across the territories of the German Empire and the Habsburg Monarchy (again, two different worlds). Eve Klein, Hélène's mother, was born in Alsace but grew up in Osnabrück. She left Germany before Hitler came to power, met Georges Cixous in Paris and moved with him to Algeria. In 1938, her grandmother, who had initially stayed in Osnabrück, followed them there with other family members, which was possible only thanks to the fortunate circumstance that Alsatians had the right to French citizenship. Unlike those family members who did not make it out of Europe, they were spared deportation and death in the Nazi concentration camps. Hélène Cixous grew up in Oran in a polyglot family in which, in addition to French, Spanish, and Hebrew, a lot of German was spoken, but in which, in addition to the experience of expulsion, the Holocaust played a major part.

Hélène Cixous wrote about the German part of her family only late in her life. In three compelling books (*Eine deutsche Autobiographie, Osnabrück, Meine Homère ist tot…*) she also allows a kind of Germany to appear in Algeria. For example, she recalls her childhood encounters with Jewish refugees from Germany, Austria, and Hungary who briefly stayed in Algeria in transit to America and elsewhere, looking lost as they sat on the benches in the parks of Oran, speaking German to one another.[14] For her, Germany, embodied by the presence of her grandmother, was 'a mixture of Nazism and family legend' that lived on in Algeria and in the young girl's imaginary world.[15] Cixous expresses this connection in *Eine deutsche Autobiographie*, resorting to a characteristic play on words: 'Every time I'm on the point of saying: Al – Algeria, Germany [Allemagne], my two countries arise. They are so dissimilar so connected, they mingle with and in me and only understand each other through their experiences of suffering and hatred over which love has triumphed.'[16]

Cixous thereby brings together not only the two countries, but also Oran and Osnabrück. For in both cities there rages 'a terrible battle between good and evil', by which Cixous means 'the relationship to the other': 'For me, Oran and Osnabrück were like twins. With different racisms, different types of antisemitism.'[17] Algeria was by no means free of prejudice and resentment. On the contrary, the country was founded on racism. There was colonial racism, the dominant form, directed against the Arab population. There was the racism of the Arabs against the Jews and of the Jews against the Arabs. And last but not least, there was the antisemitism of the French Algerians, which increased under the Vichy regime from 1940 onwards.

Antisemitism is also at the heart of a childhood experience that Cixous had to endure in Oran in the early 1940s. It belongs to the category of 'key events' – Cixous herself even speaks of a 'primal scene'.[18] It took place on the Place d'Armes, i.e. the site where her grandfather's shop stood, and actually consisted of several events from around 1940. At the beginning of the Second World War, Cixous's father was called up as a military doctor in the French army and stationed in Tunisia. With his appointment as an officer came a number of privileges for the family, such as the opportunity for young Hélène to gain entry to the so-called Cercle militaire, an exclusive garden on the Place d'Armes reserved for the officers' relatives. With its extensive grounds, it had long been an object of the child's desires. Once she had won admission, however, it quickly became the scene of antisemitic hostility. She was insulted and spat on as a 'little Jewess.' The paradise garden turned out to be a hell of exclusion. In any case, her visits there soon came to an abrupt end: when the anti-Jewish Vichy laws came into force, her father was prohibited from practising medicine – a result of the ban on Jews from the professions. He was

thrown out of the army, obliged to take down his doctor's practice sign, and forced to do menial podiatry instead. Like all Algerian Jews, the family were stripped of their French citizenship in October 1940, leaving them stateless.

Hélène Cixous has told this story of being thrown out of the Cercle militaire, which she experienced (more or less consciously) as a three-year-old, many times, in very different ways. The story appears in literary and essayistic texts and most recently in a long autobiographical conversation with her German publisher Peter Engelmann in 2017. There, her childhood experience is given a psychoanalytic interpretation: according to Cixous, being thrown out of the Cercle militaire was a 'historically overdetermined primal scene', a 'primal cell of psychic configuration' in which 'everything was connected for me' and 'absolutely everything was contained'.[19] The expression 'overdetermination', which goes back to Sigmund Freud, describes in its simplest form the multiple determination and polysemantic nature of psychic processes. Dreams as well as neurotic symptoms are overdetermined in that they are usually caused and shaped by a plurality of distinguishable (unconscious) wishes and motives. In a somewhat free interpretation of Freudian terminology, Cixous describes her experience in the scene of the Cercle militaire as being 'a monstrous overdetermination in which historical, political, moral, and affective circumstances were at work'. The act of expulsion forms a junction at which all the personal and familial threads of life, and all the great historical periods, are interwoven. Cixous's talk of the 'primal scene' also comes directly from the vocabulary of psychoanalysis. In Freud, it describes a shocking as well as arousing experience in childhood (the child's real or imagined observation of parental sexual intercourse). For Cixous, the primal scene

Palm trees in the Cercle militaire, Oran, Algeria, late 1930s.

again becomes a traumatic and at the same time identity-forming moment: being thrown out of the Cercle militaire represents humiliation, stigmatization, and uprooting, but also a decisive moment in the development of her personality and her subsequent life.

The psychoanalytical impact of this interpretation is unsurprising. For Cixous, psychoanalysis has always been an important reference point. But it is interesting to see that she goes beyond the relatively narrowly defined boundaries of psychoanalytic interpretation and draws decidedly aesthetic conclusions from her primal scene. As a writer and philosopher, she certainly gives the matter a special and by no means self-evident twist when she claims that her entire thinking and writing also have their 'origin' in her experience of the scene. 'My primal scene has become a philosophy', says Cixous in conversation with Engelmann, thereby revealing its full significance for her: being thrown out of the Cercle militaire became the catalyst for a constant reflection on what she had experienced, a way of processing it in her memories.[20]

The hypostatization of the primal scene is not just a post hoc explanation in the quest for biographical coherence. A look at the texts in which the topos of the '*cercle*' appears in its various meanings – such as 'circle' or 'encirclement' (*encerclement*) – confirms this urge for aesthetic processing. The opening sentence of her first fictional text, *Dedans*, reads: 'Ma maison est encerclée.' This sentence, as she later described elsewhere, literally 'fell' upon her when she began to write. What is still somewhat implicit in this award-winning novel from 1969 becomes explicit in the essayistic text 'Mon algériance' from 1997. There, Cixous begins a philosophical reflection on the fateful effects of inclusion and exclusion, starting with a description of being expelled from the Cercle militaire, which closely followed her being granted access. Paradoxes such as the sentence 'being inside also meant being outside', of which there are many examples in the text, show that Cixous never writes without a certain delight in wordplay, which some see as a virtuoso method of deconstruction while others see it as a form of literature that is difficult to access.[21]

Cixous talks a lot about the factors that shaped her identity, about past experiences, influences, and contexts. Just as important to her, however, is the question of what can be made of this 'humus' of experiences and memories. It never remains a mere depiction or even preservation of what has happened. It is always a matter of processing the wounds suffered and translating them into texts, transforming what has been experienced into literature and theory. She is still an uprooted person trying to cope with her past, but her attempts now express themselves in writing and script, in a field, says Cixous, 'in which, in a way, the opposite of what is inherited arises, namely something new, unique: this, fed by what is inherited, produces new effects.'[22] Having been exiled from her worlds, Cixous first said to herself: 'The only salvation lies in writing. That was the only world in which one could dwell without being chased out.'[23]

Oran, the city in which it all began, was certainly not one of those worlds in which one could stay after the events of the Vichy period. At the end of the Second World War, Cixous's father decided to leave the city for Algiers. The family moved to the immediate vicinity of a poor district (Clos Salembier), where tens of thousands of Algerians lived in sometimes miserable conditions without water or electricity. Cixous called Clos Salembier, which lay at the bottom of a slope, the 'cauldron of the damned.'[24] It was one of these slums that the budding sociologist Bourdieu visited at the end of the 1950s, in the middle of the Algerian War, to research the catastrophic living conditions of the uprooted Algerian population.[25] The Cixous family lived outside the settlement, but were valued by its Arab residents because Cixous's mother worked there as a midwife. In retrospect, Cixous was grateful to her father (he died of tuberculosis in 1948) for finding her a new home on the fringes of Algiers and society. During the Second World War, she had been reminded 'at every moment that, at one moment or another, we will, by decree, be waste and rubbish.' In her new surroundings, the young Hélène learned that this applied not only to her family and the Algerian Jews, but also, and in particular, to the Arab population, which was systematically oppressed by the French colonial power. Slums are often called *bidonvilles* in French: the word derives from the custom of using discarded canisters (*bidons*) as building materials for makeshift shanty settlements. For Cixous, growing up near one of these *bidonvilles* meant 'never forgetting that we were kin to those doomed to have the *bidon* as their city and abyss as their horizon.'[26]

But the central place of destiny for Cixous always remained Oran. It was a purported paradise that seemed irrevocably lost, but was never forgotten for that very reason. Cixous remembered her birthplace in a literary way: if writing is the only world in which one can stay without being chased away, then there could be a new place for Oran in that world, including, of course, all the feelings resulting from the experience of loss. This, at least, is how we can interpret the poetic opening scene of 'Mon algériance', in which Cixous relives her childhood in Oran:

> In the smiling, happy little girl that I was, I hid (from others and from myself) a secret, restless, clandestine little girl who knew full well that she had actually been born somewhere else. The dark feeling of having appeared there by chance, of not being from any 'here' by inheritance or descent; the physical sensation of being a delicate mushroom, a spore that sprouted overnight and clings to the earth only with hasty, delicate roots. Another feeling in the shadows: the unshakable certainty that the 'Arabs' were the true descendants of this dusty, fragrant soil. But when I walked barefoot with my brother along the warm paths of Oran, I felt my body plant caressed by the hospitable palms of the ancient dead of the land and the storm in my soul subsided.[27]

Passages like this are the essence of Cixous's literature. They make the slide from idyll to a feeling of being uprooted accessible, and they show how writing can transform pain into consolation and fragility into certainty.

Departures

One of the results of practising deconstruction as a method is that one develops a certain aversion to rigid determinations and instead prefers to pursue ambiguities and differences. For Cixous, undecidability is a great philosophical good. This applies to questions of ethnic origin, national identity, and sexual difference as well as to the interpretation of one's own life path.[28] Cixous never tires of emphasizing that she never really left Algeria as she always dreamed of arriving in Algeria one day, while she never really arrived in France because the country did not allow her to arrive.[29] This 'in-betweenness' in the 'unfinished elsewhere' is a fundamental feature of her 'Algériance': 'Leaving Algeria and not arriving is, without calculation, also a way of not having broken with Algeria. I have always been happy that I was spared any "arrival".'[30] The real story of Cixous's departure and arrival is somewhat more mundane. Cixous left Algeria for Paris in 1955 immediately after finishing school. At the time, she had no special relationship with France, or rather with the French mainland. It was simply the easiest way of escaping Algeria. For her, being in Paris meant first and foremost 'freedom from Algeria' and secondly the chance to adopt 'an imaginary nationality which is literary nationality'.[31] In accordance with her motto that salvation must be sought in language, Cixous studied English at the Sorbonne, and made rapid progress: in 1959, at the age of twenty-two, she passed the *agrégation*, the admission to a higher position in the French university system, a qualification both coveted and notoriously difficult to obtain. Compared to Algeria, the first years at the university were for her associated with two particularities: on the one hand, she felt that antisemitism was much less pronounced in Paris than in Algiers, which also freed her to some extent from the 'obligation of the Jewish identity'. On the other hand, in Paris, and especially at the university, she was confronted with a chauvinism that she had not known in this form in Algeria, where she had grown up in an environment of women. In France, says Cixous, she 'abruptly learned that my unacceptable truth in this world was my being a woman. Right away, it was war. I felt the explosion, the odour of misogyny.'[32]

Another war, this time between the French army and the Algerian liberation movement, had broken out some time before. Cixous had been able to leave Algeria in time (the Algerian War had already begun in November 1954, but escalated only towards the end of 1955). Her family had stayed there. Her brother Pierre openly supported Algerian independence and thus became the target of the French-Algerian terrorist organization the OAS. When Pierre ended up on their death list, he fled to join Hélène in France. After Algeria gained independence in 1962, he returned, but was arrested again, this time by the new Algerian authorities, and fled to France a second time.

Cixous's mother and grandmother remained in Algeria until the early 1970s, which was unusual. Most Algerian Jews resettled in France, along with the other French Algerians, by 1962 at the latest.

Around the same time, in the early 1960s, Cixous met Jacques Derrida – a momentous encounter that developed into a close friendship and a lifelong philosophical dialogue. Cixous and Derrida later dedicated numerous texts to this connection, in which they called their counterparts 'H. C.' and 'J. D.' and let it be known that they 'authorized' each other to write.[33] A remarkable constellation like this is rarely encountered with such intensity in the history of philosophy. It becomes even more remarkable when one realizes that the two central figures of deconstruction both had Jewish-Algerian roots.

Cixous and Derrida share a striking number of biographical similarities. Derrida, like Cixous, was born into a Jewish family in Algeria and grew up there in extremely fraught colonial conditions. He too experienced the shock of antisemitism at first hand during the Vichy years and associated this with a key event that left a permanent mark. Like Cixous, Derrida turned his back on his homeland at the first opportunity to study in Paris. And like Cixous, he too developed an ambivalent relationship with France. On the one hand, both felt very attracted to the French language and literature. On the other hand, both were suspicious of French attitudes to national and cultural identity. They had both become acquainted with the colonial and fascist depths of the Grande Nation quite early on.

At the same time, their Algerian experiences were valuable precisely because of their differences. Cixous and Derrida experienced the Vichy regime in Algeria differently because of their age. When the anti-Jewish school laws were announced in 1942, Derrida was expelled from his lycée by his headmaster. Cixous, who was seven years younger, never even started school. Instead, as she describes, she 'went to school in a madame's dining room, where a crowd of forbidden little Jews were piled in together, organized by age group.'[34] Her main shock therefore had less to do with her school experience, as in Derrida's case, than with the violence inflicted on her father when he was banned from practising as a doctor – a humiliation that burned much more intensely in the young girl. The Cixous family became impoverished overnight.

Given all these shared experiences, one can assume that Cixous's and Derrida's Algerian origins also played a key role in the friendship. But it is also true that, initially, these topics were not discussed openly between them. Nevertheless, they definitely had an effect in the background. When Cixous and Derrida met for the first time in 1963 in the Brasserie Balzar in the Latin Quarter, they spent hours discussing their love of literature and, above all, James Joyce, the subject of Cixous's doctoral thesis.[35] There was no mention of the Algerian War that had just ended, their family fates, or the old wounds of antisemitism. Cixous often emphasizes this fact when it comes to her connection to Derrida – not so much to downplay the importance of the Algerian 'wounds and memories' that had 'always accompanied' the two of them, but to emphasize that the defining 'stage' of their exchange was from the beginning the discussion of language, and in particular the French language.[36] It was a shared departure: Cixous followed Derrida on the philosophical paths of deconstruction, and Derrida followed the poetic paths of literature laid out by Cixous.

After their first meeting in the brasserie, the new friends naturally exchanged views on Algeria. But decades passed before it became a common theme for them, in texts written specifically for the subject. If we can believe Cixous, this was largely due to Derrida, who, according to her, only began to accept 'in the fourth act of his life' that questions of Judaism and Algerian origin, from which he had previously kept his distance, were working away within him.[37] Derrida, as is well known, gave an account of his time in Algeria only in the 1990s.[38]

It was different with Cixous. She too certainly found it difficult for a long time to speak and write publicly about 'the Algerian issue', as she calls it.[39] She too did so much more freely and more frequently from the 1990s onwards. But, unlike Derrida, Cixous nevertheless took the first steps towards processing the situation in the mid-1970s, making her first attempts to discuss Algeria and many of the themes connected with it in writing. Clear traces of this confrontation can be found in *The Newly Born Woman*. In this book, written together with the writer Catherine Clément and one of her first texts on feminism, Cixous describes – among many other things – what it meant for her personally to grow up as a Jewish girl in colonial Algeria. Even in 1975 she was obviously capable of expressing herself clearly: in Algeria she had 'learned to read, write, scream and vomit.'[40] This statement comes at the beginning of a passage in *The Newly Born Woman* that spans several pages and is entitled 'The Murder of the Other.' It is worth quoting a longish excerpt from it, because it shows how Cixous combines the narration of a specific experience with a comprehensive reflection on, and interpretation of, the colonial oppression prevailing in Algeria:

> Today I know from experience that one cannot imagine what a French-Algerian girl was like; one must have been one, lived through it. One must have experienced the 'French' at the 'height' of their imperialist delusion, who behaved in a country inhabited by human beings as if it were actually populated by inhumans, born slaves. I learned everything from that first spectacle: I saw how the white (French), superior, plutocratic, civilized world based its power on the oppression of populations that suddenly became 'invisible,' like proletarians, migrant workers, and minorities who do not have the right 'colour.' Women. Invisible as human beings. But who of course continued to be perceived as tools – dirty, stupid, lazy, devious, etc. Thanks to a devastating dialectical magic. I saw that the great, noble, 'progressive' countries established themselves by expelling the 'foreign,' excluding it, not rejecting it but, rather, enslaving it. A common gesture of history: there must be two races – the masters and the slaves.[41]

Cixous compares colonial oppression with capitalist exploitation, racism, and sexism and assigns all these forms of oppression to Hegel's famous master–slave dialectic. Ironically, for Cixous, Hegel's dialectic is part of the problem, since the 'dialectical magic' produces 'history' and thus also the history of capitalist exploitation, colonial oppression, patriarchy, and Eurocentrism – including all the corresponding relationships of difference between bourgeois and proletarian, man and woman, colonizer and colonized.[42]

This is a deliberately simplistic interpretation and critique of the master–slave pattern, but one that does not miss its mark. At the end of the passage about the 'murder of the other,' Cixous lets it be known that she is concerned with the elaboration of the other:

> With the terrible simplicity that organizes the movement established by Hegel as a system, society plods along before my eyes, reproducing the mechanism of the death struggle in perfection: the reduction of a 'human being' to a 'nobody', to the position of the 'other' – the unstoppable plot of racism. There must be an 'other' – no master without slaves, no economic-political power without exploitation, no ruling class without cattle under the yoke, no 'French' without Kanaks, no Nazis without Jews, no property without exclusion – an exclusion that has its limits and is part of the dialectic.[43]

It has often been said of Cixous that her works are apolitical precisely because of their literary nature, or that they lack a political theory. In passages like these, one can see that her critics have not read them very carefully.

New worlds

What is remarkable about Cixous's reflections in *The Newly Born Woman*, in addition to their content, is the time at which they were expressed. Anti-capitalist, anti-racist, and feminist positions, as well as a reference to Hegel's master–slave dialectic, may not have been uncommon in 1975. But the connection of these individual strands to a 'philosophy of the other' certainly was. Even more unusual was Cixous's open reference to colonialism and Algeria. In the 1970s, it was downright taboo in France to mention the bloody French colonial past in Algeria and elsewhere in public, in such a negative way, let alone to problematize it. Most left-wing intellectuals also adhered to this unwritten rule. We need to say it loud and clear: neither Derrida, Foucault, Barthes, Lyotard, Rancière, nor other representatives of French Theory dared to denounce the French colonial past as directly as Cixous did at this time – more than a decade after the end of the Algerian War and long before their respective upwellings of remembrance in the 1990s. This raises the question of how we can understand in historical terms Cixous's insistence on speaking openly about it so comparatively early. Cixous may have learned, as she wrote in 1975, to 'read, write, scream and vomit in Algeria' – but where did she learn to write such sentences?

To answer this question, it is worth taking a detour via the academic and political biotope known as 'Vincennes'. This was the name of the experimental university on the outskirts of Paris, built in just a few months in the autumn of 1968 after the May protests in Paris. It has gone down in history as the 'red university'. Cixous was a professor of English literature here from 1968 until her retirement in 2005. What is less well known is that she was also directly involved in the founding of the entire university. The Centre universitaire expérimental de Vincennes was a kind of concession by the French government to the protest movement, which had demanded reforms to the system, including more say in university matters and better study conditions. As a new university centre with an experimental character, Vincennes was to test out a resolution passed by the French parliament in the autumn of 1968, which stated, among other things, that some of the state's powers in the area of higher education should be transferred to an elected council of lecturers and students.[44] At the instigation of the dean of the Sorbonne, Cixous, who had already been appointed professor in Nanterre in 1967, was commissioned to initiate the founding of the university. Together with two male colleagues, she formed the founding trio. Cixous was primarily responsible for the development of the humanities. It was a pretty challenging task: in just a few months, they had to bring an entire university to life from scratch (and on a more or less democratic basis), with a new programme, staff, and students.

Vincennes quickly became a left-wing showcase project. The aim was to create a social space in which both the idea of an academic council and different social and lifestyle concepts were to have their rightful place. Many things about it would be different: there were evening classes, a kindergarten, and access to university was possible even without a high school diploma. The composition of the students was accordingly diverse, with a high proportion of women, workers, immigrants from the former colonies, and foreign students. Politically, the university was home to a wide variety of left-wing movements from the 'post-revolutionary' 1968 era – the Communist Party was by far the most right-wing force among all the Maoist, Trotskyist, and anarchist positions. From 1970 onwards, Vincennes was also a gathering place and breeding ground for social movements such as the women's movement (MLF), the gay liberation movement (FHAR), and the Third World movement. Last but not least, new paths were also taken in academic terms, with the creation of departments for film, theatre, psychoanalysis, urbanism, and computer science, all based on the American model. Each department attracted its own intellectual avant-garde. For example, the philosophy department, led by Foucault on his return from Tunis in the autumn of 1968, welcomed a who's who of the emerging French Theory scene.[45] The fact that philosophers such as Deleuze, Lyotard, Rancière, and Balibar, to name just a few, were given academic tenure at Vincennes early on, and were able to develop their theories in freedom, was also partly thanks to Cixous.

For Cixous, the environment of Vincennes – after the hardships of the founding – naturally also offered its own intellectual freedom. Here, right from the start, she had the opportunity to reflect unhindered on questions of sexuality and gender differences in research and teaching – something that was almost impossible at the Sorbonne or in Nanterre before May 1968, as Cixous emphasizes.[46] Initially, the discussion of feminist perspectives took place within the narrow framework of her work as an English scholar. This changed in 1974, when Cixous founded the Centre d'études féminines in Vincennes. As an interdisciplinary research institution, the Centre for Women's Studies was the first of its kind in Europe and played an important role in establishing the field in the 1970s and 1980s – long before Judith Butler coined the category of gender in the late 1980s, a term that was added to the centre's denomination only in 2006. Cixous got the idea for such a centre from the US, where she had been a regular guest professor at Cornell and Buffalo since 1970, and where Women's Studies already existed.[47] An anecdote about Cixous relates that, after one of her stays in the US, she came to her seminar in Vincennes one day and announced that the English literature department would from now on, i.e. with immediate effect, be called the Centre for Women's Studies.[48] It was probably not quite that quick and easy. It is more historically correct to say that the centre owed its creation and institutional stability to the interdisciplinary collaboration of several academics working in Vincennes and interested in questions of feminism. And it was able to flourish only with the help of the presence of political activists. The Mouvement de libération des femmes deserves special mention here. The MLF's first meeting and women's march took place in Vincennes in May 1970. The protestors marched across the campus with slogans such as 'We are all hysterical! We are all frustrated! We are all lesbians!' – an ironic appropriation and transformation of clichés, but also a reminder of the social humiliations associated with them.[49]

Many different forms of feminism emerged in the sphere of Vincennes and the MLF in the early 1970s. One can even go a step further and say without exaggeration that almost all the leading protagonists of contemporary French feminism came from Vincennes, including: the writer Monique Wittig, who studied there and founded a feminist circle; Antoinette Fouque, who led the group 'Politique et Psychoanalyse'; and Luce Irigaray, who was a professor of psychoanalysis there. As in any major movement, there were strong alliances as well as groups that were at odds with each other. There was agreement on the general aim of breaking through male domination and of participating in sociopolitical debates such as the issue of the ban

An alternative course on 'Un[heim]lichkeit': Hélène Cixous at the University of Vincennes, 1975.

on abortion, a ban that the Minister of Health Simone Veil rescinded at the end of 1974. The conflicts arose when it came to the question of the 'correct' political and theoretical orientation. In theoretical terms, the most burning question was that of a feminism of equality versus a feminism of difference. Supporters of a feminism of equality stood for the equality of the two sexes in the tradition of Simone de Beauvoir: they saw gender as a social construction and fought to overcome difference. The feminism of difference, on the other hand, was based on the biological and cultural differences between the sexes, and sought to strengthen the uniqueness of the female sex and thereby dissolve the hierarchy between the genders.

Cixous was clearly on the side of a feminism of difference. Indeed, she was its defining figure. She represented an approach that was not coloured by essentialism, but oriented towards linguistic deconstruction and pluralization. She addressed the binary opposition of man and woman not only in order to destroy the dominant signifier of the masculine that prevails in this opposition, but also to displace the opposition itself and to bring to light the many spaces of female sexuality that remained 'stuck in the dark.' So 'bisexuality' was for her a crucial theme from an early stage. For Cixous, as she says in 'The Laugh of the Medusa,' there is 'no generalizable woman,' no uniform 'representative type,' but rather the inexhaustible 'imaginary world of women' in the plural, the 'infinite wealth of their individual natures.' One simply cannot, Cixous continued, speak of '*one* female sexuality.'[50] She thus rigorously rejected the feminism of equality as found in de Beauvoir. Cixous had little sympathy for the existentialist philosopher from an older generation who made a media comeback in 1975 after giving her very first television interview under the title 'Pourquoi je suis féministe' ('Why I am a feminist').[51] Cixous considered de Beauvoir to be a bourgeois figure and bad writer, and she was appalled by the title of her work *The Second Sex* precisely because it seemed to place the female sex second and thus remained caught within a patriarchal logic.[52]

Cixous's most important contribution to the feminist discussions of these turbulent years was the concept of *écriture féminine*.[53] Cixous sketched the first outlines of this concept in 1975 in 'The Laugh of the Medusa' and *The Newly Born Woman*. In both texts, which also represented a poetics of her own writing, she consciously refused to define the concept. In 'The Laugh of the Medusa,' she says:

> It is impossible to *define* a female way of writing, that is an impossibility that will continue to exist, because one will never be able to *theorize*, define, or code this way of writing, which does not mean that it does not exist. But it will always go beyond the discourse determined by the phallocentric system. It takes place elsewhere and will take place elsewhere than in those areas that are subordinate to the philosophical-theoretical origin. It will only allow itself to be thought of by the subjectivities that reduce all automatisms to ruins and hurry along borders, never subject to any authority.[54]

'Let the feminine way of writing be thought of by the subjectivities' – if one had to undertake a description of *écriture féminine* despite all the reservations about attempts at a definition, then this passage would be a good starting point. Here, it becomes clear where Cixous wanted to allow feminine writing to take place: not in theory, but in a place where subjective desires and experiences have their place right from the start. This was not directed against any philosophy or theory, but rather against the 'phallocentric system' that predominated in philosophical discourse which, according to Cixous, had for centuries suppressed all other forms of thinking and writing in the name of rationality and the logos, and had discriminated against women in particular. According to Cixous, this suppressed space, with all its negated desires, experiences, and identities, had to be regained. To do this, a language and writing of its own was needed – *écriture féminine.* A liberating, pleasurable, spontaneous, embodied and, above all, literary form of expression that would find ways out of the restrictive cultural patterns of patriarchy and enable 'women to HAVE THEIR SAY':

> It is essential that women write with their bodies, that they invent the invincible language that breaks down barriers and classifications, and rhetoric, rules, and codes. That it floods, penetrates, and overrides the last reserve of discourse, even that discourse that does not mind having to utter the word 'silence.'[55]

For Cixous, the figure of the laughing (and no longer frightening) Medusa was emblematic of the irresistible call to leave behind the speechlessness and silence imposed on women and to respond to that 'write!' by opening up a new space based on one's own desires, senses, and experiences. Could it be that this 'call of the Medusa' also accompanied or even gave rise to Cixous's preoccupation with her Algerian origins and the French colonial past, which began at exactly the same time? To return to the question I posed above of how Cixous's comparatively early openness in speaking about Algeria can be understood historically, there is no getting around the Medusa and *écriture féminine*. When Cixous wrote in *The Newly Born Woman* in 1975 that she had learned to 'read, write, scream and vomit' in Algeria, and in doing so had used her own autobiographical experiences to criticize the colonial oppression prevailing there, this was also a performative expression of this liberating writing, which sought new ways out between literature and theory. And it was an act that came about only because it was guided by a feminist perspective that raised questions about different yet comparable forms of oppression.

Cixous's reference to Algeria was therefore closely linked to her academic, feminist, and political projects in 1970s Vincennes. However, it is important to differentiate here: the anti-capitalist, anti-imperialist, and anti-racist traditions in the left-wing milieu of Vincennes certainly played an important role, but ultimately they could not have been the sole decisive factor – otherwise, other philosophers at Vincennes would also have expressed themselves more decisively about Algeria, something that they did not do at the time. It was only the connection with *écriture féminine*, which also arose in the biotope of Vincennes, that enabled Cixous to open up her own experience as a woman with Algerian-Jewish roots and in this way to 'make the necessary breakthroughs and transformations in her own history', as Cixous demanded for herself and everyone else.[56]

This detour by way of Vincennes also shows that it would not be entirely accurate to view its environment as merely an 'external context' that influenced Cixous's thinking and writing from the outside and, to a certain extent, historically. That is certainly true, but on closer inspection it becomes clear that to a large extent Cixous created that environment herself. The founding of an entire university with great intellectual, social, and political freedom; the creation of a centre for women's studies; the conception of a new literary genre and the various collaborations with Jacques Derrida, Catherine Clément, and many others – all these projects also represented, in this sense, the founding and opening up of new worlds. It seems almost as if these collective undertakings of the 1970s were also distant responses to the betrayal of Oran, that traumatic primal scene in which Cixous was thrown out of her supposed idyll and the Algeria of her childhood was turned into a hellish paradise. The painful memory of expulsion from the Algerian paradise was sometimes more, sometimes less present in the new worlds of Vincennes with its feminist and theoretical circles, but it never completely disappeared. However, this memory was always accompanied by a life-affirming, creative, laughing, and joyful attitude, which Cixous unmistakably represents with her life and her texts. In the end, it is probably both pain and joy that give Cixous's life and work its decisive turn. She says it herself: 'Happy artists are those who have experienced horror.'[57]

ÉTIENNE
BALIBAR

7

LESSONS IN ANTI-RACISM

Étienne Balibar

Since at least the campaign for the 2017 presidential election, Emmanuel Macron has ceased to be on good terms with his former university professor Étienne Balibar. During his 'Jupiter-like' rise to the French presidency, Macron – who liked to portray himself as an 'intellectual in politics' and a former assistant to the philosopher Paul Ricoeur – boasted that, during his philosophy studies at the University of Nanterre in Paris, he had been 'very inspired' by the Marxist philosopher Balibar, under whom he eventually wrote his thesis on Hegel.[1] When the journalists from *Le Monde* asked Balibar about this, he replied bluntly but 'sincerely' that he simply could not remember any of his supervisee's work, and certainly hadn't kept it. Balibar stressed that although he had 'no particular hostility' towards the politician, he found 'the staging of his philosophical education', which Macron himself or his entourage had organized, 'absolutely obscene'.[2] He was not entirely wrong. The news that spread through the media claiming that Macron was a close student of Ricoeur was, even on the most charitable interpretation, not true. The versatile Macron worked for a short time in publishing before becoming a banker, and had merely been tasked with proofreading one of Ricoeur's books. Informed of Balibar's reaction, Macron let it be known that he was disappointed and hurt by the behaviour of his once admired mentor. He regretted Balibar's memory lapse, describing it as an 'almost psychiatric case'.[3]

In June 2020, another confrontation between Macron and Balibar occurred when, in the wake of global expressions of solidarity with the American Black Lives Matter movement, protests against police violence and racism spread. The murder of George Floyd in the United States provoked especially strong reactions in France because the circumstances of the crime were reminiscent of the case of the young Adama Traoré, who in 2016 was pinned to the ground by French police and finally suffocated. Since then, the Comité vérité et justice pour Adama (Committee for Truth and Justice for Adama), founded by the deceased's sister, has not only called for the case to be investigated legally, but has also denounced systematic police violence in France.[4] Macron commented on the protests, but without naming the deceased, the Comité, or the demonstrators – many of whom were descendants of immigrants from the colonies. According to the president, it was unacceptable to speak of police violence in a constitutional state. He also described the discussions about structural racism as 'racialized' ('*racisé*') – a remark that was particularly popular with the middle class and the right[5] – and insisted that 'no traces or names will be erased from history' and 'no statues will be torn down.'[6] He had a scapegoat ready for any inflammatory tendencies: 'The academic world is guilty. It has promoted the ethnicization of the social question in the belief that this is a good road to follow. But the result can only be separatist and amounts to splitting the Republic in two.'[7] The response from the academic world, or at least from those academics who felt they were the targets of Macron's tirade, was not long in coming. In a joint statement in *Le Monde*, well-known university advocates of anti-racism – including Balibar, Achille Mbembe, and Sandra Laguier – not only rejected the accusation that they had provided the intellectual framework for the protest movement, but also struck back: 'Macron is not fighting against racists, but against anti-racists. The president seems to have seen nothing, heard nothing, and understood nothing of what has happened in the last weeks.'[8]

It is no coincidence that the philosopher Étienne Balibar was one those to object in this way. Born in 1942, he is considered one of the most important left-wing voices in the fight against racism in France. He can look back on a long series of interventions in public debates about migration, colonialism, and nationalism. Since the

1970s, he has been tirelessly committed to defending the interests of migrants living in France. This ranges from his early criticism of living and working conditions in the *banlieues* to demands for more recognition for illegal immigrants (*sans-papiers*) and young people with no prospects, as well as suggestions on how to rethink questions of citizenship, secularism, and cultural identity. What is special about Balibar is that he repeatedly supports his political engagement with philosophical analyses of how racism works and considerations of democratic theory. For him, political engagement and work on theory are two practices that make sense only in combination. This is evidenced above all by his main theoretical work on racism, *Race, Nation, Class: Ambiguous Identities*, written together with the sociologist Immanuel Wallerstein, but also by books such as *Violence and Civility* and *Equaliberty*, in which Balibar develops his project of a political philosophy of radical democracy. Balibar was long known to most people as a loyal student of the Marxist philosopher Louis Althusser. He is now also known as a philosopher of anti-racism and a theorist of radical democracy.

Balibar's commitment to questions of anti-racist practice and theory is by no means a given for a philosopher of his generation. Outside of relatively minor left-wing currents, racism hardly played a role as a philosophical topic in the French theoretical landscape of the second half of the twentieth century. In this respect, one must agree to an extent with the Cameroonian philosopher and political scholar Achille Mbembe, whom we have already met, when he claims that neither of the two major movements that deconstructed racism in the twentieth century (the US civil rights movement and the fight against apartheid) had any influence on the works of the most famous French intellectuals, with a few exceptions such as Sartre, de Beauvoir, and Derrida.[9] Mbembe does not even exclude from his criticism the pioneers of poststructuralism whom he admires, such as Foucault. Balibar, on the other hand, would certainly be one of the exceptions on Mbembe's list. This raises the question of where Balibar's special anti-racist impetus comes from. If we look at the stages of his commitment, it becomes clear that these draw on his youthful experiences during the Algerian War and his subsequent lengthy stay in Algeria. Reason enough, then, for us to examine selected stages in Balibar's career from the 1960s to the late 1980s – stages that reflect the political history of France and its decolonization.

1961 – beatings and protests

The first stage finds us in the late phase of the Algerian War, and it begins with a beating. One of Balibar's first ever political actions landed him in hospital. On 19 December 1961, numerous unions and student associations in Paris called for a large demonstration against Charles de Gaulle's Algerian policy and for immediate peace in Algeria. Balibar was assigned to the Jeunesse Communiste security service and was responsible for coordinating the crowds of protestors – until he came up against the special forces of the Paris police prefect (and former Nazi collaborator) Maurice Papon. They beat the demonstrators and stewards with wooden clubs and iron-clad carbines. Balibar was relatively lucky: while the police apprehended other injured people and gave them 'special treatment' at the station, he was pulled out of the huge crowd by friends and taken to the Saint-Antoine hospital. When he arrived there with a bloody head, he heard the doctor on duty say: 'Serves him right. What the hell was he doing there?!'[10]

Indeed, what *was* he doing there? Balibar thought he knew better than the doctor, who, as Balibar put it, was the 'poor parrot of his class discourse'.[11] Like many of his left-wing peers, Balibar was convinced that it was absolutely necessary to take to the streets to protest against the war. He was nineteen years old, had begun studying philosophy at the École normale supérieure in 1960, and had joined the Communist Student Union (UEC) and then the French Communist Party (PCF) in 1961. For a young left-wing student like him, it was therefore almost a given that one ought to stand up for anti-colonialism, anti-imperialism, and anti-fascism. There were concrete reasons for adopting all three positions: the colonial situation in Algeria, which was based on capitalist exploitation and racist discrimination; the imperialism of the French state, which insisted on maintaining its colonies by force; and, finally, the fascism of the French underground Organisation armée secrète (OAS) which, in its attempt to stop Algeria seceding from the French 'motherland', did not shy away from terrorizing its own compatriots with bombings and assassinations. In short, there were enough reasons for left-wing students to decide that this political mix could no longer be tolerated, and to rebel against it.[12]

However, a bad conscience also played a part in Balibar's anti-war commitment. This had less to do with being left-wing per se, which was often based on a moral struggle against social injustice, but more with Balibar's privileged situation and the resulting feeling that he had to pay off a certain debt.[13] Because of his studies, he was spared from military service. Had he been a worker or a peasant, he would have had to choose between war and desertion. So he was left with the more comfortable choice between doing nothing and getting involved. This

Paris, 27 October 1960: student demonstration against the Algerian War.

was a privilege that other ENS pupils such as Bourdieu and Derrida did not want to (Bourdieu) or could not (Derrida) take advantage of at the time. They were both older than Balibar, had completed their studies earlier, and were called up for military service in Algeria at the height of the war.

But you didn't necessarily have to go to Algeria to experience the violence that resulted from the war.[14] It was also clearly felt on the French mainland: the OAS and the FLN kept the country on tenterhooks with countless bomb attacks that brought France to the brink of civil war. The police were no less violent. On 16 October 1961, they carried out a massacre of Algerian demonstrators who had defied the curfew imposed on them. Hundreds of Algerians were killed; many of them were thrown into the Seine. On 8 February 1962, nine people died during a demonstration organized by the PCF against the fascist OAS terror. They had fled from the onrushing police into the entrance of the nearby Charonne metro station and were then crushed by the crowd or beaten to death by police wielding rubber batons.

These two events aroused different reactions: while around a million people paid their last respects to the dead of Charonne (who included eight trade unionists), the night-time massacre of the Algerian demonstrators in the Seine was ignored – the press did not even report on it. For Balibar, these two violent incidents and the different ways in which they were dealt with were formative experiences that shaped his political consciousness and to which he later returned again and again. On the one hand, they showed him the extent to which French society was able to ignore state-condoned violence and everyday racism towards the Algerian population. On the other hand, the events made him aware of the extent to which the fascist Vichy past, the colonial question, and the ideological struggles between communists and Gaullists had determined the political reality of France in the 1950s.

Balibar's experience was common among those of his generation. As a result of these social conflicts, large sections of French youth became alienated from the state and were radicalized. The 'Algerian generation' was formed: a cohort of left-wing students and activists who became politicized for the first time in their lives during the Algerian War, showed solidarity with the Algerian independence movement, and denounced the French power apparatus. Their importance for the history of politicization in France can hardly be overestimated. The new positions and forms of protest they shaped in opposition to the orthodox viewpoints of the old communists and socialists (who were part of the government at the time) formed an important basis for the student protests of the late 1960s. One must not forget that when the 'Vietnam generation' took to the streets in Paris in May 1968, denouncing US imperialism and championing the anti-colonial liberation struggle, the Algerian War and the left-wing anti-war protests had ended only six years earlier.[15]

This formative experience perhaps also explains why Balibar, as a young member of the 'Algerian generation', remained committed to the Algerian cause even after the end of the war. In this regard, he was quite different from the majority of the older, more established French intellectuals at the time, who had played a special role in the conflict because they were able to exert a not insignificant influence on public opinion. During the war, both left-wing and right-wing intellectuals had participated with great passion in public debates on the Algerian question. But when the war ended and Algeria gained independence in the summer of 1962, they immediately dropped the subject and fell silent, whether they were relieved or angered by the outcome. The whole Algerian question seemed to have been settled at once.

The best example of this intellectual renunciation was Jean-Paul Sartre, the man who had supported Algeria most loudly, legitimized the violence that the insurgents there had unleashed, taken on all comers, adopted a stoical attitude to the numerous attempts on his life by the OAS, and did all of this with the fury that was familiar and expected from this great intellectual. But with the securing of Algeria's independence, the whole matter was, so to speak, done and dusted as far as Sartre was concerned. Even though at this point it was not yet clear what future Algeria – decoupled from its colonial rulers but still battered by their bloody rule – and a now reduced France were heading for, Sartre was now occupied with other arenas of the 'world revolution', such as Cuba. There was nothing more for him to say about the case of Algeria. Until his dying day in 1980, he never dealt with the country again.

In a certain way, Sartre and many other intellectuals consciously or unconsciously made a move that, on a larger scale and under different circumstances, was mirrored in the forgetfulness of the entire French post-war society.[16] In France, a veritable collective amnesia settled over the preceding years, which had not even been perceived as war years by the French people as a whole. The 'events' in Algeria were euphemized: most people viewed them as a legitimate fight against an armed uprising on the very territory of the French Republic. This perhaps made it all the easier to suppress the situation and quickly return to business as usual in 1962. People no longer wanted to hear anything about the Algerian drama and French guilt, or to be reminded of the torture, deportations, and massacres that had been committed, of the centuries-long colonial rule, and even less of the bitter and final loss of empire that the decoupling of Algeria represented for their 'glorious' nation. From then on, the focus was on the famous 'retreat to the Hexagon' – a doctrine primarily associated with the journalist Raymond Cartier, who had already criticized the waste of public funds in the colonies in the 1950s and called for an economic policy focused on the mainland.[17] The spirit of Cartierism spread quickly in the 1960s, with the French economic miracle, and set the majority of French people on a new national course. But Balibar took a quite different path. He turned right round and travelled to the heart of the former colony – to its capital, Algiers.

1965 – next stop: Mecca!

Balibar lived in Algeria for two years. After completing his studies at the ENS, he took a position as a lecturer at the University of Algiers in 1965 and taught philosophy there until 1967. His stay in Algiers came about as part of an agreement between France and Algeria intended to promote educational exchange between the now separated countries. Such lectureships in former French colonies were not uncommon, and for many Parisian intellectuals they represented a welcome opportunity for a temporary taste of something different – Roland Barthes, Simone de Beauvoir, and Michel Foucault also gained their colonially tinged experiences abroad in this way. In Balibar's case, however, the decision to go to Algeria was rooted in more than just a desire for a change of scenery, and was not even remotely connected with a neo-colonial attitude. For him, it was a left-wing commitment to a recently decolonized country that was enjoying renewal and a surge of optimism.

For Balibar was not going just anywhere. He was going to the 'Third World capital.'[18] A brief look at the history of Algeria after 1962 makes it clear how Algiers became the centre of the global South. After independence, Algeria quickly rose to become a sought-after player in the world. While independence was still being celebrated extensively at home, and the question of power within the FLN had already been decided in favour of Ahmed Ben Bella, the country was enjoying its hard-won sovereignty in foreign policy. Ben Bella was received by John F. Kennedy in the summer of 1962, but an even bigger welcome from Fidel Castro awaited him in Cuba. Algeria attracted worldwide attention because of its victorious struggle against an old European colonial power. In being seen as a successful example of revolutionary decolonization, it fulfilled a certain role-model function for those countries and regions that were still striving for autonomy. At the beginning of the 1960s, fifteen African states had already achieved their independence, but for many others, especially in southern Africa, the process of decolonization had only just begun. The Algerian government saw itself as a supporter of all liberation movements that were still fighting for their freedom. Algeria opened its doors to all the 'wretched of the earth,' to quote Algeria's official 'Ambassador for Africa,' Frantz Fanon.

For a good decade, Algiers was home to a wide variety of revolutionary organizations and groups from all over the world. From the influential magazine *Révolution africaine* to the national liberation movements for South Africa, Namibia, Rhodesia, Mozambique, Cape Verde, Angola, and South Vietnam, they all had their base in Algiers[19] – a total of around twenty organizations, including Yasser Arafat's PLO and the international branch of Elridge Cleaver's Black Panther Party.[20] *Alger, la Blanche*, as the city was called after the white façades of its houses, became *Alger, la Rouge*, 'Red Algiers,' an international contact point for revolutionaries and liberation fighters. One of these fighters, Amílcar Cabral from Guinea, also wrote the most famous description of Algiers' golden years: 'Muslims make pilgrimages to Mecca, Christians to the Vatican, and freedom fighters to Algiers.'[21]

When Balibar arrived in Algiers in the summer of 1965, there was definitely still a hint of global revolution in the air. None other than the Cuban revolutionary Che Guevara made a celebrated stopover there in the same year, before setting off on his legendary Congo expedition, with Algerian support. In Algeria itself, however, the initial magic was already fading. That same summer, Houari Boumédiène seized power with the help of the military and had his old FLN comrade Ben Bella and other opposition members arrested. In terms of foreign policy, everything remained the same, but under Boumédiène the country would later change significantly. The coup took place almost silently, and quite a few residents of Algiers even thought that the tanks rolling through the streets were part of a film set. In the weeks before, the Italian director Gillo Pontecorvo had shot large-scale war scenes in the middle of Algiers' old town for his anti-colonial cult film *The Battle of Algiers*, a neorealist piece that shows key episodes from the War of Independence. But Pontecorvo had long since dismantled his film set by the time of the coup.[22]

Why did Balibar make the pilgrimage to this revolutionary Mecca? His still young academic career in France was certainly not helped by his choice of Algeria. His presence in the country was more idealistically motivated: it can also be understood as a way of helping with academic reconstruction. The French had left the Algerians with a desolate higher education system: during the colonial period, the country's only university had been a haven for colonial racist science and reactionary cliques who shared intellectual and political responsibility for the oppression of the Algerian population. Pierre Bourdieu, who had worked there a few years previously, would have had a thing or two to say about it. In addition, the university had been literally destroyed: in the very last days of the war, the OAS had used phosphorus bombs to reduce the university library to rubble and ashes, in line with its 'scorched earth policy', thereby destroying a large part of the written knowledge available in the country.[23]

The university had to be rebuilt and ideologically reoriented by the new Algerian state. In this process, it was enthusiastically helped by former anti-colonial activists from France who continued to sympathize with Algeria. The left-wing French who had recently arrived in the country were called *pieds-rouges* – an ironic reference to the term *pieds-noirs*, used to describe the French Algerians of the colonial era.[24] Balibar, like the sociologist Monique Gadant and many others, was one such *pied-rouge*.[25] The young ENS graduate brought with him above all a proven knowledge of Marxism, but he also had something special in his luggage: his volume *Reading Capital*, edited with Louis Althusser, Jacques Rancière and other ENS comrades, was published in 1965, and soon became the world's best-known interpretation of Marx. Althusser's structuralist reading of Marxist theory was, as Michel Foucault reported from Tunis at the same time, extremely popular among students in North Africa.[26] Accordingly, during his time as a lecturer in Algiers, Balibar taught what he had done before and would later do in Paris, namely Marxist philosophy in the style of Althusser.[27]

It is difficult to reconstruct how Balibar's stay in Algeria specifically influenced him and to what extent it was reflected in his work in the following years. This has a lot to do with the circumstances of his stay: he did not write any philosophical texts in Algeria that could testify to a theoretical processing of his experiences there, which is not surprising given his tender years and his focus on political activism. But even in his subsequent theoretical works, no Algerian 'residues' can be found. Rather, a continuity in the engagement with questions of Marxist theory can be observed in the Althusser circle, which extended into the late 1970s – Balibar remained loyal to Althusser and the PCF for a very long time. Even in the aftermath of the student revolt of May 1968, epistemological reflections on the nature of the class struggle were more important to him, at least in philosophical terms, than questions arising from France's colonial legacy.

On closer inspection, Balibar's stay in Algeria seems to have been more a lived experience than a source of theoretical insight – an experience that did not as yet affect his philosophical engagement but was initially of a political nature. What Balibar brought with him when he returned to France in 1967 was mainly, in addition to a knowledge of independent Algeria, a sensitized view of the postcolonial situation in France itself. The special situation of the Algerians and other immigrants living there, with their histories of immigration and their experiences of discrimination, was now clearer to him than ever. The order of the day was now support for the specific struggles of the working immigrants. The question was how these migrant struggles (and the commitment to them) could be integrated into an understanding of communist politics and Marxist philosophy. Balibar found useful answers to this question only in the 1980s, after his political commitment and his theoretical work in the field of anti-racism came together. Significantly, this convergence also required a public break with the politics of the Communist Party.

1981 – racism from the left

The new decade began with two bombshells for Balibar. In November 1980, Louis Althusser strangled his wife Hélène Rytmann in their shared apartment at the ENS. The Althusser case caused a great stir, among other things because a court case was blocked by Althusser's friends in the Paris establishment. Instead, Althusser ended up confined in a psychiatric hospital, disappearing from the public stage on which he had previously appeared in his dual role as an influential philosophy teacher and Communist Party intellectual. The incident sealed the decline of Althusserianism, which had long been the dominant movement, and marked the beginning of a period of emancipation from their intellectual mentor for Althusser's students. With the loss of his teacher as a theoretical pillar and protective force within the PCF, Balibar sooner or later had to reorient himself in questions of Marxist theory and practice.

The second bombshell came in March 1981, when Balibar was expelled from the Communist Party. The philosopher had been a sometimes harsh critic within the party since the end of the 1970s, but the final break occurred only after the PCF had increasingly presented the image of a party veering to the right in a series of xenophobic actions in the preceding months. The most notable incident was the 'bulldozer affair' in Vitry: in the presence of the media, the communist mayor of the Parisian working-class suburb had the entrance to a dormitory in which 300 workers from Mali were housed filled in on the grounds that the quota of foreigners in Vitry had long been exceeded. This occurred during an election campaign, and the ailing PCF was clearly not afraid to use right-wing slogans to publicly exploit the fears of its core electorate in its quest for every vote. Balibar reacted to the party's racist tendencies with a long essay, 'PCF: De Charonne à Vitry', in the weekly magazine *Le Nouvel Observateur*.[28] In it he asked openly: 'Is the PCF now a racist party?' For him, the 'failures' in Vitry and other communist strongholds were by no means isolated cases that could be blamed on misguided local politicians, but actions backed by a party leadership desperate to maintain its declining power at all costs.

> It is this abdication, this surrender to racism and populism, this poor man's Peyrefitte-style approach, that has suddenly been brought to light by the bulldozer operations, the administrative 'quotas' designed to limit the number of immigrants and impose the 'threshold of tolerance' wherever it is possible, and the risk, blithely accepted, of equating every North African in the public eye with a potential drug trafficker![29]

Balibar added that the Party had connived with a policy that would effectively block any further immigrants, while failing to ensure that those already in France would be protected or have any real say in their fate. The slogans on which the Party relied claimed to be defending immigrants, while they actually deprived them of agency and even tended to justify all kinds of arbitrary expulsions. The party leadership's reaction was not long in coming: it immediately threw Balibar out of the party.

If you look more closely at the text, you can see why it did so. The article is not just an intervention by a party intellectual in day-to-day politics, but also an attempt to explain and examine historically how these racist actions could have occurred in the PCF – a party that always saw itself as anti-colonial and, since the Algerian War, had consistently presented itself as such. Balibar was thus ruthlessly putting the party's alleged anti-colonialism to the test and shedding light on an unresolved past. The result of his examination: 'a long and disturbing history' full of myth-making and missed opportunities, in which one 'encounters the destructive effects of nationalism and an anti-colonialism that is often more verbal than consistent at every turn'.[30]

Balibar begins his account at one of the central places of remembrance of the Communist Party, the Charonne metro station, where eight communist trade unionists had been killed during the protests of 8 February 1962. In order to prove its anti-colonial commitment during the Algerian War, the party had since repeatedly and quite rightly made reference to these dead comrades. But this memory already contained an ambiguity that bothered Balibar and whose consequences could still be felt: the party continued, as before, to glorify those who fell on that day, but never recalled the reason for the demonstration itself:

> They always only talk about an abstract and mythical anti-colonial struggle. There are many who can testify from very clear memory that if there was a unified demonstration on February 8, 1962 and, before that, December 19, 1961 …, then it was only because there had been *the terrible October 17, 1961, about which the party is silent and no one else speaks anymore.*[31]

This was a reference to the massacre of the Algerian demonstrators, whose bodies had to be recovered from the Seine the following day. Balibar not only criticizes the lack of recognition of this event, which impelled him to act as he did; behind the one-sided memory of the PCF, he uncovers completely different, and bitter, truths. For example, the party never took a clear stance on the Algerian question, but often hesitated and sometimes tolerated the war for nationalist reasons; its demonstrations always opposed the fascism of the OAS and the imperialism of de Gaulle, but never addressed the concerns of the Algerians, let alone stood up for them. The communists and many other leftists called for solidarity at the demonstrations, but Algerian protestors with their own demands were neither invited nor really wanted there, because here too – it needs to be said loud and clear – a political culture of segregation prevailed.[32]

Balibar's conclusion: the party had 'no right to claim a monopoly on anti-colonialism' because it was never consistently anti-colonial. From Charonne to Vitry, a contrary history of missed opportunities and disappointments could be observed. He counts among these failings the party's inability to recognize the Algerians' aspirations to independence during the war, but also its subsequent ignorant attitude towards the immigrants, who mainly came from former French colonies.

> The opportunity to create an organic unity in the class struggle between the French workers and the immigrant workers was missed. For both, internationalism remained ... a matter of calculating converging interests, instead of becoming a common practice in which the participants gradually get to know each other, overcome their contradictions and begin to envisage a common future.[33]

Balibar's choice of words reveals a great deal of Marxist-utopian pathos, but this does not diminish the sharpness of his analysis: on migration issues, the Communist Party actually followed nationalist interests most of the time, and its appeal to the internationalism of the working class was just decorative.[34] The roots of current party politics, Balibar argued, lay in such inconsistencies and blind spots: 'Consequently, we should not be surprised if it suddenly turns out that it too is permeated by the worst temptations of moralism and racism that threaten French society.'[35]

In view of this threatening scenario, Balibar also saw what was at stake for his party, which was already in decline in 1981: the danger that its flirtation with racist resentment would lead to slogans such as 'They need to go, they're taking our jobs away from us' becoming part of its usual repertoire, that a 'gangrene' would develop that would slowly but surely eat into the party with no one knowing where it would end. 'But who it will benefit is already quite clear: when it comes to mobilizing those who are nostalgically waiting for a "France of the French", there are other forces that are better prepared and more "credible" than the Communists. And their posters are already stuck to every wall.'[36] Balibar was to be proved right in this assessment. In the 1983 French regional elections, the far-right Front National (FN) of Jean-Marie Le Pen achieved one of its first significant electoral victories. The PCF suffered heavy losses.

Think what you will of Balibar's 1981 article: many of his comments could be dismissed as those of a disappointed communist who had been a member of an ossified, Moscow-loyal party for far too long and was now attempting to make up for this with a belated, compensatory zeal in an act of (self-)critique. One could just as well speculate that Balibar, who had long been one of the best-known opposition figures within the party and was now more isolated than ever after the

Althusser scandal, may even have deliberately provoked his premature expulsion with this article. Both points may be true, but it would still be too simplistic to understand the text merely as the expression of an intellectual's personal alienation from his party.

The essay offers more: the questions and problems Balibar discusses are, from today's perspective, extremely topical and far from being resolved. He addresses fundamental shifts in France's political culture that continue to have an impact today. In drawing attention to the left's dangerous flirtation with racist reflexes and the possible shifts in electoral support towards the Front National, his essay is an early problematization of developments that have been increasingly troubling the French and European public in view of the electoral successes of right-wing populist parties in recent years. One of the best-known books often cited in discussions about the characteristics and causes of right-wing populism (and the role that left-wing parties play in it) is the bestseller *Returning to Reims* by the French sociologist Didier Eribon. Interestingly, Eribon makes the migration of voters from the PCF to the FN, predicted by Balibar, the heart of his auto-sociobiographical reflections. Drawing on his own family history, he addresses the question of why large parts of the working class, who previously viewed the PCF and other left-wing parties as their natural political representatives, have increasingly voted for the FN since the 1980s. Anyone searching for a historical echo of Eribon's retrospective narrative will find what they are looking for in Balibar's text.

Balibar's essay contains another important point, which can undoubtedly be applied to current conditions. It is the discovery – one that is not easy to prove even on closer inspection and becomes clear only after a meticulous analysis – that there might also be something like a problem of structural racism among leftists. By exposing the internal contradictions of the PCF with regard to its double-edged anti-colonialism, Balibar draws attention to a general blind spot that can affect not only one aging party, but also the entire political left. His warning: do not believe that as a leftist you are automatically exempt from racism or protected from it. Racism does not always come only from the right, as one might expect. It can also be rampant on the left, where, even though it may be more hidden and subtle, it is no less problematic and exclusionary. Racism, as we know, has many faces. Demonstrating this has become a leitmotif of Balibar's anti-racist commitment and thinking since his 1981 essay.

1988 – a new theory for a new racism

The Vitry affair was merely the harbinger of a whole series of xenophobic and racist incidents that occurred in the early 1980s. During this phase, France increasingly had to contend with racially motivated acts of violence, unsolved murders, and controversial police operations, which subsequently led to the emergence of anti-racist protest movements such as SOS Racisme and La marche pour l'égalité et contre le racisme (March for equality and against racism).[37] The decade had actually begun with an upwelling of hope, when, with the election of François Mitterrand as French president in 1981, a socialist government came to power with a liberal integration and migration policy. But not much of this was left by 1983 at the latest, as Mitterrand made his neoliberal-conservative turn in the wake of a persistent economic crisis. At the same time, the FN made advances at the ballot box. The party's electoral successes initially remained local and relatively manageable. But Le Pen was already beginning to have an impact with slogans like 'Two million unemployed are two million immigrants too many' that helped shape the country's political agenda. The FN received ideological support from the so-called Nouvelle Droite (New Right) – a collective term for the right-wing extremist intellectuals who had enjoyed a rapid rise in popularity since the late 1970s. By adopting theories of popular nationalism and the incompatibility of cultures, they gave themselves a bourgeois veneer that many people found less racist. The philosopher Alain de Benoist was considered the mastermind of this New Right. Generously supported by conservative circles in the Parisian cultural establishment, de Benoist quickly managed to make right-wing ideas socially acceptable in France and across Europe, with bestsellers and numerous media appearances.[38] The ascendency of these New Right thinkers was unmistakable testimony to the fact that Paris, once the preserve of die-hard left-wing intellectuals, had within a few years become 'the capital of European intellectual reaction', as the British historian Perry Anderson noted in 1983.[39]

Race, Nation, Class, which, as mentioned above, Balibar wrote together with the American sociologist Immanuel Wallerstein, also belongs to this context of a resurgence of racist discourse. Published in French in 1988 and translated into numerous languages, the book quickly became a standard work in international research on racism and is still considered an important reference point today.[40] It grew out of a series of seminars that Balibar and Wallerstein held together at the Maison des Sciences de l'Homme in Paris between 1985 and 1987. In the years following his expulsion from the PCF, Balibar had intensified his anti-racist commitment and regularly intervened in political debates. He wrote articles on voting and citizenship law and on France's colonial legacy, and was one of the first to call for the 'decolonization of France'.[41] Parallel to his political commitment, however, as a philosopher Balibar was also confronted with a fundamental problem that required theoretical and historical reflection rather than activism: Why is racism still on the rise? Why is it still so strong, or becoming so strong again, forty years after the defeat of Nazism, thirty years after formal decolonization, and twenty years after the recognition of civil rights for the African-American population of the United States? Why can't it be defeated?

Balibar also noted the lack of theoretical tools needed to understand and explain the phenomenon of a racism that was increasing worldwide. One thing was clear to him: Marxism was no longer sufficient as the sole explanatory system. With only a fossilized theory that plasters the world with major and secondary contradictions and explains history as a class struggle, the phenomenon of racism could not be adequately addressed conceptually. Rather, it required a modified vocabulary, different categories, sharper historical analyses, and, last but not least, new perspectives that could shed light on the different political experiences and dimensions of colonialism, nationalism, and global capitalism. In short, a new theory was needed – one which, it should be noted, was not born from an anti-Marxist impulse but still understood by Balibar as a contribution to Marxist debate.[42]

With Immanuel Wallerstein, Balibar had exactly the right intellectual partner for this project. At the time, Wallerstein was primarily known for developing his so-called world systems theory – a large-scale attempt to describe the emergence and functioning of capitalism on a decidedly global scale, even before 'globalization' became a buzzword. He was also a leading expert on anti-colonial liberation movements and their often rocky paths to independence. In the 1950s and 1960s, he had researched the processes of transformation in African nation states.[43] Wallerstein was not as yet an expert on racism, but he nevertheless had the aura of a nonconformist left-wing scholar who was influenced by the 1968 protests at Columbia University as well as by the anti-racist movements in the United States and South Africa. His reputation was certainly enhanced by the fact that he was one of the few people who had had the pleasure of engaging in long and detailed conversations with Frantz Fanon: first in the summer of 1960 in Accra, Ghana, where Fanon often stayed as the Africa ambassador of the provisional Algerian government, and where Wallerstein was conducting field research, and a second time in the autumn of 1961 in a hospital in Washington, DC, where Fanon was being treated in the final stages of his leukaemia after completing his work on *The Wretched of the Earth*.[44] Wallerstein was subsequently one of the first to try to make fruitful use of Fanon's work for sociological research.[45] In addition to his scholarly interest in the further development of Marxist theory, he also shared with Balibar his roots in the international milieu of left-wing activists and intellectuals – whether from Paris, New York, or Algiers – involved in anti-colonial movements.[46]

Race, Nation, Class ultimately became more of an academic essay than a systematic theory. The book is a dialogue between two authors who, from one text to the next, exchange their sometimes divergent views and work out their different positions. Each text is determined by the focus on a specific question: What is the specificity of contemporary racism? Why does it still exist despite massive critique and many struggles? How is racism connected to capitalism and the rise of the nation state? When do conflicts between social groups and classes become racist? The remarkable thing about the book is that Balibar and Wallerstein discuss these questions of racism, capitalism, and the nation state as interconnected and historically conditioned categories. As conscientious Marxists, they remain true to the principles of historical-materialist analysis and do not abandon the category of class. But the real intellectual momentum is now sought elsewhere – wherever racism is commonly related to capitalism, the nation, or any of the other large historical formations that make up a society, such as class, work, gender, community, identity, or the state.

Where does the uncanny strength of racism lie? For Balibar and Wallerstein, it can ultimately be explained only in terms of structural causes: 'To the extent that what is in play here – whether in academic theories, institutional or popular racism – is the categorization of humanity into artificially isolated types, there must be a violently conflictual split at the level of social relations themselves.'[47] Racism, according to their thesis, is neither a mere prejudice, nor a passing episode, nor an archaic relic, but a social relationship that is inseparably linked to the actual structures of this world and is reproduced in them – as a kind of internal complement to the bourgeois, capitalist, nationalist, sexist, and exploitative world. Racism cannot therefore be reduced to an attitude or mindset that could be quickly remedied by circulating enough anti-racist ideas and engaging in educational work. Rather, it is the historical product of social divisions (the division of labour, the division of the world into centre and periphery), and is itself historically and structurally rooted in the emergence of homogeneous national state principles and global capitalist economies.

There is a special significance to talking about racism. One of its peculiarities: it is, comparatively speaking, very difficult to conceptually summarize the phenomenon to be observed and explained – to determine what racism actually is and how it works. Balibar and Wallerstein are also faced with this challenge, hence the somewhat tentative and essayistic character of their statements. In the first essay in the volume, 'Is there a "neo-racism"?', Balibar offers a long but precise description of racism that can certainly compete with contemporary attempts at a definition:

> Racism – a true 'total social phenomenon' – inscribes itself in practices (forms of violence, contempt, intolerance, humiliation and exploitation), in discourses and representations which are so many intellectual elaborations of the phantasm of prophylaxis or segregation (the need to purify the social body, to preserve 'one's own' or 'our' identity from all forms of mixing, interbreeding or invasion) and which are articulated

> around stigmata of otherness (name, skin colour, religious practices). It therefore organizes affects ... by conferring upon them a stereotyped form, as regards both their 'objects' and their 'subjects'. It is this combination of practices, discourses and representations in a network of affective stereotypes which enables us to give an account of the formation of a racist community ... and also of the way in which, as a mirror image, individuals and collectivities that are prey to racism find themselves constrained to see themselves as a community.[48]

'Is there a "neo-racism"?' is important not only in terms of its enlightening and organizing aspects, but also in terms of diagnosing the times. Even before the main argument of the intertwining of race, nation, and class is touched upon, Balibar directs his full attention to the analysis of the immediate present. The title indicates the question: in terms of the issues it addresses and its social significance, to what extent is it appropriate to speak of a 'new racism' that cannot be reduced to pre-existing models? In France, Balibar notes, racism against Jews, immigrants, and others has of course existed for a long time, and a number of theories have been developed to explain this in the past, such as anthropological racial theories. However, since the Second World War and the experiences of the Holocaust, apartheid regimes, and colonialism – in the course of which the concept of race finally fell into disrepute and was scientifically refuted – a fundamental change in the categorical theory of racism can also be observed. Balibar finds evidence of this post-war break in the way in which 'the category of immigration [functions] as a substitute for the notion of race'.[49] He is primarily looking at the racism and discrimination that was typical of the time, directed against immigrants who came to France as part of recruitment quotas and postcolonial migration. A new historical context of reference opens up: according to Balibar, the new racism is a racism of the era of decolonization, characterized by migration movements between the former colonies and the colonial metropolises.[50]

What is new about this racism is primarily that, where immigration is concerned, it seems to get by without recourse to the traditional concept of race, forging instead a stronger ideological connection with the concept of culture. Balibar, together with others, coined the terms 'racism without races' and 'cultural racism' to describe this change.[51] It is a racism whose dominant theme is no longer biological inheritance, but the ineliminability of cultural differences. A racism that, at least at first glance, no longer postulates the superiority of certain groups or peoples over others, but seems to limit itself to asserting the harmfulness of any blurring of boundaries and the incompatibility of cultural ways of life and traditions. In other words, it is a racism in the more inoffensive guise of culture.

In his essay Balibar did not name anyone who had played a part in this ideological drift, but perhaps that was not even necessary. It did not take much imagination to see that the 'new racism' was primarily based on the concepts of the aforementioned 'New Right'. One thinks of the representatives of ethnopluralism or the cultural circle theory, who expressly recognized cultural diversity but then all the more vehemently rejected the 'mixing' of cultures in Europe, a mixing primarily caused by migration. At the time, Alain de Benoist was playing this game like no other. This was particularly evident in an interview with the German news magazine *Der Spiegel*, where de Benoist, instead of talking about exclusion, preferred to propagate his idea of a cultural 're-rooting' of Europe. By this he meant 'that ethnic groups become aware of their cultural history again, and people learn to live with an awareness of their past and future'. In the conversation, he countered the accusation of racism with a feigned anti-racism: 'In many articles against racism, I have always emphasized that history is more important than biology, culture more important than nature.'[52] The fact that almost every issue of his own magazine preferred to quote German authors from the Nazi era on matters of culture and race was lost in this culturalist argument.

The shift from biological to cultural arguments for racism should not, however, be seen as a one-way street or a complete displacement. On the one hand, Balibar shows that there were already symbiotic links between biological and cultural arguments in earlier forms of racism, such as in antisemitism or in the French colonial ideology of the civilizing mission.[53] On the other hand, he points out that biological remnants do not really disappear, especially in cultural racism, since talk of the cultural differences between people is still based on supposedly biological-natural characteristics such as skin colour or ethnic origin. What has changed, however, is that over time the content and ideological emphasis has shifted more towards cultural themes, because the purely biological argument has become socially unacceptable and is now ruled out. The form of racist discourse remains almost the same, despite the change in category. The concept of culture has the same function of exclusion as the concept of 'race'. This preference for a cultural racism without races, however, produces a new effect that is very powerful: if people do not speak explicitly about racism and races, then the accusation of racism no longer holds water, because only an argument conducted in purely biological terms is considered racism. In this way, racism is masked and de-thematized.[54]

With his observations on and conceptualizations of the new racism, Balibar provided a useful tool for 'knowing one's enemy'. In order to combat racism, it was necessary to know exactly how it manifests itself, how it functions, and how it changes. At the same time, his statements can be read as an attempt to understand why anti-racism in particular had such difficulty identifying the new guises of racism. For Balibar, the weakening of the anti-racist position was one of the most dangerous political consequences of the changes. He blamed this on 'reverse racism' on the right, by means of which the common arguments of anti-racism were increasingly turned against it.[55] A dominant strategy here involved taking literally a culturalism that had traditionally provided the arguments for anti-racism. For example, in the 1980s, the anthropologist Claude Lévi-Strauss, who had become famous for showing that all cultures are equally complex and equally necessary for the advancement of human thought, suddenly found himself (whether voluntarily or involuntarily) being read strategically by right-wing thinkers and yoked to the idea that 'cultural mixing' and the elimination of cultural distances would lead to the spiritual death of humanity, and even threatened its biological survival.[56]

Another reverse effect was to derive supposedly intuitive and logical explanations of racist behaviour from this ethnopluralism, for example the following: if irreducible cultural difference forms the truly natural environment of man, then any blurring of this difference must necessarily trigger defensive reactions and lead to interethnic conflicts and more generally an increase in aggressiveness. Aggressive behaviour towards people from other cultures then no longer appears to be racist, but rather a completely human and natural defensive reaction. Such chains of argument often led to a demand for the 'right to difference' – an expression that was originally found in the political slogans of migrants and other minorities and was now being hijacked in order to, so to speak, pull the rug out from under anti-racism.[57] In Balibar's eyes, the new racism always appeared as a meta-racism that claimed to have learned its lessons from the conflict between racism and anti-racism, and presented itself as a politically viable theory of the causes of social aggression. This meta-racism found its most succinct forms in the claim that it is only anti-racism that creates racism, and in the thesis of reverse discrimination against white people.[58]

Balibar's essay on neo-racism, which already enjoyed a prominent position in the architecture of the entire book, continued to have a certain life of its own among readers even after the publication of *Race, Nation, Class*.[59] The concept of racism without races became a popular phrase in academia, as it seemed, on what had previously been relatively uncertain empirical ground, to grasp and explain prejudices and expressions that were based on cultural differences rather than on biological hierarchies (and thus masked their racism). The topos of cultural racism in particular has since circulated in academia, among the public, and on the activist anti-racist scene – being sometimes more, sometimes less oriented towards Balibar's own positions and background. Nowadays, it is particularly prevalent in analyses of anti-Muslim racism, since culturally and religiously connoted patterns of perception play a prominent role in exclusionary prejudices and violence against Muslims. The spread of Balibar's concepts in this field is obvious, since he had already had in his sights racist ideas about Arabs and Muslims in France when he was endeavouring to describe and explain the new racism of the 1980s. Nevertheless, there is no reason to limit these concepts to historical or national contexts. It is precisely their ubiquitous applicability, parallel to the growing social awareness of different forms of racism, that makes them so successful.[60] Balibar's theory – this much seems clear – has lost little of its descriptive power. It hit the nerve of the times in the late 1980s, and it still does so today.[61]

JACQUES
RANCIÈRE

8

DISIDENTIFY YOURSELVES! Jacques Rancière

In a book exploring the colonial experiences of French intellectuals and the effect of those experiences on their thinking, we cannot omit the little exceptions and variations. In addition to those who stayed more or less voluntarily in a North African country for a limited period of time (Barthes, Lyotard, Foucault, Bourdieu, Balibar), and those who turned their backs on their Algerian homeland as soon as they could, but after a while returned to their biographical origins (Cixous, Derrida), there is another type of philosopher who holds a similarly great potential for fascination. We are talking about those French thinkers who were born in the colonies, moved to France as children along with their parents, but subsequently kept quiet about their colonial origins in partly European settler families. Examples of this type of unforthcoming intellectual include Louis Althusser, born in 1918 in Birmandreis near Algiers, and, with some qualifications, Alain Badiou, born in 1937 in Rabat, Morocco.[1]

The philosopher Jacques Rancière should also be included in this illustrious group of intellectuals with similar backgrounds who have no urge to speak about their colonial origins. His 'colonial' story is quickly told: Rancière was born in Algiers in 1940, but spent only two years in Algeria. In 1942, the family moved first to Marseilles and then three years later to Paris. It is worth pointing out that they decided to leave Algeria, which was under Vichy rule and had been largely spared from the Second World War, for the German occupation zone, moving in the opposite direction to many other migrants and refugees, who mostly went from Paris via Marseilles to the wider world. However, nothing more precise can be said about Rancière's early childhood in colonial Algeria. The philosopher – a visible presence in French public life and willing to provide information on many other topics – has so far barely commented on this, and there is little to suggest that this might change.[2] While other public figures such as Jacques Attali have published their Algerian memoirs in old age, 'Algiers', understood as code for a philosophical reflection on origins, remains a blank space in Rancière's work.[3]

Apart from his origins, much in Rancière's academic and political career is reminiscent of Étienne Balibar. Both philosophers belong to the generation that experienced its political awakening in the course of the Algerian War. Early on, they even followed an identical trajectory: like Balibar, Rancière arrived at the ENS in 1960 and joined the Communist Student Union (UEC) the same year. A short time later, at the ENS, he made a formative acquaintance with Louis Althusser, who introduced him to Marxist philosophy. In 1965, the legendary Althusser circle produced the collective work *Reading Capital*, to which Rancière contributed a central essay. Following the events in Paris in May 1968, Rancière, like Balibar, was involved in setting up the philosophy department at the experimental university of Vincennes, where he taught as a professor until his retirement in 2000.[4]

In the 1970s their paths then diverged. Rancière set out on a different road after radically distancing himself from Althusser, the Communist Party, and orthodox Marxism. In *The Lesson of Althusser* (1974) he dismissed Althusser's thinking as a 'philosophy of order' and 'conceptual police'. However, this move away was not followed by a reactionary anti-Marxism, as was common in the mid-1970s among disillusioned leftists, in particular the 'New Philosophers' around André Glucksmann and Bernard-Henri Lévy.[5] Instead, driven by a desire for concreteness and activism, Rancière began a long and intensive phase of engagement with the history of the French workers' movement. *The Nights of Labor* (1981) was an expression of this philosophical immersion in the social history of workers' emancipation.

In the 1990s, he turned to aesthetic-political questions; to date, this preoccupation has led to around twenty books on cinema, literature, the sensual, and the visual. Despite this diversity of topics, political philosophy was and remains the centre of gravity of Rancière's thinking. Everything here revolves around the question of how the political can be thought and understood in all its diversity, be it in workers' strikes, in educational contexts, or in films. This is always linked to the demand to uphold, implement, verify, or refigure the principle of equality in political struggles. In his main work of political philosophy, *Dis-agreement* (1995), Rancière expressed it as follows: 'Nothing is political in itself for the political only happens by means of a principle that does not belong to it: equality.'[6]

The same period in which Rancière developed the central tenets of his theory of the political also saw an event that will be the focus of what follows, as it highlights the theme of France's recurring colonial past and holds a special place in Rancière's work. He may not have wanted to comment publicly on his family's origins, but in the early 1990s, in the course of pursuing his interest in modes of political subjectivation, he began to speak about events and experiences that took place during the Algerian War. One date from the final phase of the war was of particular importance: 17 October 1961.

On this day – which, as we have seen, was also key for Balibar, but let's describe it in detail here again – one of the bloodiest massacres in French colonial history took place, not in Algeria or in some other distant overseas territory, but in the middle of Paris, the capital of the colonial empire. The French branch of the FLN had called for a peaceful, albeit unauthorized, demonstration for the lifting of the curfew – for several weeks, the approximately 400,000 Algerians living in the greater Paris area, already exposed to severe racism and reprisals by the security forces, had been forbidden to leave their homes after 9 p.m. The Paris police, incited by recent FLN assassination attempts on police officers, were of the unfounded opinion that the protest would be dominated by violent demonstrators; on the instructions of their police prefect, Maurice Papon, they reacted with extraordinary severity. Before the approximately 30,000 demonstrators could even reach the intended squares and boulevards, many of them were turned away or attacked and bloodily beaten. Around 12,000 people were arrested in the process, taken to collection points on the outskirts of the city, and crammed together for days in inhumane conditions. The situation escalated when the police radio incorrectly reported that an officer had been shot, and the motto Papon had already issued at the beginning of October, 'For one policeman, ten Algerians', was repeated.[7] It was an invitation to unbridled violence. According to estimates, around 200 people were killed by the security forces. They were beaten to death with monstrous clubs, shot, and thrown into the nearby Seine – some of them still alive.

The shameful way this crime was dealt with in the aftermath was also shocking. The extent of the police violence and the actual number of

'This is where they drown the Algerians': graffiti on the parapet of a Paris quay wall on the left bank of the Seine, between the Pont des Arts and the Pont Saint-Michel, not far from the police headquarters. The inscription refers to the massacres that the Paris security forces carried out against Algerian demonstrators on 17 October 1961. It was probably created by members of the Committee for Peace in Algeria on 5 November 1961, and was painted over by the authorities on the same day. No newspaper would publish this photo at the time for fear of censorship and seizure. It was not published until twenty-five years later.

deaths were not reported in the media. There were indeed attempts at critical reporting to begin with, but censorship, news blackouts, police cover-ups, and a simple a lack of interest prevented public awareness of the case.[8] The events became taboo and were quickly forgotten by most people. Only decades later, and only slowly, did public discussion and processing of the Paris massacre begin. Its official recognition by the French government, and condemnation as a state crime, came only in 2011.

Rancière was twenty-one years old at the time of the massacre. Since the events were an open secret in left-wing student circles, it can be assumed that Rancière also knew about them early on. However, knowledge of the injustice that had occurred did not stop him, like many others, from turning a blind eye to it for decades. When he responded to the massacre and the Algerian War in the early 1990s – ten years later than Balibar – the work of remembering could no longer be separated from his philosophical interpretation of the events, nor from the theoretical framework he had developed in the meantime. The reference to certain experiences from the time of the Algerian War went hand in hand with the development of concepts such as disidentification, a central building block of his political philosophy. We can imagine this as a kind of exclusivity agreement: when Rancière talked about the concept of disidentification in the 1990s, the key words 'Algeria' and 'the Paris massacre' always came up. And whenever he mentioned 'Algeria' and 'the Paris massacre', he was talking about disidentification. It was a strange connection that needs to be explained. Was this a case of a historical experience being translated into philosophical reflection that then led to the theory, or was the experience subsequently incorporated into the already existing theory? How did this connection come about and why at this point in time? How did theory emerge here? And what significance did the Algerian War and the Paris massacre have in this context? The larger the biographical gap marked 'Algiers' becomes, the more significance is accorded to the two central texts in which Rancière described his perspective on the Algerian War. These are what we will be discussing below.

Against identity

Sometimes it seems easier to talk about one's own background when one is abroad. In any case, it is rather curious that Rancière broke his decades-long silence on the Algerian War, not in France, but in a foreign country. It was in the United States that he addressed the massacre of 17 October 1961 for the very first time, while also presenting his philosophical concept of disidentification in a particularly clear form. The occasion for this was a high-profile conference that took place in New York in November 1991 under the title 'Questioning Identity', referring to the then virulent question of identity politics.[9]

In the United States, identity politics and multiculturalism had increasingly become the subject of long and heated debates at universities and in the public sphere. The arguments focused on diversity and political correctness as well as on questions of the recognition and representation of ethnic minorities. The conference aimed to critically examine the theoretical problems arising from this form of identity politics.[10] The list of invited guests was impressive. The shooting stars of the contemporary theory scene were gathered: Judith Butler, Cornel West, Chantal Mouffe, Ernesto Laclau, Homi K. Bhabha, Slavoj Žižek, Joan Scott and, last but not least, Jacques Rancière. They all represented, in their own specific ways, certain leading discourses of the time, be they political philosophy, feminist and queer theory, postcolonial theory, or African-American studies. Rancière, whether deliberately or not, was the only guest from France to represent 'French Theory', which was very popular in North American universities at the time and so could not be left out.[11]

It is interesting that the organizers invited Rancière – someone who did not really claim to be a representative of the poststructuralist current within French Theory. Rancière had kept his distance from the postmodern and deconstructive approaches that flourished in the exchange between Paris and the American universities. He was even less interested in the topics and questions that so preoccupied his colleagues in the United States. What surprised him most was the importance that 'minoritarian' and 'communitarian' politics had assumed there.[12] He was referring in particular to multiculturalism. According to the conference discussions, this was based on the principle that every minority has an inherent right to its own culture or subculture, to heroic narratives that give it a sense of self-respect and empowerment, and such cultures should be better represented in the larger or dominant culture, but should not be integrated into or merged with it. Rancière felt that this way of making questions of identity and the commitment to existing identities ever more virulent was a 'current dead end' in political discourse.[13] To the thinker of equality, who gave priority to universal principles and values, such discussions seemed absurd. The focus on particular interests seemed to him to lose sight of the bigger political picture.

Rancière's scepticism towards identity politics and multiculturalism had less to do with a rejection of the concerns of minorities than with his specific understanding of politics and the question of what it actually means to be a political subject. He therefore used his entire lecture, entitled 'Politics, Identification, and Subjectivization', to convey to those present the advantages of his own political philosophy. Key words of his thinking were highlighted, such as the distinction between 'police' and 'politics'. Rancière's argument was as simple as it was provocative: it is more important to focus on political modes of subjectivization than on natural identities. To illustrate this, he attempted to conceptualize the gap between identity and subjectification, or, as he put it: 'the gap between the "police" community, which is defined as a community of certain identities, places and functions, and the political community as a subjectification process that dissolves this allocation of places and identities'.[14] The central process of this political subjectification, according to Rancière, consists in the act of disidentification, i.e. in the collective rejection of collective identities and attributions.

It was at precisely this point, in dealing with the idea of disidentification, that Rancière had the opportunity to return to the experiences that had led his generation in France into political activism. On the one hand, there was the Algerian War, and on the other, May 1968. The Algerian War, like the Vietnam War later for May '68, was an experience of massive disidentification with the national forces and identities that suppressed the decolonization movements. According to Rancière, this disidentification reached its peak with the Seine massacre of 17 October 1961. In his words:

> As far as my generation is concerned, politics was based on the impossible identification with the Algerians who were beaten to death and thrown into the Seine by the French police in October 1961 in the name of the French people. We could not identify with these Algerians, but we could question our identification with the 'French people' in whose name they were murdered. It was therefore possible for us to act as political subjects in the space or gap between two identities, neither of which we could adopt.[15]

These sentences were significant in several respects. Firstly, the retelling of this episode from the time of the Algerian War served as an illustrative example of a successful political subjectification of one's own milieu. Rancière describes how a previously ill-defined group of people (he did not specify who 'we' were, but presumably he meant the young French students of his generation) became political at the moment when, although unable to identify with the Algerian demonstrators, they became alienated and disidentified from the French state, and finally took to the streets in protest against the war.

But the scene he recounted was more than an example used to illustrate a political theory. After briefly mentioning the events of October 1961, Rancière immediately derived a threefold definition of the political: first, that political subjectification is never simply the assertion of an identity, but first of all the refusal of an identity imposed by the police or some other order; second, that it is usually realized in the form of demonstration and protest; and third, that it involves an impossible identification that places the subject between given identities. In return, however, this definition also meant that Rancière did not understand identity-based self-assertion as political, but rather located it in the realm of 'police order'.[16]

Rancière's emphasis on disidentification did not fail to have its effect in the New York context of the conference. His aim was to develop an understanding of politics in relation to the emergence and self-assertion of previously unrecognized groups, and to avoid the pitfalls of an identity politics based on the American model aimed at minority rights. In his efforts to distance himself from identity politics, Rancière came closer to a republican universalism traditionally prevalent in France, a universalism that is fundamentally wary of multiculturalism, which it describes pejoratively as *communautarisme*. In this universalist reading, 'identity politics' designates the particular self-assertion of a minority group that gathers under the banner of a supposedly stable common identity and resolutely separates itself from the rest of society. According to Rancière's radical understanding of politics, it could therefore not be considered political. This blanket rejection proved to be quite problematic.[17] For other participants in the conference, such as the postcolonial theorist Homi K. Bhabha, identity politics and multiculturalism were not a matter for negotiation, but an inescapable intellectual horizon. To them, Rancière's plea for disidentification must have seemed like a fatal step back into the old patterns of Eurocentric universalism. This was not the French poststructuralism that people had hoped for.

In the sometimes lively discussions about identity, diversity, and political correctness that followed the lecture, Rancière's reference to the massacre of October 1961 played no role. He had dealt with the event relatively briefly and then quickly moved on from it. In addition, most of those present did not know much about what had happened in France in the early 1960s – the massacre of the Algerian demonstrators had received hardly any publicity in France, let alone internationally. This raises the question of why Rancière decided to speak about the massacre and his formative experiences during the Algerian War for the first time in New York, and precisely at that moment. The fact that the lecture was given in the autumn of 1991 provides a clue: in France only a few weeks earlier, on 17 October 1991 to be precise, on the occasion of the thirtieth anniversary of the Paris massacre, the first tentative attempts had been made to remember the repressed event and to initiate a long-overdue reappraisal.[18] These attempts met with considerable opposition and triggered a wave of indignation in France. Rancière certainly knew about these new efforts, but he was also aware of the dangers involved in addressing the horrors of the Algerian War and the French colonial past. The fact that he chose what was, from a French perspective, a rather remote place for his first statement on those horrors was perhaps due to this fact. Sometimes, as I said, it is easier to talk about one's own affairs in a foreign country.

The cause of the other

Four years passed before Rancière spoke for a second (and last) time about the French colonial past and the massacre of 17 October 1961. This time, the occasion was an event on home soil, and one with a decidedly French-Algerian focus. In May 1995, Algerian and French intellectuals gathered at the Maison des Écrivains in Paris for the conference 'France-Algérie. Regards croisés' to discuss the past and future of French–Algerian relations. The speakers on the French side were Rancière, Balibar, Lyotard, and the sociologist Monique Gadant, all of whom had an obvious connection to Algeria in their biographies. On the Algerian side were scholars now living and researching in France, namely the philosopher Sidi Mohammed Barkat, the historian Mohammed Harbi, and the ethnologist Tassadit Yacine.[19] In keeping with the title of the conference, the aim was to look in 'both directions' at the turbulent and violent history that had entangled the two countries. However, the shadow of current violence also hung over the proceedings. In Algeria, a civil war had been raging since December 1991 between the government and Islamist groups, plunging the country into a chaos that lasted for more than ten years and resulted in up to 200,000 deaths. The conflict was followed very closely in France. This was due to the large number of Algerian intellectuals who found refuge there and reported on the terror, as well as to the large Algerian community in France, which was affected by the civil war because of family ties. The ongoing spiral of violence on the other side of the Mediterranean also sparked sympathy in the rest of French society. The reports of torture and executions – often heavily mediatized – awakened painful and sometimes buried memories of the time of the Algerian War. Shocking elements of that earlier war resurfaced in this latest one, in particular the violence against civilians and the spread of terror to French soil, as occurred in 1995 with a series of attacks on the Paris metro.

At the conference there was plenty of opportunity to discuss the past and present of the French–Algerian relationship. With a view to this troubled history, many contributions strove for the usual virtues displayed at such events, such as a willingness to engage in dialogue with respect and empathy for the other side. It was a matter of identity and otherness, of self and other. The first thing that strikes one about Rancière's contribution, entitled 'The cause of the other', is his refusal to accept these – often morally motivated – efforts to include an 'other' position. 'To speak of the cause of the other', he says, 'appears to refer politics to something it does not want to be, and which it is right not to want to be, namely ethics.' Rancière – who in his political philosophy strictly separates morality and politics and insists that moral considerations do not offer access to social normativity – seeks to show instead that there is a 'concern for the other' that is not that of ethics, and not its opposite either, but is 'truly political'.[20]

Anyone who thinks that, after this somewhat brutal elimination of the moral question in favour of a political issue unspecified here, there is a direct path to the otherness called 'Algeria' is mistaken: the opposite is the case. At any rate, Rancière clearly finds it difficult to talk about Algeria at all – that is, to call the country and its inhabitants by name, to objectify it by means of a discourse so that it could then be described from a French perspective as somehow 'Algerian' or 'other'. This is also surprising because Rancière gives his lecture a title – 'The cause of the other' – which implies precisely this debate with and about Algeria as an 'other'. But at no point is he concerned with explicitly articulating or including Algerian positions and issues, or with allowing them to speak for themselves. Rancière takes a different path: for him, speaking about the relationship between France and Algeria means first and foremost speaking about France's relationship to itself, and then about the otherness contained in this non-identical relationship, an otherness that is constantly negated and split off. Approaching the relationship between France and Algeria in this way ultimately means problematizing France's inner otherness as disidentification.[21]

We should definitely keep this point in mind when reading 'The cause of the other' if we wish to avoid major misunderstandings, as for instance when he describes the system of alterity he is studying in the French-Algerian context as his 'French Algeria', 'without provocation', as he emphasizes – something that could then be seen as provocative, because 'L'Algérie française' was the name for the occupied territory 'French Algeria' during the period of colonial rule.

The question at the core of Rancière's essay is similarly vague: 'My concern is, rather, with the reflexive gaze we turn back on ourselves when we consider an *other* whose presence or absence modifies the meaning of the adjective "French" and distances the "French" political subject from him or herself.' This does not, of course, refer to the agency of Algerians who might have initiated or shaped a political process during the Algerian War. Nor does it refer to those on the French left who expressed solidarity with the Algerian independence struggle and wanted a different France – it is significant here that Rancière, in his look back at the 1960s and the Algerian War, dismisses the positions of anti-colonial intellectuals such as Sartre, Fanon, and Bourdieu as hyper-moral self-appropriations of and over-identifications with the Algerian independence movement. Looking back, Rancière said that the question of the fight against the Algerian War and the French government had raised a completely different dilemma for him: 'in what sense, if not an ethical sense, could the cause of the Algerians be our cause?'[22] In other words, it was all about him and his generation, and nothing else.

At this point in his remarks, Rancière turns his attention to the events of 17 October 1961. They lie at the heart of his memory and his interpretation. The day on which the Algerian demonstration in Paris was brutally suppressed was an obvious and yet concealed historical 'turning point' in two respects: firstly, it was a traumatic trigger (albeit not recognized as such at the time) for the subsequent anti-war demonstrations in the autumn and winter of the same year; secondly, it was a key event in the politicization of a generation, 'a moment when the ethical aporia of the relationship between "mine" and the other was transformed into the political subjectivation of an inclusive relationship with alterity.'[23]

Rancière identifies the essence of the impact of this day with reference to three relationships that, according to him, significantly shaped the situation at the time and were entangled in questions of the visibility and invisibility of oppression: 'the relationship between Algerian militants and the French state; that between the French State and "us"; and that between the Algerian militants and "us".

It is important to emphasize here that Rancière defines this 'us' in a footnote as 'a political generation taken as a whole'.[24] This 'us' has a bitter aftertaste, because, by this standard, Algerian activists, despite their French citizenship, do not belong to Rancière's political generation. At the same time, this 'us' enables Rancière to present his interpretation of the events and the history of political subjectification contained therein. From the point of view of the French state, according to Rancière, the Algerian demonstrators appeared visibly as militant political actors and entered the public space of France as French citizens. This process, which was intolerable from the state's point of view, was stopped by the police, and even made invisible when they cleared the public space, brutally eliminated the activists, and imposed a news blackout.

What to some people might look like a fall into complete invisibility seems for others to be an opportunity for political visibility. That is how we have to understand Rancière, for better or for worse. For him, it was precisely the withdrawal of visibility caused by a police operation that first illuminated or even created the political stage of his own generation. Only on this basis was a political subjectification possible that functioned neither as an 'external aid for the other's war' nor as 'an equation of the cause of the war with our cause', but as a kind of 'dis-agreement':

> This political subjectivation was primarily the result of a disidentification with the French state that had done this in our name and removed it from our view. We could not identify with the Algerians who appeared as demonstrators within the French public space, and who then disappeared. We could, on the other hand, reject our identification with the State that had killed them and removed them from all the statistics.[25]

Disidentification as the climax of the political – the sentences quoted are reminiscent of Rancière's New York statements, right down to the almost identical wording, and not without reason: the rest of the argument builds on the well-trodden paths of 1991. As at that time, following a dense description of the political significance of the Seine massacre, he draws philosophical conclusions such as that the cause of the other as a political figure is above all the disidentification of a certain self.

Impossible solidarity

There is, however, one peculiarity that distinguishes the text 'The cause of the other' from the New York statements: Rancière does not present his theses on disidentification in an identity-political context, as was the case in the US, but turns to the topic of citizenship, a traditional theme in French discourse. There, what is called *citoyenneté* was and is often used to place questions of national identity on the agenda. But for the political philosopher Rancière it expresses first and foremost a politics of difference, namely 'a special relationship between the self and the other.' To illustrate this, Rancière points to fatal contradictions in the history of French citizenship. According to him, many disagreements can be traced back to the 1875 Code de l'indigénat – a law that sought to provide a legal definition of Frenchness in the era of colonial conquests by distinguishing between French citizens of European origin (*citoyens*) and French subjects in the colonies (*sujets*). When independence movements arose in the colonies after the end of the Second World War, France, hoping to contain decolonization efforts and save its empire, removed the distinction between *citoyens* and *sujets* by granting everyone the same French nationality. That this was true only on paper, however, was already apparent during the Algerian War, when Algerians living in France were given the official designation 'Français musulman algérien' ('French Muslim Algerian'), thus making them 'others' again.[26]

For Rancière, France's police officers in particular had made clear 'the entire distance' between the self and the other on that day in October 1961, by distinguishing, in their act of oppression, between those who had a right to appear in public space and those who did not. There were not just French people and others. There were French people only because there were others. In Rancière's words: 'The State therefore made it possible to subjectivate the self-difference of our citizenship, or a gap between juridical citizenship and political citizenship … This did not create a politics for the

Algerians. But in France it did create a political subjectivation.' This statement must be savoured: Rancière goes so far as to argue that this distance was not subjectifiable (i.e. not political) for the Algerian 'fighters involved in a war of liberation', because they were simply 'determined to win their Algerian identity through war'. He continues: 'We, on the other hand, could subjectivate it as we were caught between two definitions of citizenship.'[27] As if in a kind of reversal of perpetrator and victim, in this reading the French are 'caught' and are political subjects precisely for that reason, while the Algerian demonstrators remain apolitical subjects because they are identity-political fighters.

Rancière's turn to the topic of citizenship may have been valid and produced its own theoretical yield. To give just one example, it gives him an opportunity to include colonial-historical questions much more firmly than usual within the abstract philosophical relationship between self and other. But this opening cannot disguise the fact that there seems to be something wrong with Rancière's conception and approach. The most problematic aspect is his talk of 'we' and the 'other'. This problem has already been hinted at, but must be described in more detail here: Rancière's way of relating this 'we' to the entirety of a (French white) political generation and the 'other' to the (in his eyes Muslim and apolitical) Algerian demonstrators is so strange that he has to face the uncomfortable question of why he draws such a firm distinction in the first place and then maintains it to the end. In a philosophical analysis dealing with abstract categories, this is understandable and comprehensible. But the 'others' or the 'other', insofar as they are associated with dead Algerian demonstrators, can no longer be an exclusively philosophical category. At the point in time when 'the other' is propounded as a philosophical term, it is always also a political category that threatens to be reproduced. Although Rancière sees the internal contradictions of French citizenship and shows its oppressive effects, he to some extent intensifies these contradictions by pretending that the Algerians simply disappeared and became invisible.[28]

In line with Rancière's own approach, wherein regimes of visibility and other divisions of the sensory domain belong to the essence of politics and require historically precise scrutiny, the historical case of the Seine massacre should also be treated accordingly. But for Rancière, the Algerians – in contrast to the French – always remain abstract and nameless shapes. Even where they figure as demonstrators, their political actions and thoughts are reduced to the invisible faces and bodies of the murdered. But what about their rebellion? After all, the moment of protest is a central component of politics for Rancière. For him, however, the Algerians seem to be merely identity warriors who cannot disidentify and who therefore cannot become political subjects. In reference to Marx's statement 'They cannot speak. They must be represented', Rancière sounds as if he wants to say of the Algerians: 'They cannot disidentify. They must remain others.' But that isn't all: the Algerians must also remain others because only as others – not as victims, note, because for Rancière 'fear and pity' are, as we know, 'not political affects' – do they become the cause of a completely different disidentification and politicization, namely that of his generation. Rancière himself finally admits this, with a touch of cynicism: 'One might therefore say that the political profits from this "cause" of the other were reaped here, and one might express the paradox in the ethical teminology of an unpaid debt.'[29]

Rancière's talk of 'we' and the 'other' reveals a rather one-dimensional understanding of the possibilities for political connection between different social groups. The events during and after the Algerian War seem to have unfolded as if there could be no political relationship between the young French anti-war generation and the Algerian citizens other than through the state, and even then only as a negative disidentification. Real solidarity – so we must understand Rancière to be saying, and so he basically wants to be understood – was ultimately impossible. Rancière thereby ignores other forms of interaction and even solidarity with the Algerian cause, especially among contemporary intellectuals. One thinks of Jean-François Lyotard, who became a supporter of and 'suitcase carrier' for the FLN, not out of identification but out of solidarity. This activist alliance of relatively privileged French people with the Algerian independence movement certainly had its own blind spots and limited impact. Nevertheless, it can be claimed that, as French citizens, the 'suitcase carriers' were able to build a more concrete and closer relationship with the alterity system called 'Algeria' than Rancière was retrospectively prepared to grant with his idea of disidentification.[30]

There are various other examples that cast Rancière's generational narrative in a different light and call it into question: Pierre Bourdieu, who, in a civic act of political education, tried to describe the injustice seen in Algeria with scholarly precision and sought to make his findings public; or Étienne Balibar, who belongs to the same political generation as Rancière but evidently demonstrated a different concept of commitment and solidarity when, like many other *pieds-rouges*, he went to the University of Algiers to help in academic reconstruction after Algerian independence.

The field of possible and actual connections was, in any case, broad and diverse. The more one becomes aware of this, the more Rancière's thesis of the impossibility of solidarity falls back on him biographically and theoretically. What was actually wrong with him, the *pied-noir*, the native son of Algiers? 'La cause de l'autre' reads in part like an attempt to retrospectively legitimize a shameful political attitude, a lack of interest in the Algerian struggle. The fact that this is expressed in terms of a linguistically abstract philosophy that tolerates no morality or ethics in politics shows once again how strongly the political emotions of the past shape theory, and how strongly theory is compelled to conceal the political emotions of the past. 'La cause de l'autre' expresses something that characterized Rancière from the time of the Algerian War up to the 1990s and beyond: an inability to show solidarity.

Colour-blind

Apart from the prologue in New York, 'La cause de l'autre' remains Rancière's only notable engagement with the past of the Algerian War and the legacy of French colonialism. Some of the ideas developed at the French-Algerian meeting did find their way into *Dis-agreement*, published the same year, but these were more self-quotations than newly raised questions.[31] Since then, he has been relatively quiet – at least on the subject of the colonial past or postcolonial questions. On related topics such as migration and racism, however, Rancière regularly campaigns for groups marginalized in France such as the Roma and the *sans-papiers*. Exposing and combating racism, whether it be structural, as in the state, or party political, as in the Front National, is a recurring theme in Rancière's political interventions – this is particularly evident in his numerous articles and essays published in daily newspapers over the last thirty years.[32]

However, this commitment did not prevent Rancière from taking very controversial positions within the anti-racist left on certain political events. For example, in the autumn of 2005, after provocative statements by the then Interior Minister Nicolas Sarkozy and the brutal deaths of two boys fleeing from the police, young people in the French suburbs rioted; the disturbances lasted for weeks and the government declared a state of emergency – drawing, incidentally, on a law brought in during the Algerian War. Rancière commented on these riots several times, each time dismissing the actions of the suburban youth as apolitical and based on identity. In the spirit of the republican principle of equality he upholds, Rancière claimed to have noticed that the protestors, most of whom came from immigrant families, made no 'real political proposal' that demonstrated the ability to 'think not only for themselves but for everyone.'[33] He also emphasized that the young people were reinforcing identities assigned to them from outside instead of questioning them, and concluded that the revolt lacked political subjectivization precisely because of this lack of disidentification. In this sense, Rancière refused to show solidarity with the demonstrators because their actions did not meet his own political standards. This can certainly be called consistent. It would then be equally consistent to ask why Rancière unquestioningly and unconditionally granted this capacity for disidentification and political subjectification, which he denied to young people, to every worker and trade union struggle, no matter how small.

Rancière never made a secret of the fact that he was more interested in the workers' struggle for emancipation than in any other socio-political struggle, but it remained unclear why this focus should imply a decades-long exclusion of colonial and postcolonial topics. In an interview with the cultural scholar Sudeep Dasgupta in 2008, Rancière offered some clarification in this regard. When asked how his theory of the political subject, developed using the example of the French labour movement, related to the current boom in identity-based positions such as the hybrid conceptions of the subject in postcolonial studies, Rancière answered with a laugh: 'As you may know, I am French. In France there is no identity politics and no postcolonial studies.' According to Rancière, these topics were systematically ignored in France. He was not entirely wrong in this observation: at that time there was no tradition of postcolonial studies at French universities. For Rancière, this circumstance meant realizing, with a sense of relief, that 'I never had to deal with the topics that are important in other countries.' Even though he hinted that some commentators would 'certainly see connections between my preoccupation with identity and subjectivity and the problems of postcolonial studies', he made it clear that this preoccupation was never an attempt to 'deal with questions of identity politics or postcolonial identities and so on.' He did not think much of terms like 'hybridity' anyway.[34] Rancière was, as he made very obvious on this occasion, no friend of postcolonialism.

Rancière's clearly defined positioning, set against the background of the international impact of his text 'La cause de l'autre' in the meantime, drew criticism from a postcolonial perspective. The list of accusations is long, but essentially focuses on two points of criticism. The first was formulated most clearly by the American anthropologist and historian Ann Laura Stoler. She considers Rancière's position to be a classic expression of 'colonial aphasia' – a kind of speech block that can be traced back to collective repression in French society and that has affected many left-wing luminaries of French Theory. In this reading, Rancière proves to be particularly incapable of locating himself biographically and theoretically in the space of the French post-colony. According to Stoler, he not only rejects a 'more intimate' engagement with the 'racialized colonial situation' into which he was born; he also shows himself unable to deal adequately with the colonial entanglements that underlie the objects of his theory.[35]

Following Stoler's quite justified but somewhat simplistic findings, a second criticism has been formulated, one of a philosophical nature that focuses more strongly on Rancière's universalism. In this reading, proposed for example by Niklas Plaetzer, Rancière's unwillingness to take into account his own position as a 'white French philosopher' in the postcolonial metropolis is interpreted as the effect of a 'difference-blind universalism.'[36] This refers to a universalism that, while it rejects traditional universalisms with their transcendental attempts at ultimate justification and places much more emphasis on the articulation of claims to equality, nonetheless blatantly ignores its own particularity and situational relevance. In the present context, this means that Rancière's concept of equality refers to a 'normative Eurocentrism' because he universalizes a very specific emancipation narrative – the story of white French workers who insist on equality – and sees that as a feature of politics in general. 'Difference blindness' arises precisely when, due to such unexamined premises, other particular struggles cannot be seen or are not allowed to fit into the picture of politics. Postcolonial criticism also relates the problem of Rancière's difference blindness to his interpretations of the pro-Algerian demonstration of October 1961 and the post-migrant youth protests of 2005. His polemical interventions in this regard failed to achieve their emancipatory goal because they systematically ignored the entanglement of French universalist discourses of liberty, equality, and fraternity in the reproduction of colonial hierarchies. Ultimately, according to Plaetzer, Rancière falls into the same self-contradiction as conservative representatives of French republicanism, who criticize the discourses introduced by non-white actors as identity politics, but at the same time have no problem with 'defending their universalism as a French peculiarity.'[37]

This form of postcolonial criticism prefers to operate with concepts from the field of American critical race theory, such as critical whiteness, white ignorance, or racialized colour blindness. In relation to Rancière, it ultimately comes down to accusing him of being an old white man.[38] However, French idiosyncrasies can only be explained to a limited extent in this way. It is therefore all the more important to emphasize here that the self-contradictions of universalism mentioned above are primarily homemade and inherent in the self-imposed ideals of the French Republic. According to its constitution, France is an indivisible and secular republic that guarantees the equality of all citizens before the law, without distinction of origin, race, or religion. By definition, then, it recognizes no skin colour and no religion, is universalistic by principle, and is therefore consciously 'colour-blind' – for example, no collection of official statistical data on ethnic and religious affiliations is permitted. The social reality is, as we know, quite different, and anything but colour-blind. It is therefore not surprising that the French state (and with it state-centred philosophies such as Rancière's) has great difficulty in dealing adequately with the real inequalities – be they privileges or discrimination – within French society. Rancière's self-contradictions are also France's self-contradictions.

As accurate as the criticism of Rancière may be, it should not be ignored that there are also constructive sides to his theory of the political. His equality thinking in particular has inspired numerous analyses of political struggles in the recent past, in which marginalized groups and their protests (the Gilets Jaunes, Black Lives Matter) were central.[39] Rancière's conception of politics always circles around the point of rebellious disagreement on equality issues, around the 'share of the shareless'.[40] This obviously finds an echo wherever, in the name of a universal right, a certain group of people rejects a hegemonic feature attributed to them and claims precisely this share for themselves in the mode of public protest.

Rancière's criticism of identity politics is also astonishingly topical. His scepticism towards overly entrenched identity-political positions, which he expressed in New York in 1991, is certainly highly relevant to current discussions on the topic. This has a lot to do with the fact that the entire New York conference, with its critical reflection on 'identity', points in a compelling manner to a problem that is again emerging today under changed political and media conditions; it may be a problem that never really disappeared. Rancière's continued unease with identity politics is not a sign of a reactionary politics from the right, but rather a reminder from the left that, in the struggle for justice, reference to the category of identity can lead to a theoretical and political dead end. In his eyes, identity always runs the risk of assuming an ethnic, social, or cultural rootedness that fills it with content; it thereby also runs the risk of falling on the side of a hegemonic, order-imposing, 'police'-enforced power. A theory that relies on pre-formed identities ultimately loses its critical and political dimension.[41]

The question of what to make of Rancière's concept of disidentification remains open. The struggle for recognition can, as is well known, be understood as a demand by an already formed subject for recognition of its identity. Claims by minority groups, for example, are understood as claims to have their identity respected. But according to Rancière, we can also understand them as claims to 'not have this identity *attributed to them*'.[42] Disidentification as a way out of the jungle of identity politics? At first glance, it is surprising that this central proposal by Rancière has not received any significant attention in most current debates, which also reveal an undeniable frustration with the excesses of identity politics and have triggered demands for less rather than more identity. After careful consideration, it also becomes clear why this is the case: the concept of disidentification became caught up in contradictions when it was used to legitimize and explain the politicization of a generation during the Algerian War. But the idea of disidentification is not to be ruled out just because it didn't work in this case. Every policy – even one seeking to promote the recognition of identities and groups – would do well to generate a disidentifying moment in its positioning, from which political subjectification can emerge. In the end, it is this idea of a progress from identities to subjects that Rancière seems to be urging on us, based on his preoccupation with the philosophical effects of the Algerian War. Disidentify yourselves! And become political subjects.

9

WHO'S AFRAID OF THEORY?

French Theory is currently going through a tough time. After decades of hovering at the zenith of academic and intellectual circles, it's now in a bad way. In the op-eds and cultural debates of today, a growing number of voices sharply criticize the representatives of French Theory, seeing them as the intellectual originators of destructive social phenomena such as 'fake news', 'cancel culture', 'wokeness' and 'identity politics.' Poststructuralism and postmodernism had frequently been written off in the past, by critics on both left and right.[1] One could even say that these polemics actually helped propel thinkers such as Michel Foucault, Jacques Derrida, and Jean-François Lyotard to their position as the stars of international theory. But the criticism that has emerged in recent years has a special significance, not least because of the increasing distance in time: it has taken on the form of a historical tribunal.

Dead philosophers are now being held accountable for the political legacy of their old ideas. The accusations are serious: the postmodern relativization of truth and reason is deemed ideologically responsible for the post-truth age, with its unchecked spread of alternative facts, anti-science conspiracy theories, and populist demagogues. The more recent debates in identity politics over making marginalized groups visible and regulating language in terms of political correctness can also be traced back to poststructuralist concepts that consider identity to be something ascribed and constructed, and that problematize language as essentially a practice of violence. In plain terms, the poststructuralists are to blame for the dogmatism of left-wing identity politics because they launched ideas and concepts that were subsequently used by 'woke' activists in the fields of gender studies, queer theory, postcolonialism, and critical race theory to enforce bans on speaking and thinking.[2] Fantasy reigns supreme in these historical genealogies and attributions of blame. Ultimately, one thing always seems clear: the verdicts, as is usual in show trials, have already been decided in advance.

Let's be clear from the start: many of these accusations against French Theory are based (intentionally or not) on grotesque misreadings, insinuations, and resentments. They neither stand up to close scrutiny nor do they deserve it. The arguments, if they are arguments at all, are usually too crude, and the way they have been cobbled together can be seen through quickly and easily.[3] One could therefore laugh at these attacks, dismiss them as mere historical nonsense, or simply ignore them – if they weren't so politically effective. On the one hand, they have significantly changed the public image of French Theory. Appearing so prominently in leading media, and reproduced there in a continuous loop, it is no surprise that these distorted representations are actually believed at some point – especially by those for whom such depictions are their first contact with French schools of thought. On the other hand, these attacks are embedded in a larger political agenda that goes beyond mere academic theory. They have become a popular tool for conservative and right-wing movements that, in their ideological fight against 'gender', 'postcolonialism', and 'anti-racism', also exploit the history of ideas in an attempt to get certain theories banned. Seen in this way, the historical tribunal is therefore not just a matter of putting the history of ideas to a show trial, but a symptom of current anti-intellectual, anti-liberal, and authoritarian developments. At stake is not only the political legacy of French Theory, but also the dispute over sociopolitical buzzwords and phantasms such as 'identity politics' and 'cancel culture'.

Given this starting point, it is urgently necessary to look more closely at the current debates about French Theory and to put a few things right in the historical record. This does not mean providing an apology (since this would follow the logic of the opponents of theory, who divide the world into two ideological camps), but rather refusing to leave the mapping out of the intellectual field to those who use theory tribunals exclusively to pursue their political agenda – or those who have already simply given up thinking. To this end, we need first to trace some basic features and functions of this highly specific political discourse via concrete examples, and then to understand why and how works by figures such as Derrida or Foucault became entangled in current debates and dragged into the dock. Such an approach, one that strives for clarification, is not only based on the demand for historical accuracy; it is also linked to the hope that we can assess – somewhat more clearly than the critics who mistakenly think they know what's what – how far these French philosophers are still important today and why we should continue to read them.

False enemies

The theory bashing I have mentioned is an international phenomenon that pops up at regular and seemingly ever shorter intervals, particularly in the United States but also in France and Germany. In France in recent years, theory bashing has been at the heart of the new culture wars, reaching even into the highest government circles. To take one particularly relevant example among many: in January 2022, accompanied by much media hype, a conference entitled 'Après la déconstruction' ('After Deconstruction') took place at the Sorbonne, organized by the 'Observatoire du décolonialisme et des idéologies identitaires' (also known as the 'University Ethics Observatory'), among others. This is the name of an association of around one hundred French university teachers who, as they themselves write, are concerned about the abuses of 'identity and communitarianism and their effects at the university', by which they mean above all the postcolonial and anti-racist positions that they dislike.[4] Similar to its German counterpart, the 'Network for Academic Freedom', this 'Observatory' acts like a right-wing think-tank that, in the name of scholarly objectivity, seeks to put a stop to 'ideological' and 'polarizing' tendencies in science and in the public sphere, but in fact itself agitates and polarizes in completely political ways. This was also true of the conference in question, which brought together several well-known scholars and intellectuals from the anti-woke camp, in panels on topics such as gender, race, intersectionality, and cancel culture, to discuss these different discourses under the unexamined collective term 'deconstruction.'[5]

This was by no means the last of the over-generalizations and simplifications: 'deconstruction' was an umbrella term that loomed larger than all other labels such as poststructuralism, postmodernism, French Theory, or 1968 thinking, and included philosophers such as Pierre Bourdieu, Michel Foucault, Jacques Derrida, Hélène Cixous, Gilles Deleuze, and Étienne Balibar. What in reality consists of different and partly conflicting approaches and discourses was presented and staged here as a homogeneous theory – necessarily so, otherwise its 'menace' would not have registered so intensely. The general finding was that deconstruction had produced a nihilistic, militant, and therefore dangerous way of thinking; it had become the theoretical arm of an ideology that 'invades knowledge, paralyses culture, and terrorises public opinion under the pretext of a new moral order.'[6] The aim of the conference, in contrast, was presented as an unbiased stocktaking, simply striving to 'restore science and culture,' as the conference subtitle put it, after all the nihilistic destructiveness of deconstruction. But the openly displayed 'anti-' character of the event (anti-woke, anti-gender, anti-postcolonial), and the absence of other or opposing positions that might have made expert contributions to the whole issue, made it abundantly clear that the aim here, in the cultural struggle against 'wokeness,' was to exaggerate the supposed political effects of deconstruction as much and as conspiratorially as possible, so as to discredit it as definitively as possible. This also meant killing two birds with one stone: not only did the conference aim to liquidate deconstruction as a theoretical project, throwing it on the scrap heap of the history of ideas; it also aimed to enforce yet again the anti-deconstructionists' right-wing agenda and interpretive sovereignty at French universities.

The conference had a particular political explosiveness as it took place in the lecture halls of the venerable Sorbonne, and was directly supported financially by the French Ministry of Education. The Education Minister Jean-Michel Blanquer even opened the proceedings with a welcome speech, ennobling it, in a sense, with his presence. During his five-year term in office, Blanquer was a determined and leading critic of what he called (without further specification) the 'woke' movement in France; here, he was in line with President Emmanuel Macron, who had previously taken a similar position when he labelled anti-racist positions as an 'ethnicization of the social question', 'un-republican', and 'separatist', and blamed the academic world for their spread.[7] Macron and Blanquer agreed above all that France's political discourse was in danger of becoming 'Americanized',[8] by which they meant that a certain type of identity politics was threatening French republicanism. In his speech at the Sorbonne, Blanquer spoke of the need to fight against the enemies of the Republic at the level of ideas. On this battleground, deconstruction appeared to be a successful theory to which young people in particular were receptive, which had already caused havoc in the United States, especially in its universities, and which was now threatening France 'like a virus' from abroad. In the middle of the pandemic, and just a few weeks before the outbreak of the Russian war on Ukraine, Blanquer thought he knew where the two main enemies of the French Republic came from: 'The anti-democrats may come from the East, but the deconstructionists come from the West.'[9] He admitted, albeit through gritted teeth, that France, with the success of 'French Theory', bore a certain responsibility for the worldwide spread of deconstruction. 'But since we have transmitted the virus', he said, 'we must now also provide the vaccine.'[10] In his eyes, this meant defending freedom of expression in universities and schools, upholding republican ideals such as equality and secularism, and above all taking action against ideas that did not fit with these ideals – all in all, a symbolically powerful attempt to restore nothing less than the republican order in the educational system and society.

Blanquer's discourse-policing manoeuvre did not go unchallenged in public. In the academic world, many felt that his appearance at this event was a scandalous overstepping of boundaries. After all, he was addressing this forum as a senior representative of the French state, not just someone voicing a private opinion. The sociologist François Dubet asked in the daily newspaper *Le Monde*: 'How can it come about that the state says which schools of thought are acceptable and which are not?' He saw a 'soft McCarthyism' on the horizon.[11] Indeed, the minister's speech was an extraordinary attack on the autonomy of scholarship, as well as a classic performative contradiction: in the name of academic freedom at universities, it amounted to nothing less than a political interference in academic freedom. While Blanquer viewed the need to speak out on 'woke' topics as a republican struggle for freedom, and promoted it with state resources, for him, all attempts to analyse racist and colonial structures in society were to be either limited or banned. You could talk about freedom, but when it came to racism and colonialism, silence was the order of the day.

This was less a matter of tunnel vision than of political calculation. During his time as minister, Blanquer had filed a lawsuit against a French teachers' union because it had used the term 'state racism' when publicizing one of its educational workshops on anti-racism – in Blanquer's eyes, in a republic where everyone is equal, there could be no racism on the part of the state.[12] In the end, the lawsuit was quietly dropped, as was the much-heralded commission of inquiry that was to be set up by the Minister of Higher Education, Frédérique Vidal, to home in on postcolonial activities at universities and the alliance between left-wing groups and Islamist movements ('*islamo-gauchisme*') that Blanquer claimed was an issue.[13] The national research centre CNRS, which was asked to carry out the investigation, refused to do so, making it clear in an official statement that the term '*islamo-gauchisme*' did not correspond to any 'scholarly reality'.[14] Even if the lawsuit and the commission of inquiry were both unsuccessful, the political calculation worked: combative words were uttered, and accusations of Islamism flew thick and fast; nor did they disappear quickly given the past history of Islamist terrorist attacks. The politicization of the scholarly terrain had reached a new level of escalation, and the damage done to academic research, which was already under pressure, was as great as possible, with little effort on the part of the aggressors.

The same fate befell deconstruction, or rather French Theory, with the hubbub surrounding the Sorbonne conference. After 'deconstruction' had been set up as a monstrous straw man, to be shot down with great aplomb, hardly anyone involved in the media hype surrounding the 'wokeness' debate was inclined to give proper airspace to a discussion of what 'deconstruction' actually was, let alone to defend it. What stuck with many was the vague feeling that French Theory must have had a malevolent impact on the confusing and worrying tendencies of their own present. It was not until a year later, in January 2023, that some of the remaining protagonists of deconstruction, old companions of Derrida, and others who had been the target of criticism, gathered for a small counter-event in Paris: they included Étienne Balibar, the New York philosopher Avital Ronell, and the gender researcher Anne Emmanuelle Berger (the daughter of Hélène Cixous). The event was tellingly called 'Who's Afraid of Deconstruction?', but the main aim was to give a voice to those who sought to maintain the intellectual legacy of deconstruction in one form or another.[15] This time, the conference was barely noted in the media. Apparently, when it comes to mobilizing the public, bashing theory is more effective than defending it.

False friends

'Deconstruction' has become a veritable phantasm. Like the key words 'gender' and 'identity', it triggers in public opinion a bundle of fears and anxieties about social and moral disintegration.[16] But one question remains unanswered in this rather emotional process: why is it that deconstruction, and in particular Jacques Derrida, are so often the focus of attention? In the numerous indictments – to employ the image of the historical tribunal again – Derrida's name is always to be found. This needs to be explained: it is by no means a mere coincidence. Within the ranks of the poststructuralists, Derrida is undoubtedly one of the most popular targets. Like no other, his philosophy stands for the downgrading of absolute, universalistic truth claims and for a fundamental questioning of the metaphysical certainties of a Western, hegemonic reason. Derrida's argument is that Western thought, from Plato via Rousseau to Claude Lévi-Strauss, fell hopelessly prey to the illusion that language can provide us with privileged access to reality – an illusion that he describes as logocentrism, ethnocentrism, or phallocentrism, and considers to be a 'a blinding and misunderstood symptom of the crisis of European consciousness.'[17] Derrida thus not only represents the central concerns of the larger French theoretical movement. He is also considered a key inspiration for work in the field of postcolonial theory, which, in the spirit of deconstruction, examined the canonical texts in the history of European culture and knowledge for moments of 'epistemic violence' and implicit hierarchies.[18] It cannot be emphasized enough: without the influence of Derrida (and other figures of French Theory), large parts of postcolonial thought and its emergence in the 1980s cannot be understood. Anyone who today reads or re-reads the classics of postcolonial studies and cultural studies – by authors such as Homi K. Bhabha, Gayatri Chakravorty Spivak, or Stuart Hall – will soon realize how present Derrida's work is in these texts.[19]

The postcolonial and feminist theorist Gayatri Spivak deserves special mention here. A literary scholar who teaches at Columbia University in New York, Spivak translated Derrida's *Of Grammatology* into English in 1976 and, as a mediator and interpreter of his work, contributed significantly to Derrida's success in US universities.[20] She became an icon of postcolonialism with her groundbreaking essay 'Can the Subaltern Speak?', which deals with the question of whether and how the subaltern – meaning marginalized and oppressed groups in postcolonial societies, such as Indian women – can raise their voices, i.e. make their perspectives and political concerns visible.[21] In order to dissolve these subaltern positions and give them access to political spaces of negotiation, Spivak proposes a 'strategic essentialism', that is, a way of thinking and acting in which certain identities or cultural characteristics are consciously emphasized in order to strengthen common interests and form alliances.[22] This essentialism is strategic (and therefore necessarily simplistic or reductive) in that it describes the collective, performative, and politically oriented reaction of postcolonial actors to homogenizing and naturalizing attributions of identity.[23]

Since Spivak's 1988 essay, 'strategic essentialism' has become a catchphrase in the theory and practice of social movements. At the same time, because of Spivak's admission that political practice cannot be carried out without essentialization and identity politics, it is also a welcome gateway for the criticism that sees a renaissance of the category of identity in deconstruction. However, there is a fundamental difference in time and content between Derrida's ideas and Spivak's concepts. For example, 'strategic essentialism' is a reaction to a completely different problem – the situation of colonized or formerly colonized subjects – and it was already being formulated by Spivak in critical opposition to French theories. But this fact is often ignored. What needs to be addressed in the objection that we are dealing here with the ideological core of identity politics are suspicions about its origin, especially when Derrida is said by his accusers to have paved the way and sown the seeds.[24]

It is important to keep this brief reception history in mind. Only in this way can the more recent invectives levelled at French Theory – and some of the oddities in the debates, especially those in Germany – be understood. Curiously, the criticism of Derrida is often voiced by people who in the past were influential mediators of the French theoretical movement at German universities. Their own enthusiasm for theory seems to have waned with age, and they are shocked to discover that the Derrida they once lauded to the skies has – without them noticing – become the academic reference point for feminist, queer, and postcolonial discussions that they are reluctant to engage with. Derrida is also subjected to a revisionary assessment, and this time, not surprisingly, he falls from grace. His work is simply declared to be a 'fair weather philosophy' that has no connection to reality, and is shelved as the kind of criticism that 'could only flourish in the shadow of a stable liberal society,' one that no longer exists in this form, in view of the bans on thinking and speaking.[25] It is highly doubtful, however, whether colonial Algeria and crisis-ridden post-war France were actually stable liberal societies with no restrictions or bans of their own. As we saw in the chapter on Derrida, a certain philosophy grew up under the Algerian sun, in the fateful shadow of war, violence, hatred, and exclusion.

Apart from this peculiarity, with German devotees of Derrida belatedly turning tail, most of the commentary in Germany has run a similar course to the French and American debates. This testifies more to resentment towards current schools of thought and political discussions than to any informed knowledge of old philosophical texts. Some voices from the bourgeois-conservative camp express their frustration with 'wokeness' and 'identity politics' and seek out those intellectually responsible, denouncing the 'cultural hegemony of deconstructionism at the universities'.[26] Here, too, it is claimed that 'deconstructionism' is a homogeneous theory that displaces and suppresses everything else. With the best will in the world, one cannot say this is true, since the popularity of Derrida's texts in contemporary seminars is currently rather limited. Others, however, attempt to redeem French Theory by laying the blame, not on Foucault and Derrida, but on their 'false friends'[27] – theorists such as Judith Butler and Gayatri Spivak, and so-called 'social justice warriors' who have misunderstood the critical thinking of the French writers and misused it in a moral-ideological struggle for sexual, migrant, and postcolonial identities.[28] At first glance, these may look like rescue attempts aimed at setting out clear differences. But the chauvinistic-nostalgic tone of many of these articles reveals that poststructuralism and postcolonialism are being played off against one another. Even these statements are based on sometimes explicit, sometimes implicit disappointments, which quickly turn into denunciations and are ultimately deployed against French Theory itself. The same story is told again and again with regard to Derrida: he played an irresponsible game with identities and differences and, out of narcissism, accepted the way his postcolonial admirers filtered a strategic essentialism out of the legacy of his work, an essentialism that then led to the hardening of the discourse of identity politics. Ultimately, we should not be surprised – so the argument goes – that Derrida's terms have now also been adopted and exploited by right-wing identitarians.[29]

Now, one can think of Derrida and his philosophy what one will. There are understandable reasons to find the notorious obscurantism and mannerism of his thinking alienating, and to reject the difficult language of his texts. There are also good reasons to take a closer and more historically inflected look at the line of reception from poststructuralism to postcolonialism and to ask what role Derrida himself played in the appropriation and expansion of the deconstructive method by Spivak and co. A certain academic need for recognition certainly played a part. But if there is one thing that finds neither a place nor an echo in Derrida's philosophy, however hard one looks for it, then it is the idea that he was ideologically partly responsible for the current dispute about identity politics and the question of who is allowed to say what, when, and how – because, so his accusers claim, as the originator of the poststructuralist-postcolonial complex, he inaugurated a school of thought in which identities were made into inescapable and fixed characteristics. In all seriousness, we have to recognize that such positions have picked the wrong target. For with Derrida, the opposite is the case: his thinking fights with all its might against the idea of overly fixed identities and group affiliations, and more generally against the dominance of the logic of descendance and origins. Instead, there is a vigorous emphasis on the constructed nature of self-relations and identities, an emphasis that can be observed in many poststructuralist authors. Nor should this be confused with postmodern arbitrariness: rather, it is closely linked to historical contingency and cultural influences.

What is special about Derrida is that this philosophical debate is so strikingly authenticated by his own biography. As we have seen, his life and work constituted an intellectual rebellion against questions of identity, especially the idea of group identification, as well as a sustained plea for the endurance of contradictory, ambiguous, and overlapping identities. Derrida is a good example of how difficult but at the same time fruitful it is to play the game of identities. From him we can learn how to break down identities into individual parts, conceal them, and hide them, but also how to bring them out again and again, work on them, and shift them somewhere else so as to foster difference. Derrida was very uncomfortable with identities and group affiliations; he was a thinker who sought to destroy such categories, and who always carried out this work of demolition against the background of his own dramatic biography in colonial, Jewish, Algerian, and French contexts of origin. It was an attempt at mastering a situation by someone who had felt overmastered by it.

A summons from the past

In the previous pages, I have dealt with the case of Derrida in detail for two reasons: not only because he is so often in the dock and has to take the blame for his philosophy of deconstruction while representing an entire generation of theorists, but also because the rectification

– the necessary correction of the distortions and misreadings that accompany these accusations – also requires its appropriate place. While judgements are summarily passed and receive a great deal of attention, their processing requires significantly more time and reflection, for which there is usually not much public time available. But the greater the enthusiasm for political judgement, the more scholarly contextualization and differentiation are needed. As soon as this work is done – as soon as the distortions and false claims have been cleared up – such an approach leads to a worthwhile insight: we gain not only a better understanding of the political drama currently being staged with, and at the expense of, French Theory, but also a clearer view of the issues being socially negotiated in this drama. With Derrida, the phantasmal aura of the key word 'identity' can be viewed in a completely different way and applied to our own time. Given the many different motives and interests that are interwoven in the discourse on identity, we may well conclude with Derrida that we should not make things too easy for ourselves with this category: there are no natural and mutually immobile 'identities,' be they national, ethnic, cultural, religious, or gendered. This insight, also gained from a study of Derrida's Algerian biography, must be upheld and stated firmly to all those who either invoke such identities or think they have a problem with the identities of others.

Derrida is not the only one for whom the pitfalls of identity are a major theme. Many of the other protagonists discussed in this book have also grappled with the ways in which identities are constructed and the demands they make. Hélène Cixous, drawing on Derrida theoretically – though she developed these insights earlier and more intensively than him – has even made questions of identity a main reference point in her autobiographical writing. How are we shaped by identities? How can we question them, resist them, or even escape them? Cixous deals with these questions within the framework of her *écriture féminine*, always careful not to think of identity in an essentialist way, but rather to break down binaries, reject fixed categories, and highlight the possibility of multiple identities. For example, by questioning phallocentric prejudices in culture and society, she enables an analysis of the construction of gender identities. As early as 1975, in 'The Laugh of the Medusa,' she argued that gender identities were by no means fixed, but rather had to be thought and lived dynamically and plurally as forms of possibility between the sexes. What is discussed and experienced today as 'gender fluidity' was already laid out *avant la lettre* in Cixous's argument.

The category of identity also plays an important role in Étienne Balibar's theory of racism – significantly, his book *Race, Nation, Class*, co-authored with Immanuel Wallerstein in 1988, has the subtitle *Ambiguous Identities*. Both underline their concern to discuss questions of racism, capitalism, and the nation state as historically conditioned, interrelated, but sometimes contradictory categories of identity ('social formations'). The contradictory nature of racism is evident in the formation of national and ethnic identities as well as in the ambiguous effectiveness of dominant ideologies. Balibar in particular shows the role that racism plays in the identity of an individual and a nation and how, in a mirror image, the individuals and collectives exposed to racism are also forced to see themselves as a community. For Balibar, racism – regardless of whether it takes a scholarly or institutional form or is widespread in the population – is a social practice that categorizes humanity into artificially isolated types. In order to understand racism, however, it must be related to other large historical formations that make up a society, such as class, work, gender, community, nation, and state. Here, interestingly, Balibar and Wallerstein are paying homage to an explanatory approach that has similarities with arguments based on 'intersectionality' – a concept that emerged just a few years later in American black feminism, drawing attention to the overlap and simultaneity of various categories of discrimination such as race, gender, and class.[30] Balibar and Wallerstein also use images of overlap when they speak of 'ambiguous identities'. They incorporate gender relations and sexism into their analysis, even if the category of 'gender' does not ultimately receive the same epistemic status as race, nation, or class and does not appear on the cover of the 1988 book.[31] Today, Balibar is one of the few French voices to welcome the import of concepts and ideas from US debates, be they intersectional, feminist, or postcolonial, because, according to him, they could pave the way to an 'anti-racist and decolonized Fifth Republic'.[32]

By far the most radical criticism of the concept of identity can be found in Jacques Rancière. Already in the early 1990s he felt that the virulent discussions of identity politics in the United States represented a dead end for political discourse. In this respect, the frequent claim that the ideological evil of today's confused identity politics can be traced back to French Theory, of all things, can be easily refuted, at least in the case of Rancière. To the thinker of equality who gave priority to universal principles, the obsession with identity politics seemed like an absurd position that had lost sight of the bigger picture of politics due to its focus on particular interests. In his eyes, identity politics is not political enough – a view he continues to take and also brings to bear in current debates. He argues for focusing less on existing and thus quasi-natural identities, and more on political modes of subjectification. According to Rancière, in order to be political, what is mainly needed is disidentification: the rejection of collective identities and ascriptions, the impossible identification of the self with the other. The concept of disidentification, a central building block of Rancière's political philosophy of dis-agreement, has been received in different ways, as was shown in detail in the last chapter. On the one hand, with his categorical rejection of the concept of identity, Rancière comes close to a certain republican universalism prevalent in France, one that refuses to take the political concerns and situations of minority groups seriously and makes no attempt to address them. On the other hand, his egalitarian thinking has inspired numerous analyses of political struggles in the recent past, struggles in which marginalized groups and their protests were centre stage. Wherever a certain group of people rejects a hegemonic attribution in the name of a universal right and claims a share in the equality of a society, Rancière's ideas are always worth being taken up and discussed.

Cixous, Balibar, and Rancière developed these different ideas against the background of their own situations and experiences in colonial and postcolonial contexts. The colonial world of the 1950s and 1960s shaped both their political engagements and their philosophical theories, which they began to formulate somewhat belatedly in the following decades. Cixous constantly made contributions to feminist discourse in France with her multi-fractured identity and her origins as a Jewish French-Algerian woman. Balibar's critique of racism, a critique that is unique in France, cannot be understood without reference to the police violence he suffered during the Algerian War and his formative experience as a so-called *pied-rouge* in independent Algeria. And Rancière's concept of disidentification can be understood as a retroactive attempt (by a French thinker born in Algeria) to capture theoretically the crime committed by the Paris police in October 1961, a violence that had long been forgotten, and link it to his own politicization and alienation from the French state.

In each of these cases, we are dealing with a world that lies far back in time, the world of decolonization, colonial wars, and intense violence in the centre of Europe and on the other side of the Mediterranean. This world seems quite different from ours. On the other hand, the interpretations and positionings of these three intellectuals – and the conclusions they drew from their respective situations – have an undiminished validity. They connect seamlessly to today's constellations of problems. The social, political, and theoretical circumstances may have fundamentally shifted since then, but as long as racism, sexism, nationalism, and the legacy of colonialism have not been remedied and therefore still require in-depth criticism, the issues these theorists raised will remain fixed points for critical and emancipatory thinking – despite, or precisely because of, reactionary attempts to settle accounts with the protagonists of French Theory and to delegitimize their philosophies.

CONCLUSION
The Strangers

They sat in Parisian cafés smoking and debating freedom. If the latest stories are to be believed, they particularly enjoyed drinking apricot cocktails.[1] Such has been one of the dominant stereotypes of French intellectuals since the middle of the twentieth century. Another, no less common image is that of the intellectuals who, taking to the streets of Paris in May 1968, picked up megaphones and expressed their solidarity with the student protestors. In a third cliché, the glorious history of the French intellectual is told on a grand scale as part of the *Trente Glorieuses* – the name given to the economic miracle between 1945 and 1975, when France enjoyed a remarkable cultural heyday in literature, film, theatre, art, science, and philosophy.

But what if these three decades were not always so glorious? After all, in exactly the same period, France experienced the fiasco of decolonization and found itself plunged into a deep political crisis with the bloody Algerian War, a crisis that it was able to overcome only with great difficulty and at considerable moral cost. What if the fundamental historical event that shaped the various schools of French thought and theory was not May 1968, but rather the collective experience of the Algerian War and decolonization?[2] And, finally, what does it mean when we become aware of the fact that French intellectuals did not just sit around in Parisian cafés, but also sometimes hung out in Algiers, Tunis, or Casablanca?

The colonial background of those years illuminates the less glorious side of the *Trente Glorieuses*. In these pages, I have tried to gauge the extent to which the historical effects of colonialism also extended to French Theory and its influential figures. I began by showing that the experience of the Algerian War marked a turning point in the lives of most French intellectuals, for whom it represented an immediate biographical reality. The protagonists discussed in this book were all undoubtedly against the war and colonialism, but their positions and the contexts for those positions were different. For example, Lyotard, who had just returned from Algeria, joined the so-called 'suitcase carriers' network right at the beginning of the war, secretly supporting the Algerian independence movement by transferring money and smuggling weapons. Bourdieu spent most of the war in Algeria, first as a conscripted soldier, then of his own free will as a university researcher, endeavouring to show the public how colonialism and war had destroyed the foundations of an entire society. Balibar and Rancière experienced the Algerian War as young Parisian students who were spared conscription. Both were committed opponents of the war and took to the streets to protest; Balibar was beaten up by the police at one of these demonstrations. The older Barthes, despite his obviously critical attitude towards the French colonial system, was reluctant to join other left-wing intellectuals in their attempt to influence public opinion on the Algerian question through petitions and protests. Instead, he sought to intervene as an intellectual by carrying out a linguistic analysis of political power ideologies. Foucault also kept a low profile, but he did so for other reasons: he felt that General de Gaulle, who returned to power in 1958 and was hated by many leftists, represented a historic opportunity for both Algeria and France. Foucault never expressed his views on the Algerian War publicly. For Derrida and Cixous, the war was one more disaster in their already conflict-ridden homeland. They were both against the continuation of French colonialism in principle, but also knew that Algerian independence could mean the loss of their homeland for their Jewish families, something that proved to be true at the end of the war.

Despite all the differences, there is nevertheless an astonishing similarity in these diverse perceptions and positions. All of these intellectuals were looking for an answer to the same question: how can one adopt a halfway moral stance in the face of such suffering and all the chaos of war? One very striking feature evident in almost every case was the widespread feeling of guilt that the protagonists expressed with regard to the colonial situation – the constant feeling that they had to pay off their debt in some way and do something about the injustice being perpetrated. The omnipresence of this question of individual and collective guilt is by far the most remarkable insight that an examination of their respective intellectual biographies has brought to light.

Another striking feature that runs through the preceding chapters is the large number of key moments of awakening that these French intellectuals experienced against the backdrop of the South. These had less to do with the Algerian War as such than with their earlier or subsequent experiences in colonies or former colonies. This was clearly demonstrated by Barthes, who, in a kind of epiphany, fantasized about becoming a novelist in Casablanca one hot Saturday afternoon in April 1978. On the Tunisian beaches of Djerba and Sidi Bou Said, Foucault not only had flashes of inspiration for key sentences, which would help shape the fame of his books; he also experienced a kind of baptism of fire in questions of political engagement during the student protests at the University of Tunis. Lyotard owed his entire political and intellectual 'awakening' to his stay in Constantine, Algeria, before the war began. Algeria enabled Bourdieu to 'accept himself', deriving from his time there not only a greater knowledge of his own social origins, but also the freedom and courage to take new scholarly paths. For Derrida and Cixous, on the other hand, their key experiences in Algeria lay in a distant childhood. They were a matter of antisemitism under the Vichy regime, of exclusion, insults, and deep wounds that would not heal easily and therefore shaped their thinking and writing all the more.

As different as these individual key experiences were in their significance for the writers' respective lives, and to some extent in the ways they played out, they all testify to a deep need to link their own intellectual existence and its transformation to fateful moments in a foreign land. As is well known, when we travel and when we hear or tell stories we are on a journey of self-discovery. In these cases, the fact that the key moments took place in foreign lands left a colonial aftertaste because the various locations were sometimes exoticized, as we have seen above all in the cases of Barthes and Foucault. But, taken as a whole, the claims of having lived through a key experience were by no means crude cultural appropriations or lofty lip service. The guilt that many of the protagonists of this book felt towards the colonized countries and their societies was primarily fuelled by the fact that they were there on the spot: the shocking immensity of the injustice was right before their eyes, and they felt a sense of shame at the behaviour of the French state. In a certain way, this feeling of indebtedness (French *dette*) was always also accompanied by a kind of gratitude (also *dette*) for having garnered experiences that had opened their eyes.

I have argued that these colonial experiences were not limited to life stories or political-moral attitudes, but were also reflected in theories and individual works. Many well-known works of French Theory are more easily understood against the historical background of colonialism. For example, the everyday mythologies that Barthes deciphered in his book of the same name were not limited to familiar French national symbols such as the Tour de France or the Citroën DS. The articles in which Barthes dealt with the contemporary myths of French colonialism are at least as many and varied. Colonialism is omnipresent in *Mythologies*. Anyone who wants to understand how it functioned as an ideology in everyday life in the 1950s (and how postcolonial myths still function today) should read the book with these aspects in mind. Lyotard's central postmodern insight, namely that the end of the grand narratives had been reached, can still be understood as a criticism of modern ideologies of progress in science and Marxism, but Lyotard found the first historical clues to the contradictions and decline of Western modernity in colonial Algeria, when as a school teacher he witnessed the educational ruins of the French civilizing mission. And anyone who wants to understand Bourdieu's theory of habitus beyond the conventional examples of social reproduction among the French bourgeoisie should take a look at how he came to conceptualize the phenomenon on the basis of his ethnological observations of Kabyle (and Pyrenean) society.

At the same time, our survey of individual theoretical structures has clearly shown that not everything was conceived, processed, and spelled out in advance in North Africa. Many colonial experiences and events were incorporated into the writers' respective theories only after a considerable delay. Sometimes, as in the case of Bourdieu, this was a result of the usual latency period in theory-building processes – the wheels of theory grind slowly, as is well known. Sometimes it stemmed from a more or less successful attempt to retrospectively certify or authenticate a theoretical life's work that had grown in the meantime, by drawing on one's own biography and historical experiences. With the exception of Barthes and Foucault, who both died in the 1980s, it was mainly in the 1990s that the other six protagonists of this book spoke about their past and their colonial experiences and residencies in the colonies. From this point on, Bourdieu, Lyotard, Derrida, Cixous, Balibar, and Rancière wrote texts, some autobiographical and some historical, in which they reflected on and analysed this formative period. At the same time, we need to emphasize that, with the exception of Cixous, none of them has written an authoritative book on Algeria.[3]

There is something special about the memoirs mentioned: although they refer to a past colonial and wartime phase that stretches from the 1940s to the 1960s, the memoirs themselves were written in the very specific historical context of the 1990s, and should therefore be situated differently. The conditions under which Algeria and the colonial past were discussed changed fundamentally in the 1990s. In addition to the fact that we are dealing with the memories of intellectuals looking back from a much later phase of their lives, there is a larger historical and explanatory context: this preoccupation with past events occurred at a time in France when a gradual public remembrance and reappraisal of the Algerian War, the atrocities committed there, and the colonial past as a whole was being undertaken, albeit only hesitantly and slowly. At exactly the same time, Algeria sank into a bloody civil war (1991–2001) marked by Islamist terror and repressive state countermeasures on the part of the military regime. This conflict, which was closely followed in France, particularly affected those intellectuals with a colonial connection. Above all, with its terrorist attacks and atrocities, this 'other Algerian War' reopened the old wounds of the war of independence.[4] For Derrida and Cixous, the religiously charged civil war meant, not least, a renewed loss of their homeland.

Before this collective remembering of the decolonization period began – timid though it was, and inevitably accompanied by polemical debates – collective silence and forgetting had prevailed in France for decades. It is almost a cultural law that the collective memory of past crimes and injustices begins only after they have been systematically hushed up and tabooed. Just as French society remained silent for decades about its colonial past, the protagonists of French Theory – with the exception of Balibar and Cixous – did not exactly cover themselves in glory when it came to engaging in the politics of memory in public. In this respect, they were also children of their time. The forms of this silence were as varied as the reasons for it: Derrida long remained silent because the traumatic experiences that connected him with his Jewish-Algerian origins and military service represented a kind of personal and epistemological obstacle to speaking and writing about them openly. Rancière, born in Algeria to French-Algerian parents, may have had other reasons for keeping quiet about the subject for so long – especially when one takes into account that the *pieds-noirs* encountered a well-nigh hostile host society on their forced mass migration to France in 1962. In Foucault's case, we find a form of silence that can seem neo-colonial given his hedonistic practices and ideas of the good life, but that can also be interpreted as an ethic of restraint in matters that did not concern him or should not have concerned him – as a foreign university lecturer, he was not allowed to interfere in internal Tunisian affairs. When Foucault returned to post-revolutionary Paris in the autumn of 1968, he exchanged this ethic of restraint for an ethic of relentless commitment to situations in which he could actually make a difference.

The colonial amnesia in French society is also an important reason why the colonial dimensions of French Theory remained unnoticed there for so long. There is no other explanation for the fact that, although a vast amount of literature on French philosophy has been produced in recent decades, not a single item has been devoted to the period of decolonization or the time spent by intellectuals in the former colonies. In addition, until the 2000s there were no significant postcolonial studies in France that could have fostered the problematization of colonialism – this too was an integral result of the reflexive rejection of memory when it came to colonialism.[5] It would certainly not have won you any friends if you had linked the renown of French intellectuals with the darkness of the colonial era. The after-effects of this process of turning a blind eye reach into the present. Even today, colonialism appears in general accounts of French intellectual history only in the context of the Algerian War, where it enables some historians to sell the anti-war position of the intellectuals as a veritable heroic stance.[6] Much of this remains hagiography. In the vast majority of otherwise excellent biographies of French intellectuals, their residencies in the colonies and post-colonies mostly feature as exotic episodes that add a bit of colour to the life story, or else are quickly passed over because they don't seem worth mentioning. Where North African locations such as Casablanca, Algiers, or Tunis do appear, they are presented as if they were the natural habitats of Parisian intellectuals. I have repeatedly shown that the life and thought of intellectuals is thereby relocated to a contextless, ahistorical, and innocent space. The only tangible context is the place where their experiences were reflected on, written down, presented, published, and finally celebrated: Paris.

I have tried to tell a different story. A story that seeks out, examines, and problematizes the hitherto criminally neglected colonial roots of French Theory. I hope that this will result in a different picture of French theoretical development and a different geographical map of philosophy. It is not without irony that Robert J. C. Young, in view of the many references to North Africa made by poststructuralist theorists, has argued for speaking of a 'Franco-Maghreb theory' instead of 'French Theory'.[7] I am not sure whether 'Maghreb' is the right choice of word here, because a dominant geographical-cultural construction (France) is linked to another (Maghreb) that is no less homogenized and obscured. When they are left unexamined, such postcolonial gestures, which are not uncommon, ultimately run the danger of falling into the trap of an identitarian logic of origin.[8] Nevertheless, the idea suggests an interesting approach that has less to do with the 'Maghreb' or any kind of logic of origin than with the national, cultural, and linguistic processes of unification that lead to a philosophy or a theoretical current being exclusively labelled as 'French' and virtually purified of its specific origins – be they in Algeria, Indochina, the south-west of France, or Brittany. The term 'Franco-Maghreb theory' reminds us that many of the French theorists had made peripheral places and themes their own before they became Parisian intellectuals. These places are gradually coming to light. There is a South of theory.

To search for the colonial roots of French Theory means to ask, on a higher level, what thinking has to do with its place and its time. Does philosophy have an origin? What is the connection between a philosophy and its era? These are by no means far-fetched questions. They touch on a classic theme of philosophy, and perhaps even lead to its core. After all, in the search for the origins of philosophy, people have been asking for centuries why philosophy arose in ancient Greece, at that particular time and in that particular place. In *What is Philosophy?*, Gilles Deleuze and Félix Guattari found an answer that, in my opinion, is worth considering: they locate philosophical positions geopolitically without falling victim to a national logic of origin. They claim that the first philosophers were 'strangers in flight' who came to Athens 'from the borderlands of the Greek world'.[9] As 'emigrants' they became strangers to themselves, to their language, and to their nation. In the Greek milieu they found what philosophy is essentially about, according to Deleuze and Guattari: inventing concepts in order to better understand the world around them. The protagonists of French Theory are also strangers to me. They went to the School of the South, became strangers to themselves, to their language, and to their nation, and in doing so found their own philosophy and their own style.

Picture Credits

p. 21 Aïn Aghbel. Archive Photographique Pierre Bourdieu. Images d'Algérie, 1957–1961 © Fondation Pierre Bourdieu, Paris. Courtesy Camera Austria, Graz, Austria (above: N 088/787; below: N 088/786).
p. 22 Pierre Bourdieu during the inquiry in Aïn Aghbel. Archive Photographique Pierre Bourdieu. Images d'Algérie, 1957–1961 © Fondation Pierre Bourdieu, Paris. Courtesy Camera Austria, Graz, Austria (N 034 /147).
pp. 44–45 View of Constantine in Algeria. © Alamy/dpa picture alliance.
p. 46 Jean-François Lyotard at the Lycée d'Aumal. © Anciens des Lycées de Constantine (alyc.fr).
p. 81 View of the Dar Zarrouk palace. © CAP/Roger-Viollet.
p. 85 Foucault in Tunisia. Copyright © Archives Michel Foucault/IMEC.
p. 89 The Club Méditerranée. Postcard by Édition Gaston Lévy – Tunis. Personal archive of Philippe Legrand (https://collierbar.fr).
p. 94 Daniel Defert and Michel Foucault. 'Ceci n'est pas une pipe. Rue de Vaugirard chez Michel Foucault, milieu des années 1970.' © DR. Photo from *Une vie politique. Entretiens avec Philippe Artières et Éric Favereau* by Daniel Defert, Éditions du Seuil, 2014.
p. 117 Algiers, early 1959. Archive Photographique Pierre Bourdieu. Images d'Algérie, 1957–1961. © Fondation Pierre Bourdieu, Paris. Courtesy Camera Austria, Graz, Austria (N 129/7).

p. 129 Les Deux Mondes. Image from *Rootprints: Memory and Life Writing* by Hélène Cixous and Mireille Calle-Gruber. Routledge: New York, 1997, p. 181. © Routledge.
pp. 132–133 Cercle militaire. © Alamy/dpa picture alliance.
p. 144 Hélène Cixous at the University of Vincennes. © Getty Images. Photo by Hervé Gloaguen.
p. 155 Demonstration against the Algerian War. © akg-images/Paul Almasy.
p. 180 Graffiti on the left bank of the Seine. © Getty Images/Keyston-France. Photo: Jean Texier.

Notes

Introduction: In the South of Theory

1 Quoted in Schultheis, 'Algerien 1960', in Steinrücke (ed.), *Pierre Bourdieu*, p. 18.

2 Todd, *Albert Camus: A Life*, p. 378.

3 Foucault, *The Order of Things*, p. 387. More specifically, this took place on 5 January 1965. See Defert, 'Chronology', in Falzon et al. (eds), *A Companion to Foucault*, p. 31.

4 Foucault, 'La philosophie structuraliste permet de diagnostiquer ce qu'est "aujourd'hui"', in *Dits et Écrits I*, p. 584.

5 A book of such a kind that examines these locations, visits, and key events historically and collectively has not yet been published. Nevertheless, books and articles have already appeared problematizing the topic of 'colonialism and French philosophy', primarily from a postcolonial perspective. However, these have not been either historically focused or particularly site-specific. They include Young, *White Mythologies*; Ahluwalia, *Out of Africa*; Davis, 'Algeria as Postcolony?'; Ott, *Welches Außen des Denkens?*; Toscano, 'The Name of Algeria'. For the history of French sociology in colonial contexts, see the detailed study by Steinmetz, *The Colonial Origins of Modern Social Thought*.

6 I am here following Shatz, *Writers and Missionaries*, p. 4; Said, *Culture and Imperialism*, p. xxii.

7 See in particular Blanchard et al., *Décolonisations françaises*; Anderson, *La guerre civile en France*; Blanc, *Décolonisations*.

8 For the impact of decolonization on social and political life in France, see in particular Shepard, *The Invention of Decolonization.*

9 Elements of this postcolonial critique can be found in Young, *White Mythologies*; Ott, *Welches Außen des Denkens?*; Stoler, 'Colonial Aphasia'; Mbembe, 'Faut-il provincialiser la France?,' p. 163.

10 Pluckrose and Lindsay, *Cynical Theories.* For a critique from the left, see Neiman, *Links ist nicht woke.*

11 On colonial amnesia and the heritage of colonialism in French society, see Stora, *La gangrène et l'oubli*; Blanchard et al. (eds), *La fracture coloniale.*

1 An Algerian *Bildungsroman*: Pierre Bourdieu

1 Ernaux, *A Girl's Story*, p. 7.

2 Ibid., p. 9. *Djebel* is an Arabic word for 'mountain' or 'range of mountains.'

3 Chirac, 'Entretien avec Dominique Ottavioli et Guy Lagorce.' My account of the Algerian War draws partly on Eckert, 'Probelauf für einen öffentlichen Intellektuellen,' in which Chirac's comment is noted.

4 Data from the Fédération Nationale des Anciens Combattants en Algérie. See also Yacine, 'At the Origins of a Singular Ethnolosociology,' in Bourdieu, *Algerian Sketches*, pp. 13–34. For the history of the Algerian War, see especially Thénault, *Histoire de la guerre d'indépendance algérienne.*

5 Bourdieu, *Picturing Algeria*, p. 32.

6 Bourdieu, *Sketch for a Self-Analysis*, p. 37.

7 Ibid., p. 39.

8 This is not the place to quote the relevant expressions, but see Bourdieu, 'The Algerian Landing,' p. 416.

9 See Yacine, 'At the Origins of a Singular Ethnosociology'; Stora, *Appelés en guerre d'Algérie*, p. 45.

10 Quoted from Schultheis, 'Algerien 1960,' p. 18.

11 Bourdieu, *Sketch*, pp. 39 and 54. The expression 'colonial situation' goes back to the French anthropologist Georges Balandier, who, in the 1950s, was the first to attempt to grasp the essential character of colonial societies from a sociological and analytical point of view. See his 'La situation coloniale.' On the origins of this theoretical concept, see Steinmetz, *The Colonial Origins of Modern Social Thought.*

12 Bourdieu, *Sketch*, p. 40.

13 Bourdieu, *Sociologie de l'Algérie*, pp. 114ff. and p. 123.

14 Bourdieu, 'Letters to André Nouschi,' in *Algerian Sketches*, p. 319.

15 Ibid., p. 318.
16 Ibid., p. 319.
17 On closer inspection, the intrinsically provocative arrangement of the chapters is highly culturalistic, since Bourdieu reduces the social structure of Algeria to ethnic groups and thereby reproduces the centuries-old scholarly tradition of the disciplinary division of labour which he himself had criticized: ethnology is responsible for investigating traditional society, oriental studies for Arab society, and sociology for modern, European society.
18 Bourdieu, 'Letters to André Nouschi,' pp. 318–19.
19 On the University of Algiers as the 'reflection of a colonized Algeria,' see Yacine, 'At the Origins of a Singular Ethnosociology,' p. 14.
20 Ibid., p. 15.
21 Ibid.
22 See Vidal-Naquet, *L'Affaire Audin.*
23 Bourdieu, *Sketch*, pp. 53–4.
24 On the photographs and their origins, see Bourdieu, *Picturing Algeria*; Frisinghelli, 'Comments on the Photographic Documentations of Pierre Bourdieu,' in ibid., pp. 201–14; Brohm, 'Diagramm und Fotografie als Praxis des Visuellen,' in Probst and Klenner (eds), *Ideengeschichte der Bildwissenschaft*, pp. 197–218.
25 See Bourdieu, 'Algerian Landing,' p. 429.
26 Bourdieu, *Sketch*, pp. 46–7.
27 Ibid., p. 47.
28 See also Rey, *Bourdieu on Religion*, pp. 59ff.
29 See also Steinmetz, 'Soziologie und Kolonialismus'; Feichtinger and Malinowski, '"Eine Million Algerier lernen im 20. Jahrhundert zu leben"'.
30 Bourdieu, *Sketch*, p. 47.
31 Ibid., p. 48.
32 For the circumstances of his departure, see Yacine, 'Pierre Bourdieu in Algeria at War,' p. 492.
33 Aron, 'Preface' to Bourdieu, *The Algerians*, p. v.
34 Ibid.
35 Perroux (ed.), *L'Algérie de demain*; Bourdieu, 'From Revolutionary War to Revolution,' in *Algerian Sketches*, pp. 85–91.
36 Bourdieu, 'Révolution dans la Révolution'; Bourdieu, 'Les sous-prolétaires algériens.'

37 See Bourdieu, 'From Revolutionary War to Revolution', p. 87; Le Sueur, *Uncivil War*, p. 284.
38 Bourdieu, 'From Revolutionary War to Revolution', p. 87, and Bourdieu, 'Between Friends', in *Algerian Sketches*, p. 290.
39 See Bourdieu, *Sketch*, p. 59.
40 Bourdieu, *Sketch*, p. 63. See also Schultheis, 'Algerien 1960', pp. 28–9.
41 On the friendship between Bourdieu and Sayad, see Bourdieu, 'For Abdelmalek Sayad', in *Algerian Sketches*, pp. 295–300; Pérez, *Combattre en sociologues*.
42 Pérez, *Combattre en sociologues*, p. 125.
43 Ibid., pp. 174–80.
44 Bourdieu, *Sketch*, p. 71.
45 See Schäfer, 'Pierre Bourdieus algerische Gründungsszene', in Farzin and Laux (eds), *Gründungsszenen soziologischer Theorie*, p. 71.
46 The dates in brackets are those of the first French publications.
47 Bourdieu and Passeron, *The Inheritors*.
48 See Krais, 'Habitus und soziale Praxis', in Steinrücke (ed.), *Pierre Bourdieu*, p. 98.
49 Bourdieu, *Algerian Sketches*, p. 181.
50 Ibid.
51 Bourdieu, 'The Making of Economic Habitus', p. 180.
52 On this passage see also Krais, 'Habitus und soziale Praxis', p. 99.
53 Reed-Danahay, 'The Kabyle and the French', in Carrier (ed.), *Occidentalism*, pp. 61–84; Hammoudi, 'Phenomenology and Ethnography', in Goodman and Silverstein (eds), *Bourdieu in Algeria*, p. 200.
54 Bourdieu, *The Algerians*, p. 144.
55 Bourdieu and Sayad, *Le déracinement*, p. 161.
56 Bourdieu, 'Uprooted Peasants', in *Algerian Sketches*, pp. 117–45 (pp. 134–5, translation modified).
57 On the 'cleft, tormented habitus', see Bourdieu, *Pascalian Meditations*, p. 64.
58 Bourdieu, 'Uprooted Peasants', p. 142.
59 Bourdieu, 'A Lecture on the Lecture', in *In Other Words*, p. 191.
60 See Rehbein, *Die Soziologie Pierre Bourdieus*, p. 89.
61 Bourdieu, 'Der Habitus als Vermittlung zwischen Struktur und Praxis', in *Zur Soziologie der symbolischen Formen*, p. 132; Bourdieu, 'Postface' to Panofsky, *Architecture gothique et pensée scolastique*, pp. 133–67; see also Krais and Gebauer, *Habitus*, p. 26.
62 Bourdieu, *Outline of a Theory of Practice*, p. 72.

2 A Hopeless Contradiction: Jean-François Lyotard

1 See Lyotard, 'A New Phase in the Algerian Question', in *Political Writings*, pp. 187–96.

2 The descriptions found in Flaubert, Maupassant, and Dumas are cited in Stora, *Les clés retrouvées*, pp. 17–18. See also Camus, 'A Short Guide to Towns without a Past', in *Personal Writings*, pp. 153–8.

3 Lyotard, 'The Name of Algeria', in *Political Writings*, p. 170.

4 On the Sétif massacre, see Leggewie, 'Der andere 8. Mai 1945'.

5 Bamford, *Jean-François Lyotard*, p. 28.

6 Lyotard, 'The Name of Algeria', p. 170.

7 Lyotard, 'The Situation in North Africa', in *Political Writings*, p. 174.

8 For Lyotard's activities and influence as a teacher in Constantine, see also the memories of his former pupil Véga-Ritter, 'Un an d'enseignement de la philosophie entre docte Sorbonne et ravin du Rhumel', in *Les bahuts du Rhumel*, pp. 4–5.

9 Lyotard, 'The Name of Algeria', p. 170.

10 See Lyotard, 'A New Phase', p. 190. On Marcel Emérit see Yacine, 'At the Origins of a Singular Ethnosociology', in Bourdieu, *Algerian Sketches*, pp. 13–34.

11 Lyotard, *The Postmodern Condition*, p. xxiv.

12 Lyotard, 'The Name of Algeria', p. 170.

13 On the history of the suitcase carriers, see Hamon and Rotman, *Les porteurs de valises*; Leggewie, *Kofferträger*.

14 Bamford, *Jean-François Lyotard*, p. 45.

15 Ibid., p. 44.

16 Lyotard, *Peregrinations*, p. 59.

17 Lyotard, 'The Situation in North Africa', p. 175.

18 Ibid., p. 178.

19 See Lyotard, *Peregrinations*, p. 59.

20 Lyotard, *Instructions païennes*, p. 83.

21 Lyotard, 'Rules and Paradoxes and Svelte Appendix', p. 213.

22 This is the conclusion reached by Lyotard in 'The Name of Algeria'.

23 Lyotard, *The Differend*, p. xi.

24 Quoted in Altwegg and Schmidt, *Französische Denker der Gegenwart*, p. 148.

25 See Hiddleston, *Poststructuralism and Postcoloniality*, p. 87.

26 See Ramdani, 'L'Algérie, un différend', in Lyotard, *La guerre des Algériens*, p. 12.
27 Lyotard, *Phenomenology*, p. 60.
28 See Gumbrecht, 'Lyotard: Eine Maschine ohne Körper kann nicht denken'.

3 A Moroccan Epiphany: Roland Barthes

1 Du Camp, *Souvenirs littéraires*, pp. 314f.
2 See König, 'Flauberts Orient-Schock', and Mölk, 'Gustave Flaubert am zweiten Katarakt'.
3 Barthes, *The Preparation of the Novel*, p. 7.
4 Ibid.
5 Ibid., p. 8.
6 Ibid.
7 Ibid., p. 4.
8 Ibid.
9 Ibid., p. 8.
10 Ibid., p. 7.
11 See Nathalie Léger, 'Editor's Preface', in Barthes, *The Preparation of the Novel*, p. xxii; Samoyault, *Barthes: A Biography*, pp. 470–90; Morgenroth, '1978. Roland Barthes', in Zanetti (ed.), *Improvisation und Invention*, pp. 149–59; Ritter, 'Ins neue Leben schreiben'.
12 Samoyault, *Roland Barthes*, p. 263. See also Defert, 'Chronology', in Falzon et al. (eds), *A Companion to Foucault*, pp. 9–83 (p. 28).
13 Samoyault, *Barthes*, p. 321.
14 Erdur is here alluding to the 1966 play by Günter Grass, criticizing Brecht for his failure to respond adequately to the 1953 East German uprising. (Translator's note.)
15 For the circumstances of his stay in Morocco, see Samoyault, *Barthes*, pp. 320–30.
16 Barthes, 'Digressions', in *The Grain of the Voice*, p. 121. See also Samoyault, *Barthes*, p. 323.
17 See ibid., pp. 320–30.
18 Barthes, 'One Always Fails in Speaking of What One Loves', in *The Rustle of Language*, p. 299.
19 Samoyault, *Roland Barthes*, p. 324.
20 Quoted from ibid., p. 323 (translation slightly modified).
21 Ibid., p. 325.

22 Barthes, 'A Case of Cultural Criticism,' in *The Language of Fashion*, pp. 104–7.
23 Barthes, *Incidents*, p. 24.
24 Ibid., pp. 19, 28, and 36 respectively.
25 On the book's reception see Boulaâbi et al. (eds), *Roland Barthes au Maroc*; Chambers, 'Pointless Stories, Storyless Points.'
26 See especially Knight, *Barthes and Utopia*; Hiddleston, *Poststructuralism and Postcoloniality*, pp. 99–124; Boulaâbi, 'Barthes et l'Orient,' in Boulaâbi et al. (eds), *Roland Barthes au Maroc*, pp. 35–51.
27 See especially Boulaâbi, 'Barthes et l'Orient, p. 46.
28 A historically detailed and balanced assessment of sexual Orientalism in French society in the second half of the twentieth century (including a few minor Barthes references) can be found in Shepard, *Sex, France, and Arab Men, 1962–1979*.
29 See the Preface to Boulaâbi et al. (eds), *Roland Barthes au Maroc*.
30 Marty, 'Roland Barthes au Maroc,' p. 8.
31 For a nuanced view of Barthes's travel narratives, see Ette, 'Reiseberichte und Reiselandschaften.'
32 See Sarasin, *1977. Eine kurze Geschichte der Gegenwart*, p. 184.
33 See Barthes, *The Empire of Signs*; 'Digressions,' in *The Grain of the Voice*; *Sade. Fourier. Loyola*; *Mythologies*. See also Knight, 'Barthes and Orientalism.'
34 Barthes, *Mythologies*, p. ix (emphasis in original).
35 Ibid., p. xi.
36 On the German edition, see Brühmann, '"Als Diskussionsgrundlage für Großstadtbüchereien empfohlen",' in Körte and Reulecke (eds), *Mythen des Alltags*, pp. 25–40.
37 Ibid., p. 178.
38 On the publishing history of this article, see Naguschewski, 'Politik im Diskurs,' in Körte and Reulecke (eds), *Mythen des Alltags*, pp. 132–41.
39 'African Grammar' in Barthes, *Mythologies*, pp. 153–60 (p. 153).
40 For this and previous quotation, ibid., pp. 156–7 (emphasis in the original).
41 For this and previous quotation, ibid., p. 158 (emphasis in the original).
42 Ibid., p. 82. See also Sartre, 'Colonialism is a System,' in *Colonialism and Neocolonialism*, pp. 30–47.

43 For this and previous quotation, Barthes, *Mythologies*, pp. 265–6. For the way exoticism operates, see also ibid., pp. 184–5.
44 Ibid., p. 225.
45 Samoyault, *Roland Barthes*, p. 225.
46 For this and previous quotation, Barthes, *Mythologies*, pp. 271–4.

4 Enjoyment and Silence: Michel Foucault

1 See Defert, 'Chronology', in Falzon et al. (eds), *A Companion to Foucault*, p. 34.
2 Ibid., p. 43.
3 Pinguet, 'Les années d'apprentissage', p. 126.
4 Macey, *Michel Foucault*, p. 81.
5 Daniel, 'La passion de Michel Foucault'. See also Eribon, *Foucault*, p. 188. Daniel's text is an obituary published on the occasion of Foucault's death in 1984.
6 For this and the preceding quotation, see Foucault, 'La philosophie structuraliste permet de diagnostiquer ce qu'est "aujourd'hui"', p. 3.
7 Sartre, 'Jean-Paul Sartre répond', p. 88.
8 Foucault, 'La philosophie structuraliste', p. 3.
9 Quoted in Macey, *Lives of Foucault*, p. 184.
10 See Eribon, *Foucault*, pp. 279–81.
11 Ibid., p. 223 and p. 266.
12 These were Gérard Deledalle and Jean Wahl. See ibid.
13 Macey, *Lives of Foucault*, p. 77; Defert, 'Chronology', p. 37; Samoyault, *Barthes*, p. 263.
14 Daniel, 'La passion de Michel Foucault'.
15 Eribon, *Foucault*, p. 268; Macey, *Lives of Foucault*, p. 188; Daniel, *La blessure*, p. 183.
16 Eribon, *Foucault*, p. 269.
17 Ibid.; Macey, *Lives of Foucault*, p. 190; Hafsia, *Visages et rencontres*, p. 51.
18 Hafsia, 'Quand la passion de l'intelligence illuminait Sidi Bou Saïd', quoted in Eribon, *Foucault*, p. 187.
19 Flaubert, *Dictionary of Received Ideas*, p. 73.
20 Defert, 'Chronology', p. 35.
21 Foucault, *The Archaeology of Knowledge*, p. 17.
22 Foucault, 'Les hétérotopies' (7 December 1966), in *Le Corps utopique*, pp. 23–36; 'Des espaces autres', in *Dits et Écrits IV*, pp. 752–62.

23 Ibid., p. 935. In Foucault, 'spaces' and 'places' are often used interchangeably.
24 Foucault, 'Les hétérotopies,' p. 32.
25 Ibid., pp. 34–5.
26 For this and the preceding quotation, see ibid., p. 20. See also Macey, *Lives of Foucault*, pp. 186ff. See Daniel Defert, afterword to Foucault, *Le Corps utopique*, pp. 37–61 (p. 43).
27 See Defert, ibid., p. 43.
28 Foucault, 'Le corps utopique' (21 December 1966), in *Le Corps utopique*, p. 9.
29 Defert, 'Chronology,' p. 34.
30 Ibid., p. 35.
31 Fons Elders, 'Preface,' in Foucault, *Freedom and Knowledge*, p. 7.
32 Wade, *Foucault in California*; Dean and Zamora, *The Last Man Takes LSD*.
33 Cusset, *French Theory*.
34 Foucault, 'Des espaces autres.' On the complex editorial history, see Defert, afterword to Foucault, *Le Corps utopique*, pp. 37–61.
35 Foucault, 'Des espaces autres,' p. 759.
36 See in particular Foucault's notorious 'reports on ideas' about the Iranian Revolution in 'L'armée, quand la terre tremble,' in *Dits et Écrits III*, pp. 662–9.
37 Macey, *Lives of Foucault*, p. 209; Eribon, *Foucault*, p. 192.
38 Eribon, *Foucault*, p. 192.
39 Ibid., p. 193.
40 Ibid., p. 192.
41 Defert, *Une vie politique*.
42 Ibid.
43 Pinguet, 'Les années d'apprentissage,' p. 126.
44 Macey, *Foucault*, p. 35.
45 Defert, *Une vie politique*; Macey, *Lives of Foucault*, p. 83.
46 See Eribon, *Foucault*, p. 193; Macey, *Foucault*, pp. 81f.
47 For the first thesis, see Eribon, *Foucault*, p. 83, for the second, Macey, *Lives of Foucault*, p. 205; Macey, *Foucault*, p. 83; Said, 'Diary,' pp. 42f. For a cautious position on this question, see Defert, *Une vie politique*.
48 For this and the preceding quotations, see Foucault, 'Entretien avec D. Trombadori,' in *Dits et Écrits IV*, pp. 78–9.
49 Ibid., p. 94.
50 Foucault, 'Le problème des réfugiés est un prélude au grand mouvement

migratoire du XXIe siècle', in *Dits et Écrits III*, pp. 798–800. See also de Lagasnerie, *La dernière leçon de Michel Foucault*; Preciado, 'Les leçons du virus'; Sarasin, 'Mit Foucault die Pandemie verstehen?'

51 Young, 'Foucault on Race and Colonialism.'

52 Stoler, *Race and the Education of Desire*; Spivak, 'Can the Subaltern Speak?'; Mbembe, 'Faut-il provincialiser la France?', p. 163; Stoler, 'L'éclat de Foucault dans les études (post) coloniales.'

53 Edward Said, 'Diary', p. 42.

54 For this and the preceding quotations, see ibid.

55 For a postcolonial critique of this influential conversation, see Spivak, 'Can the Subaltern Speak?'

56 Foucault, *History of Madness*, p. 33.

57 Lukács, Preface to *Theory of the Novel*.

5 Identity and Its Discontents: Jacques Derrida

1 *Derrida's Elsewhere*, directed by Safaa Fathy, France 1999, 68 minutes.

2 Ibid., at 3:08 mins.

3 Ibid., from 7:13 mins onwards.

4 Derrida, *Monolingualism of the Other*, p. 46. See also *Derrida's Elsewhere*, from 10:50 mins.

5 See in particular Oliver Precht's presentation, 'Portrait of a Philosopher (Notes on a New Biography of Jacques Derrida).' The exceptions include Peeters, *Derrida: A Biography*, and Baring, *The Young Derrida and French Philosophy*.

6 On the detailed circumstances of the name-giving, see Salmon, *An Event, Perhaps*, pp. 16–19; Thomä et al., *Der Einfall des Lebens*, pp. 294–7.

7 Derrida, *Monolingualism*, p. 1.

8 On the history of the Algerian Jews, see Stora, *Les trois exils*.

9 'Disorder of identity' in Derrida, *Monolingualism*, p. 14; for the 'earthquake', see Peeters, *Derrida*, p. 19.

10 Derrida and Roudinesco, *For What Tomorrow*, p. 4. See also Peeters, *Derrida*, p. 17.

11 Derrida, 'Circumfession', p. 186. See also Peeters, *Derrida*, p. 17; Thomä et al., *Der Einfall des Lebens*, p. 295.

12 *Derrida*, directed by Kirby Dick and Amy Kofman, USA 2002, 85 minutes. On this passage see also Derrida and Roudinesco, *For What Tomorrow*, p. 7; Bennington, 'Curriculum Vitae', p. 332.

13 See Thomä et al., *Einfall des Lebens*, p. 295; Cixous, 'Celle qui ne se ferme pas,' in Chérif (ed.), *Derrida à Alger*, p. 47.
14 Bennington, 'Curriculum Vitae,' p. 333.
15 See also Thomä et al., *Einfall des Lebens*, p. 295.
16 See ibid., p. 296; Cixous, 'Celle qui ne se ferme pas,' p. 47; Cixous, *Aus Montaignes Koffer*, p. 45.
17 Derrida, *Monolingualism*, p. 26.
18 Ibid., p. 56.
19 Ibid., p. 37.
20 Ibid.
21 Fanon, *The Wretched of the Earth*, p. 39.
22 Derrida, *Monolingualism*, pp. 39–40.
23 Ibid., p. 42.
24 Ibid., p. 41. On this passage, see also Salmon, *An Event*, p. 25.
25 Derrida, *Learning to Live Finally*, p. 37.
26 Ibid., pp. 36–7.
27 See Salmon, *An Event*, p. 32.
28 For this and the preceding quotation, see Derrida, *Monolingualism*, p. 44. See also Peeters, *Derrida*, p. 35.
29 See ibid., p. 113 and p. 120; Salmon, *An Event*, pp. 62f.
30 Quoted in Peeters, *Derrida*, p. 77.
31 Malabou and Derrida, *Counterpath: Travelling with Jacques Derrida*, p. 290.
32 Quoted in Peeters, *Derrida*, p. 58.
33 Ibid., p. 63.
34 Ibid., p. 71.
35 Ibid., p. 93.
36 Ibid., p. 99.
37 'Lettre de Jacques Derrida,' in Nora, *Les Français d'Algérie*, p. 275. Quoted here from Peeters, *Derrida*, p. 116.
38 'Lettre de Jacques Derrida,' p. 292.
39 Letter from Derrida to Nora, 30 June 1961, quoted from Peeters, *Derrida*, p. 118. For the discussion between Derrida and Nora, see also Diner, 'Algerische Ouvertüren.'
40 Todd, *Camus*, p. 378.
41 Peeters, *Derrida*, p. 118.
42 Ibid.

43 See Derrida, 'To Forgive: The Unforgivable and the Imprescriptible'; Derrida, 'Racism's Last Word.' See also Shatz, 'Not in the Mood.'
44 Derrida, 'Les voix d'Artaud,' p. 34.
45 Derrida, 'Introduction,' in *Speech and Phenomena*.
46 Derrida, *Monolingualism*, p. 88. See also Nancy, 'L'indépendence de l'Algérie, l'indépendence de Derrida,' in Chérif (ed.), *Derrida à Alger*, pp. 19–25; Huffer, 'Derrida's Nostalgeria,' in Lorcin (ed.), *Algeria & France, 1800–2000*, pp. 228–46.

6 Infernal Paradise: Hélène Cixous

1 Cixous, *Aus Montaignes Koffer*, p. 36.
2 Cixous, 'The Laugh of the Medusa.'
3 See Postl, 'Eine Politik des Schreibens und des Lachens,' in Hutfless et al. (eds), *Hélène Cixous*; Scholz, 'Hélène Cixous an der FU.'
4 See Cixous, *Die unendliche Zirkulation des Begehrens*.
5 Cixous, 'How Not to Speak of Algeria,' in *Volleys of Humanity*, p. 164.
6 Cixous, *Reveries of the Wild Woman*, p. 26.
7 See Leggewie, 'Roman nicht nur zur Stunde.'
8 Camus, 'The Minotaur, or The Stop in Oran,' in *The Myth of Sisyphus and Other Essays*, p. 116.
9 Ibid.
10 Cixous, 'My Algeriance,' in Cixous, *Stigmata*, pp. 153–72 (p. 164); Cixous, *Aus Montaignes Koffer*, p. 87.
11 Cixous, 'Interview,' *purple magazine* 24.
12 Cixous and Calle-Gruber, *Rootprints*, p. 182.
13 Ibid.
14 Cixous and Wajsbrot, *Eine deutsche Autobiographie*, pp. 65–6.
15 Cixous, *Aus Montaignes Koffer*, p. 161.
16 Cixous and Wajsbrot, *Eine deutsche Autobiographie*, p. 17.
17 Cixous, *Aus Montaignes Koffer*, p. 161.
18 Ibid., p. 83.
19 Ibid.
20 Ibid., p. 84.
21 Cixous, 'My Algeriance,' p. 159.
22 Cixous, *Aus Montaignes Koffer*, p. 99.
23 Ibid., p. 95.
24 Cixous and Wajsbrot, *Eine deutsche Autobiographie*, p. 74.

25 See Bourdieu, *Sketch for a Self-Analysis*, p. 59.

26 For this and the preceding quotation, see Cixous and Wajsbrot, *Eine deutsche Autobiographie*, p. 74 and p. 75.

27 Cixous, 'My Algeriance', p. 153.

28 See Cixous, *Aus Montaignes Koffer*, p. 75.

29 See Cixous, *Reveries*, p. 157; Cixous, *Si près*, p. 18.

30 Cixous, 'My Algeriance', p. 170.

31 Cixous and Calle-Gruber, *Rootprints*, p. 204.

32 For this and the previous quotation, ibid.

33 Cixous, *Portrait of Jacques Derrida as a Young Jewish Saint*; Derrida, *H. C. für das Leben, das heißt …*; Cixous and Derrida, *Veils*. On the 'authorization', see Cixous, *Aus Montaignes Koffer*, p. 66.

34 Cixous and Wajsbrot, *Eine deutsche Autobiographie*, p. 69.

35 Cixous, 'Ein föderales Algerien ist eine Illusion'.

36 Cixous, *Aus Montaignes Koffer*, p. 72.

37 Ibid.

38 Derrida, 'Circumfession'; *Monolingualism of the Other*.

39 Cixous, *Si près*, p. 19.

40 Cixous and Clément, *The Newly Born Woman*, p. 70.

41 Ibid.

42 Ibid., pp. 127f.

43 Ibid., p. 128. See also Young, *Postcolonialism*, pp. 411–26; Young, *White Mythologies*, pp. 32–5; Schep, *The Autobiographical Effect*, pp. 153–5.

44 On the history of the University of Vincennes see Erdur, *Die epistemologischen Jahre*, pp. 203–12; Soulié (ed.), *Un mythe à détruire?*

45 See Erdur, *Die epistemologischen Jahre*, p. 206.

46 Cixous, *Aus Montaignes Koffer*, p. 14.

47 Ibid., pp. 13–15.

48 *Vincennes, l'université perdue*, directed by Virginie Linhart, France 2016, 90 minutes.

49 Cixous, 'The Laugh of the Medusa'. See also Schwarzer, 'MLF wird 50: Allons les filles!'

50 For this and the previous quotations, see Cixous, 'The Laugh of the Medusa'.

51 'Simone de Beauvoir: Pourquoi je suis féministe', Télévision Française 1, 6 April 1975.

52 Cixous, 'Ich konnte die Frauenfeindlichkeit förmlich riechen'.

53 See Naudier, 'L'écriture-femme, une innovation esthétique emblématique'.
54 Cixous, 'The Laugh of the Medusa', p. 47 (emphasis in the original).
55 Ibid., p. 45 and p. 51 (emphasis in the original).
56 Ibid., p. 44. See also Cixous and Clément, *The Newly Born Woman.*
57 *Ever, Rêve, Hélène Cixous*, directed by Olivier Morel, France and USA 2018, 118 minutes.

7 Lessons in Anti-Racism: Étienne Balibar

1 See Truong, 'Emmanuel Macron, un intellectuel en politique?'; Cieslinksi, 'Macron philosophe: ces intellectuels qui n'y croient pas'.
2 Ibid. See also Hanimann, 'Wie philosophisch ist Emmanuel Macron'; Balibar, 'Jetzt regiert Hegel'.
3 Zitzmann, 'Ein Überflieger mit Retro-Hauch zieht ins Elysée'.
4 See Traoré and de Lagasnerie, 'Der Kampf Adama', in Loick and Thompson (eds), *Abolitionismus. Ein Reader*, pp. 288–315.
5 Fressoz and Pietralunga, 'Après le déconfinement, l'Elysée craint un vent de révolte'.
6 Pantel, 'Macron sollte die Proteste ernst nehmen'.
7 Fressoz and Pietralunga, 'Après le déconfinement'; Bouchet-Petersen, 'Antiracisme: la voix ambiguë d'Emmanuel Macron'.
8 Balibar et al., 'Emmanuel Macron engage le combat non pas contre le racisme, mais contre l'antiracisme'. See also Balibar et al., 'Pour une République française antiraciste et décolonialisée'.
9 Mbembe, 'Faut-il provincialiser la France?', p. 163.
10 See https://viewpointmag.com/2018/02/01/charonne-vitry-1981 (translation modified).
11 Ibid.
12 See Kalter, '"*Le Monde* va de l'avant. Et vous êtes en marge"'.
13 See Cailleteau, 'Zwischen Philosophie und Politik'.
14 Ibid.
15 See Kalter, *Die Entdeckung der Dritten Welt.*
16 See also Leggewie, 'Papa, was hast Du in Algerien gemacht?'
17 See Ruz, 'La force du "cartiérisme"', in Rioux (ed.), *La guerre d'Algérie et les Français*, pp. 329–36.
18 See Mokhtefi, *Algiers, Third World Capital.*
19 See *Algier – Alger, la Mecque des révolutionnaires 1962–1974*, directed by Ben Salama, France 2014, 55 minutes.

20 For the Black Panthers in Algiers, see Mokhtefi, *Algiers, Third World Capital.*
21 Quoted from *Algier – Mekka der Revolutionäre.*
22 Ibid.
23 N. N., 'Un incendie criminel ravage l'université'.
24 See Simon, *Algérie, les années pieds-rouges.*
25 Gadant, *Parcours d'une intellectuelle en Algérie.*
26 See Defert, 'Chronology', p. 35.
27 See Gadant, *Parcours d'une intellectuelle en Algérie*, p. 58.
28 Balibar, 'De Charonne à Vitry'.
29 Ibid.
30 Ibid., p. 154.
31 Ibid., p. 150 (emphasis in the original).
32 See ibid., p. 151.
33 For this and the preceding quotation, see ibid., p. 152.
34 See Reid, 'Étienne Balibar: Algeria, Althusser, and Altereuropéenisation', p. 69.
35 Balibar, 'De Charonne à Vitry'.
36 Ibid.
37 See Abdellali Hajjat, *The Wretched of France: The 1983 March for Equality*, translated by Andrew Brown (Bloomington: Indiana University Press, 2022).
38 de Benoist, *Vue de droite.*
39 Anderson, *In the Tracks of Historical Materialism*, p. 32.
40 On the reception and publishing history, see Bojadžijev and Klingan (eds), *Balibar/Wallerstein's 'Race, Nation, Class'.*
41 Balibar, 'Sujet ou citoyen? (Pour l'égalité)', in *Les frontières de la démocratie*, pp. 42–71 (p. 57), and 'Suffrage universel!' in ibid., pp. 35–41.
42 See Balibar, 'Émancipation, transformation, civilité'; Balibar and Wallerstein, 'Wie Rassismus überwinden?'
43 Wallerstein, *The Road to Independence.*
44 See Heiter, 'Immanuel Wallerstein: Unthinking Culture?', in Moebius and Quadflieg (eds), *Kultur*, pp. 708–21 (p. 709).
45 Wallerstein, 'Fanon and the Revolutionary Class', in *The Essential Wallerstein*, pp. 14–32.
46 Significantly, *Race, Nation, Class* is dedicated to Elaine Klein and Mokhtar Mokhtefi, 'common friends' and activists in the Algerian struggle for

liberation. See Mokhtefi, *Algiers, Third World Capital*; Mokhtefi, *I was a French Muslim.*

47 Balibar and Wallerstein, *Race, Nation, Class*, p. 9.
48 Ibid., pp. 17–18.
49 Ibid., p. 20.
50 Ibid., p. 21.
51 Ibid., p. 21. See also Guillaumin, *L'idéologie raciste*; Barker, *The New Racism*; Taguieff, *Force of Prejudice*; Hall, *Rassismus und kulturelle Identität*; Fanon, 'Rassismus und Kultur', in *Für eine afrikanische Revolution*, pp. 47–63.
52 N. N., 'Den alten Volksgeist erwecken'.
53 See Balibar, *Race, Nation, Class*, p. 24.
54 Ibid., pp. 34–5. See also El-Mafaalani, *Wozu Rassismus?*, pp. 18–19 and p. 124.
55 Balibar, *Race, Nation, Class*, p. 35. On this 'reverse racism', see Taguieff, *Force of Prejudice.*
56 See Balibar, *Race, Nation, Class*, p. 22.
57 See Hajjat, *The Wretched of France.*
58 Ibid., p. 9.
59 On the reception history in France, see Ajari, 'Human Sciences as a Battlefield', in Bojadžijev and Klingan, *Balibar/Wallerstein's 'Race, Nation, Class'*, pp. 22–33.
60 For example, in recent years, in the wake of European enlargement eastwards and, not least, the war in Ukraine, public awareness has grown that anti-Slavism, and racist reflexes against 'white Europeans', are largely based on cultural racism. See Heinze, 'Die Unterscheidungen sind das Problem'.
61 On the renaissance of a Marxist theory of race, see Roldán Mendívil and Sarbo (eds), *Die Diversität der Ausbeutung.*

8 Disidentify Yourselves!: Jacques Rancière

1 Some of Louis Althusser's autobiographical memories of Algeria can be found in his *The Future Lasts Forever*. Alain Badiou, who was not born into a French-Algerian family, produces a short sketch of the family conditions and environment of his childhood in his recent *Mémoires d'outre-politique (1937–1985)*, pp. 12–17.
2 One exception is the conversation with Laurent Jeanpierre and Dork

Zabunyan, in which Rancière answers questions about the Algerian War; see Rancière, *The Method of Equality.*

3 Attali, *L'année des dupes.*

4 See Erdur, *Die epistemologischen Jahre,* pp. 206–8.

5 See Erdur, 'Antimarxismus. André Glucksmann: *Les maîtres penseurs* (1977)', in Wulz et al. (eds), *Deregulation und Restauration,* pp. 126–45.

6 Rancière, *Dis-agreement,* p. 31.

7 See Chabrun, 'Octobre 1961: le témoignage d'un policier'; N. N., 'Le 17/10/1961, le massacre des Algériens'; Blanchard, '17 octobre 1961: La police française tue des Algériens'.

8 See the early and rapidly banned report by Paulette Péju, *Ratonnades à Paris.*

9 The conference proceedings, including the discussions and other accompanying material, were gathered in 'The Identity in Question', a special issue of *October* (61, 1992), edited by John Rajchman with Slavoj Žižek and Homi K. Bhabha. See also the later expanded version edited by Rajchman and published as *The Identity in Question.*

10 Rajchman, 'Introduction: The Question of Identity'.

11 On the reception of French Theory in the United States, see Cusset, *French Theory.*

12 Rancière, 'Vorwort zur deutschen Ausgabe', in *An den Rändern des Politischen,* p. 17.

13 Rancière, 'Politics, Identification and Subjectivization', in Léger (ed.), *Identity Trumps Socialism,* pp. 35–40 (p. 36).

14 Rancière, 'Vorwort zur deutschen Ausgabe', p. 17.

15 Rancière, 'Politics, Identification and Subjectivization', p. 38.

16 It is interesting to see how Rancière built up his theory. His argument suggests that the theory of political subjectivation, with its three sub-themes of refusal, demonstration, and the impossibility of identification, was already in some ways established in 1961 and was fed by a concrete historical experience that Rancière merely had to conceptualize by translating historical experiences into formal categories. In doing so, he incorporated his experience retrospectively into his theory. See also the Introduction to Honneth and Rancière, *Recognition or Disagreement.*

17 For this whole episode, see Davis, *Jacques Rancière,* p. 88.

18 See Einaudi, *La bataille de Paris*; Stora, *La gangrène et l'oubli.*

19 See N. N., 'Algérie-France. Regards croisés.' The conference proceedings can be found in *Lignes* 30.
20 For this and the preceding quotation, see Rancière, 'The Cause of the Other,' p. 27, p. 25.
21 See Balibar, 'Algérie, France: une ou deux nations?,' p. 8.
22 For this and the preceding quotation, see Rancière, 'The Cause of the Other,' p. 25, p. 27.
23 Ibid., p. 28.
24 Ibid., p. 28 and p. 32 note 6.
25 Ibid., p. 29.
26 Ibid.
27 Ibid.
28 See also Toscano, 'The Name of Algeria.'
29 For this and the preceding quotation, see Rancière, 'The Cause of the Other,' p. 30.
30 For this comparison, see also Toscano, 'The Name of Algeria.'
31 Rancière, *Dis-agreement*, p. 119.
32 Rancière, *Uncertain Times*, pp. 3–8.
33 Quoted in Gündoğdu, 'Disagreeing with Rancière,' p. 208. See also Rancière, 'Our Police Order.'
34 For this and the preceding quotation, see Dasgupta, 'Art is Going Elsewhere,' pp. 74f.
35 For this and the preceding quotation, see Stoler, 'Colonial Aphasia,' p. 131.
36 Plaetzer, 'Universalismen zwischen Politik und Polizei,' in Gebhardt (ed.), *Staatskritik und Radikaldemokratie*, p. 200 and p. 203.
37 For this and the preceding quotations, see ibid., p. 199, p. 200 and p. 203.
38 Ibid., pp. 201f.
39 See ibid., p. 192. Rancière, 'Les vertus de l'inexplicable'; Havercroft and Owen, 'Soul-Blindness, Police Orders and Black Lives Matter.'
40 Rancière, *Dis-agreement*, p. 9.
41 See also Deranty and Genel, 'Zur Einführung,' p. 39. For a nuanced understanding of identity, see Rancière, *The Method of Equality*.
42 Rancière, 'Critical Questions on the Theory of Recognition,' in Honneth and Rancière, *Recognition or Disagreement*, pp. 83–95 (p. 90, emphasis in original).

9 Who's Afraid of Theory?

1 Two prominent examples from the 1980s are Habermas, 'Die Moderne – ein unvollendetes Projekt', and Laermann, 'Lacancan und Derridada. Frankolatrie'.

2 This claim is emblematically found in Pluckrose and Lindsay, *Cynical Theories*; Thiel, 'Die neue Lust am Büßen'.

3 See Sasse and Zanetti, '#Postmoderne als Pappkamerad'; West, 'In Defence of Postmodernism'.

4 See N. N., 'Appel de l'Observatoire du décolonialisme et des idéologies identitaires'. See also Dufoix, *Décolonial*, pp. 30f.

5 Hénin et al. (eds), *Après la déconstruction*.

6 From the blurb to the conference proceedings in ibid.

7 Fressoz and Pietralunga, 'Après le déconfinement'; see also Dufoix, *Décolonial*, p. 29.

8 On growing Americanization, see Stangler, 'France is Becoming More Like America. It's Terrible'; Williams, 'The French Are in a Panic over Le Wokisme'; Zamora, 'The Culture Wars Come to France'.

9 For this and the preceding quotation, see Blanquer, 'Construire. Discours d'ouverture du colloque', in Hénin et al. (eds), *Après la déconstruction*, p. 28.

10 Ibid., p. 35.

11 Dubet, 'Le colloque organisé à La Sorbonne contre le "wokisme" relève d'un maccarthysme soft'. See also Williams, 'The French Are in a Panic'.

12 See N. N., '"Racisme d'Etat"'. See also Williams, 'The French Are in a Panic'.

13 See Le Nevé, 'Polémique après les propos de Jean-Michel Blanquer'; Enault et al., 'Hommage à Samuel Paty, lutte contre l'islamisme; Balmer, 'Der Feind steht in der Uni'.

14 See Centre national de la recherche scientifique, 'L'"islamogauchisme" n'est pas une réalité scientifique'.

15 See Alfandary et al. (eds), *Qui a peur de la déconstruction?*

16 Butler, *Who's Afraid of Gender?*

17 Derrida, *Of Grammatology*, p. 82.

18 Kerner, *Postkoloniale Theorien zur Einführung*, p. 34.

19 Spivak, 'Can the Subaltern Speak?'; Bhabha, *The Location of Culture*; Hall, 'Alte und neue Identitäten, alte und neue Ethnizitäten', in *Rassismus und kulturelle Identität*, pp. 66–87.

20 Derrida, *Of Grammatology*; Spivak, *A Critique of Postcolonial Reason.*
21 Spivak, 'Can the Subaltern Speak?'
22 On 'strategic essentialism' see Spivak, 'Criticism, Feminism and the Institution.'
23 Mackenthun, 'Essentialismus, strategischer,' in Göttsche et al. (eds), *Handbuch Postkolonialismus und Literatur*, pp. 142–4.
24 For a prominent example, see the chapter on postcolonial theory in Pluckrose and Lindsay, *Cynical Theories*, pp. 67–88.
25 Gumbrecht, 'Jacques Derrida: Ein Abgesang'; Koschorke, 'Die akademische Linke hat sich selbst dekonstruiert.'
26 Strauss, 'Lebensader in Gefahr.'
27 Kleie, 'Wer haftet für die "woke" Identitätspolitik?'
28 See also Graff, 'Makellos. Kein Fortschritt'; Bernhard, 'Wen kümmert's, wer spricht?'; Steinfeld, 'Schuld war nur der Poststrukturalismus.'
29 Scheu, 'Das Spiel der Differenzen.'
30 Crenshaw, 'Mapping the Margins.'
31 See *Intersecting Optics: A Dialogue on 'Race, Nation, Class' 30 Years On.* A filmed interview with Étienne Balibar and Immanuel Wallerstein by Manuela Bojadžijev, directed by Charles Heller and Lorenzo Pezzani, France and Germany 2018, 43 minutes.
32 Balibar et al., 'Pour une République française antiraciste et décolonialisée.'

Conclusion: The Strangers

1 Bakewell, *At the Existentialist Café.*
2 See Young, *White Mythologies*, p. 32.
3 Cixous, *Algériance.*
4 Stora and Jenni, *Les mémoires dangereuses*, p. iii.
5 Mbembe, 'Faut-il provincialiser la France?,' p. 163.
6 See Dosse, *La saga des intellectuels français*, vol. 1.
7 Young, *Postcolonialism*, p. 414.
8 See Ahluwalia, *Out of Africa.*
9 Deleuze and Guattari, *What is Philosophy?*, p. 87.

Bibliography

Ajari, Norman, 'Human Sciences as a Battlefield: The Reception of *Race, Nation, Class* in France', in Bojadžijev and Klingan, *Balibar/Wallerstein's 'Race, Nation, Class'*, pp. 22–33.

Ahluwalia, Pal, *Out of Africa: Post-Structuralism's Colonial Roots* (London: Routledge, 2010).

Alfandary, Isabelle et al. (eds), *Qui a peur de la déconstruction?* (Paris: PUF, 2023).

Althusser, Louis, *The Future Lasts Forever: A Memoir*, edited by Olivier Corpet and Yann Moulier Boutang, translated by Richard Boutang (New York: New Press, 1993).

Althusser, Louis et al., *Reading Capital: The Complete Edition*, translated by Ben Brewster et al. (London: Verso, 2016).

Altwegg, Jürg and Aurel Schmidt, *Französische Denker der Gegenwart. Zwanzig Porträts* (Munich: C. H. Beck, 1987).

Anderson, Grey, *La guerre civile en France. Du coup d'état gaulliste à la fin de l'OAS* (Paris: Fabrique, 2018).

Anderson, Perry, *In the Tracks of Historical Materialism* (London: Verso, 1983).

Aron, Raymond, *La tragédie algérienne* (Paris: Plon, 1957).

Aron, Raymond, 'Preface' to Pierre Bourdieu, *The Algerians*, translated by Alan C. M. Ross (Boston, MA: Beacon Press, 1962), pp. 5–7.

Attali, Jacques, *L'année des dupes. Alger, 1943* (Paris: Fayard/Pluriel, 2021).

Badiou, Alain, *Mémoires d'outre-politique (1937–1985)* (Paris: Flammarion, 2023).

Bakewell, Sarah, *At the Existentialist Café: Freedom, Being, and Apricot Cocktails* (London: Chatto and Windus, 2016).

Balandier, Georges, 'La situation coloniale. Approche théorique', *Cahiers internationaux de sociologie* 1 (1951), pp. 44–79.

Balibar, Étienne, 'De Charonne à Vitry', *Le Nouvel Observateur*, 9.3.1981.

Balibar, Étienne, 'Der Widerspruch hat die Grenzen des Ertraglichen überschritten! Die KPF zwischen Internationalismus und Chauvinismus', *PROKLA* 11 (1981), pp. 147–60.

Balibar, Étienne, *Les frontières de la démocratie* (Paris: La Découverte, 1992).

Balibar, Étienne, 'Algérie, France: une ou deux nations?', *Lignes* 30 (1997), pp. 5–22.

Balibar, Étienne, *Equaliberty: Political Essays*, translated by James Ingram (Durham, NC: Duke University Press, 2014).

Balibar, Étienne, *Violence and Civility: On the Limits of Political Philosophy*, translated by G. M. Goshgarian (New York: Columbia University Press, 2015).

Balibar, Étienne, 'Émancipation, transformation, civilité', radio interview, *France Culture*, 8.6.2016, www.radiofrance.fr/franceculture/podcasts/a-voix-nue/emancipationtransformation-civilite-9269617.

Balibar, Étienne, 'Jetzt regiert Hegel', *Der Freitag*, 28.3.2018.

Balibar, Étienne and Immanuel Wallerstein, *Race, Nation, Class: Ambiguous Identities*, translated by Chris Turner (London: Verso, 2011).

Balibar, Étienne and Immanuel Wallerstein, 'Wie Rassismus überwinden?', *100 Jahre Gegenwart – Journal* (Haus der Kulturen der Welt), 15.3.2018, https://journal.hkw.de/wie-rassismus-ueberwinden.

Balibar, Étienne et al., 'Emmanuel Macron engage le combat non pas contre le racisme, mais contre l'antiracisme', *Le Monde*, 22.6.2020.

Balibar, Étienne et al., 'Pour une République française antiraciste et décolonialisée', *Mediapart*, 3.7.2020, https://blogs.mediapart.fr/les-invites-de-mediapart/blog/030720/pour-une-republique-francaise-antiraciste-et-decolonialisee.

Balmer, Rudolf, 'Der Feind steht in der Uni', *taz*, 27.2.2021.

Bamford, Kiff, *Jean-François Lyotard* (London: Reaktion Books, 2017).

Baring, Edward, *The Young Derrida and French Philosophy (1945–1968)* (Cambridge: Cambridge University Press, 2011).

Barker, Martin, *The New Racism: Conservatives and the Ideology of the Tribe* (London: Junction Books, 1981).

Barthes, Roland, *Sade. Fourier. Loyola*, translated by Richard Miller (London: Jonathan Cape, 1977).

Barthes, Roland, *Empire of Signs*, translated by Richard Howard (New York: Hill & Wang, 1982).

Barthes, Roland, *The Grain of the Voice: Interviews 1962–1980*, translated by Linda Coverdale (New York: Hill & Wang, 1985).

Barthes, Roland, *The Rustle of Language*, translated by Richard Howard (New York: Farrar, Straus & Giroux, 1986).

Barthes, Roland, *S/Z*, translated by Richard Miller (Oxford: Blackwell, 1990).

Barthes, Roland, *Incidents*, translated by Richard Howard (Berkeley and Los Angeles: University of California Press, 1992).

Barthes, Roland, *The Preparation of the Novel: Lecture Courses and Seminars at the Collège de France, 1978–1979 and 1979–1980*, translated by Kate Briggs (New York: Columbia University Press, 2011).

Barthes, Roland, *Mythologies*, translated by Richard Howard and Annette Lavers (New York: Hill & Wang, 2012).

Barthes, Roland, *The Language of Fashion*, edited by Andy Stafford and Michael Carter, translated by Andy Stafford (London and New York: Bloomsbury, 2013).

Bennington, Geoffrey, 'Curriculum vitae', in Jacques Derrida and Geoffrey Bennington, *Jacques Derrida*, translated by Geoffrey Bennington (Chicago: University of Chicago Press, 1993).

Benoist, Alain de, *Vue de droite. Anthologie critique des idées contemporaines* (Paris: Copernic, 1977).

Bernhard, Andreas, 'Wen kümmert's, wer spricht?', *Die Zeit*, 20.8.2020.

Bhabha, Homi K. *The Location of Culture* (London: Routledge, 1994).

Blanc, Guillaume, *Décolonisations. Histoires situées d'Afrique et d'Asie* (Paris: Seuil, 2022).

Blanchard, Emmanuel, '17 octobre 1961: La police française tue des Algériens', *Le Média TV*, 16.10.2019, www.youtube.com/watch?v=rN9Em-phqhY.

Blanchard, Pascal et al. (eds), *La fracture coloniale. La société française au prisme de l'héritage colonial* (Paris: Éditions la Découverte, 2005).

Blanchard, Pascal et al., *Décolonisations françaises. La chute d'un empire* (Paris: Éditions de la Martinière, 2020).

Blanquer, Jean-Michel, 'Construire. Discours d'ouverture du colloque', in Henin et al. (eds), *Après la déconstruction*, pp. 26–37.

Bojadžijev, Manuela and Katrin Klingan (eds), *Balibar/Wallerstein's 'Race, Nation, Class': Rereading a Dialogue for our Times* (Hamburg: Argument Verlag, 2018).

Bouchet-Petersen, Jonathan, 'Antiracisme: la voix ambiguë d'Emmanuel Macron', *Libération*, 23.6.2020.

Boulaâbi, Ridha, 'Barthes et l'Orient: lecture d'*Incidents*', in Boulaâbi et al. (eds), *Roland Barthes au Maroc*, pp. 35–51.

Boulaâbi, Ridha et al. (eds), *Roland Barthes au Maroc* (Meknes: Éditions de l'Université Moulay, 2013).

Bourdieu, Pierre, 'Tartuffe ou le drame de la foi et de la mauvaise foi', *Revue de la Méditerranée* 92/93 (1959), pp. 453–8.

Bourdieu, Pierre, 'Révolution dans la Révolution', *Esprit* (January 1961), pp. 27–40.

Bourdieu, Pierre, 'Les sous-prolétaires algériens', *Les Temps modernes*, 199 (December 1962), pp. 1030–51.

Bourdieu, Pierre, *The Algerians*, translated by Alan C. M. Ross (Boston, MA: Beacon Press, 1962).

Bourdieu, Pierre, 'Postface' to Erwin Panofsky, *Architecture gothique et pensée scolastique*, translated by Pierre Bourdieu (Paris: Les Éditions de Minuit, 1967), pp. 133–67.

Bourdieu, Pierre, 'Der Habitus als Vermittlung zwischen Struktur und Praxis', in *Zur Soziologie der symbolischen Formen* (Frankfurt am Main: Suhrkamp, 1970), pp. 125–58.

Bourdieu, Pierre, *Outline of a Theory of Practice*, translated by Richard Nice (Cambridge: Cambridge University Press, 1977).

Bourdieu, Pierre, 'A Lecture on the Lecture', in *In Other Words: Essays towards a Reflexive Sociology*, translated by Matthew Adamson (Cambridge: Polity, 1990), pp. 177–98.

Bourdieu, Pierre, *The Logic of Social Practice*, translated by Richard Nice (Cambridge: Polity, 1990).

Bourdieu, Pierre, *Practical Reason: On the Theory of Action* (Cambridge: Polity, 1998).

Bourdieu, Pierre, *Pascalian Meditations*, translated by Richard Nice (Cambridge: Polity, 2000).

Bourdieu, Pierre, *Masculine Domination*, translated by Richard Nice (Cambridge: Polity, 2001).

Bourdieu, Pierre, 'The Algerian Landing', *Ethnography* 5 (2004), pp. 415–43.

Bourdieu, Pierre, *Sketch for a Self-Analysis*, translated by Richard Nice (Cambridge: Polity, 2007).

Bourdieu, Pierre, *The Bachelors' Ball: The Crisis of Peasant Society in Béarn*, translated by Richard Nice (Cambridge: Polity, 2008).

Bourdieu, Pierre, *Sociologie de l'Algérie* (Paris: PUF, 2009).

Bourdieu, Pierre, *Picturing Algeria*, edited by Franz Schultheis and Christine Frisinghelli (New York: Columbia University Press, 2012).

Bourdieu, Pierre, *Algerian Sketches*, edited by Tassadit Yacine, translated by David Fernbach (Cambridge: Polity, 2013).

Bourdieu, Pierre and Jean-Claude Passeron, *The Inheritors: French Students and their Relation to Culture*, translated by Richard Nice (Chicago: University of Chicago Press, 1979).

Bourdieu, Pierre and Abdelmalek Sayad, *Le Déracinement. La crise de l'agriculture traditionelle en Algérie* (Paris: Les Éditions de Minuit, 1964).

Bourdieu, Pierre et al. (eds), *The Craft of Sociology: Epistemological Preliminaries*, edited by Beate Krais, translated by Richard Nice (Berlin and New York: Walter de Gruyer, 1991).

Bourdieu, Pierre et al., *Travail et travailleurs en Algérie* (Paris and The Hague: Mouton, 1963).

Brohm, Holger, 'Diagramm und Fotografie als Praxis des Visuellen. Pierre Bourdieu', in Jörg Probst and Jost Philipp Klenner (eds), *Ideengeschichte der Bildwissenschaft. Siebzehn Porträts* (Frankfurt am Main: Suhrkamp Verlag, 2008), pp. 197–218.

Brühmann, Horst, '"Als Diskussionsgrundlage für Großstadtbüchereien empfohlen". Zu Übersetzung und Rezeption der *Mythen des Alltags* in Deutschland', in Mona Körte and Anne-Kathrin Reulecke (eds), *Mythen des Alltags – Mythologies. Roland Barthes' Klassiker der Kulturwissenschaften* (Berlin: Kulturverlag Kadmos, 2014), pp. 25–40.

Butler, Judith, *Who's Afraid of Gender?* (London: Penguin, 2025).

Cailleteau, Adèle, 'Zwischen Philosophie und Politik', *taz*, 1.12.2017.

Camus, Albert, 'The Minotaur, or The Stop in Oran', in *The Myth Of Sisyphus and Other Essays*, translated by Justin O'Brien (New York: Alfred A. Knopf, 1955), pp. 114–33.

Camus, Albert, 'A Short Guide to Towns without a Past', in *Personal Writings*, translated by Ellen Conroy Kennedy and Justin O'Brien (London: Penguin, 2020), pp. 153–8.

Centre national de la recherche scientifique, 'L'"islamogauchisme" n'est pas une réalité scientifique', https://www.cnrs.fr/fr/presse/l-islamogauchisme-nest-pas-une-realite-scientifique.

Chabrun, Laurent, 'Octobre 1961: le témoignage d'un policier', *L'Express*, 16.10.1997.

Chambers, Ross, 'Pointless Stories, Storyless Points: Roland Barthes between "Soirees de Paris" and "Incidents"', *L'esprit créateur* 34, 1994, pp. 12–30.

Chirac, Jacques, 'Entretien avec Dominique Ottavioli et Guy Lagorce', *Paris Match*, 24.2.1978.

Cieslinksi, Charlotte, 'Macron philosophe: ces intellectuels qui n'y croient pas', *L'Express*, 6.9.2016.

Cixous, Hélène, *Dedans* (Paris: Grasset, 1969).

Cixous, Hélène, 'The Laugh of the Medusa' (1975), translated by Keith Cohen and Paula Cohen, https://www.sidcot.org.uk/sites/default/files/inline-files/Cixous_The_Laugh_of_the_Medusa.pdf.

Cixous, Hélène, *Die unendliche Zirkulation des Begehrens. Weiblichkeit in der Schrift* (Berlin: Merve Verlag, 1977).

Cixous, Hélène, 'My Algeriance, in other words: to depart not to arrive from Algeria', in Cixous, *Stigmata: Escaping Texts* (London: Routledge, 1998), pp. 153–72.

Cixous, Hélène, *Portrait of Jacques Derrida as a Young Jewish Saint*, translated by Beverley Bie Brahic (New York: Columbia University Press, 2004).

Cixous, Hélène, *Reveries of the Wild Woman: Primal Scenes*, translated by Beverley Bie Brahic (Evanston, IL: Northwestern University Press, 2006).

Cixous, Hélène, *Si près* (Paris: Galilée, 2007).

Cixous, Hélène, 'Celle qui ne se ferme pas', in Mustapha Chérif (ed.), *Derrida à Alger. Un regard sur le monde* (Arles: Actes Sud, 2008), pp. 45–58.

Cixous, Hélène, 'How Not to Speak of Algeria', in *Volleys of Humanity: Essays 1972–2009* (Edinburgh: Edinburgh University Press, 2011), pp. 160–76.

Cixous, Hélène, 'Ein föderales Algerien ist eine Illusion', qantara.de, 12.5.2014, https://de.qantara.de/inhalt/interview-mit-der-philosophin-Hélène-cixous-einfoederales-algerien-ist-eine-illusion.

Cixous, Hélène, *Homère est morte* (Paris: Galilée, 2014).

Cixous, Hélène, 'Interview', *purple magazine* 24 (2015), https://purple.fr/magazine/fw-2015-issue-24/Hélène-cixous.

Cixous, Hélène, *Aus Montaignes Koffer. Im Gespräch mit Peter Engelmann* (Vienna: Passagen Verlag, 2017).

Cixous, Hélène, 'Ich konnte die Frauenfeindlichkeit förmlich riechen', *Die Zeit*, 13.10.2017.

Cixous, Hélène, *Osnabrück* (Paris: Des Femmes, 2017).

Cixous, Hélène, *Meine Homère ist tot ...* (Vienna: Passagen Verlag, 2019).

Cixous, Hélène, *Algériance. Dekonstruktion des Kolonialen* (Vienna: Passagen Verlag, 2026).

Cixous, Hélène and Catherine Clément, *The Newly Born Woman*, translated by Betsy Wing (London: I. B. Tauris, 1996).

Cixous, Hélène and Cécile Wajsbrot, *Eine deutsche Autobiographie* (Vienna: Passagen Verlag, 2019).

Cixous, Hélène and Jacques Derrida, *Veils*, translated by Peggy Kamuf (Stanford, CA: Stanford University Press, 2002).

Cixous, Hélène and Mireille Calle-Gruber, *Rootprints: Memory and Life Writing* (London: Routledge, 1997).

Crenshaw, Kimberlé, 'Mapping the Margins: Intersectionality, Identity Politics, and Violence against Women of Color', *Stanford Law Review* 43 (1991), pp. 1241–99.

Cusset, François, *French Theory: How Foucault, Derrida, Deleuze, & Co. Transformed the Intellectual Life of the United States* (Minneapolis: University of Minnesota Press, 2008).

Daniel, Jean, 'La passion de Michel Foucault', *Le Nouvel Observateur*, 24.6.1984.

Daniel, Jean, *La blessure* (Paris: Grasset, 1992).

Dasgupta, Sudeep, 'Art is Going Elsewhere. And Politics Has to Catch It. An Interview with Jacques Rancière', *Journal for Contemporary Philosophy* 1 (2008), pp. 70–5.

Davis, Muriam Haleh, 'Algeria as Postcolony? Rethinking the Colonial Legacy of Post-Structuralism', *Journal of French and Francophone Philosophy* 19:2 (2011), pp. 136–52.

Davis, Oliver, *Jacques Rancière* (Cambridge: Polity, 2010).

Dean, Mitchell and Daniel Zamora, *The Last Man Takes LSD: Foucault and the End of Revolution* (London: Verso, 2021).

Defert, Daniel, 'Chronology', in Christopher Falzon et al. (eds), *A Companion to Foucault* (Oxford: Blackwell, 2013), pp. 9–83.

Defert, Daniel, *Une vie politique* (Paris: Seuil, 2014).

Deleuze, Gilles and Félix Guattari, *What is Philosophy?*, translated by Graham Burchell and Hugh Tomlinson (London: Verso, 1994).

Deranty, Jean-Philippe and Katia Genel, 'Zur Einführung: Die Kritische

Theorie zwischen Anerkennung und Unvernehmen', in Axel Honneth and Jacques Rancière, *Anerkennung oder Unvernehmen? Eine Debatte* (Berlin: Suhrkamp, 2021), pp. 7–58.

Derrida, Jacques, *Speech and Phenomena and Other Essays on Husserl's Theory of Signs*, translated by David B. Allison and Newton Garver (Evanston, IL: Northwestern University Press, 1973).

Derrida, Jacques, *Writing and Difference*, translated by Alan Bass (Chicago: Chicago University Press, 1978).

Derrida, Jacques, 'Racism's Last Word', *Critical Inquiry* 12 (1985), pp. 290–9.

Derrida, Jacques, 'Circumfession', in Jacques Derrida and Geoffrey Bennington, *Jacques Derrida*, translated by Geoffrey Bennington (Chicago: University of Chicago Press, 1993), pp. 3–315.

Derrida, Jacques, *Monolingualism of the Other, or The Prosthesis of Origin*, translated by Patrick Mensah (Stanford, CA: Stanford University Press, 1998).

Derrida, Jacques, 'Les voix d'Artaud', *Le magazine littéraire* 434 (2004), pp. 34–6.

Derrida, Jacques, *H. C. for Life, That Is to Say ...*, translated by Laurent Milesi and Stefan Herbrechter (Stanford, CA: Stanford University Press, 2006).

Derrida, Jacques, *H. C. für das Leben, das heißt ...* (Vienna: Passagen Verlag, 2007).

Derrida, Jacques, *Learning to Live Finally: The Last Interview*, translated by Pascale-Anne Brault and Michael Naas (Basingstoke: Palgrave Macmillan, 2007).

Derrida, Jacques, *Of Grammatology*, translated by Gayatri Chakravorty Spivak (Baltimore, MA: Johns Hopkins University Press, 2016).

Derrida, Jacques, 'To Forgive: The Unforgivable and the Imprescriptible', translated by Elizabeth Rottenberg, in *Questioning God*, edited by John D. Caputo, Mark Dooley, and Michael J. Scanlon (Bloomington and Indianapolis: Indiana University Press, 2001).

Derrida, *Le parjure et le pardon, vol. II (Séminaire: 1998–99)* (Paris: Seuil, 2020).

Derrida, Jacques and Élisabeth Roudinesco, *For What Tomorrow ... A Dialogue*, translated by Jeff Fort (Stanford, CA: Stanford University Press, 2004).

Diner, Dan, 'Algerische Ouvertüren. Pierre Nora und Jacques Derrida im Widerstreit', *Romanisches Jahrbuch* 67 (2016), pp. 35–50.

Dosse, François, *La saga des intellectuels français*, 2 vols, vol. 1, *À l'épreuve de l'histoire (1944–1968)* (Paris: Gallimard, 2018).

Du Camp, Maxime, *Souvenirs littéraires* (Paris: Aubier, 1994).

Dubet, François, 'Le colloque organisé à La Sorbonne contre le "wokisme" relève d'un maccarthysme soft', *Le Monde*, 10.1.2022.

Dufoix, Stéphane, *Décolonial* (Paris: Anamosa, 2023).

Eckert, Andreas, 'Probelauf fur einen öffentlichen Intellektuellen', *Frankfurter Allgemeine Zeitung*, 22.9.2010.

Einaudi, Jean-Luc, *La bataille de Paris (17 octobre 1961)* (Paris: Éditions du Seuil, 1991).

Elders, Fons, 'Preface', in Michel Foucault, *Freedom and Knowledge* (Amsterdam: Elders Special Productions, 2012), pp. 7–8.

El-Mafaalani, Aladin, *Wozu Rassismus? Von der Erfindung der Menschenrassen bis zum rassismuskritischen Widerstand* (Cologne: Kiepenhauer & Witsch, 2022).

Enault, Marianne et al., 'Hommage à Samuel Paty, lutte contre l'islamisme: Blanquer précise au JDD ses mesures pour la rentrée scolaire', *Le Journal du Dimanche*, 25.10.2020.

Eribon, Didier, *Michel Foucault*, translated by Betsy Wing (Cambridge, MA: Harvard University Press, 1991).

Eribon, Didier, *Returning to Reims*, translated by Michael Lucey (Los Angeles, CA: Semiotext(e), 2013).

Erdur, Onur, *Die epistemologischen Jahre. Philosophie und Biologie in Frankreich, 1960–1980* (Zurich: Chronos, 2018).

Erdur, Onur, 'Antimarxismus. André Glucksmann: *Les maîtres penseurs* (1977)', in Monika Wulz et al. (eds), *Deregulation und Restauration. Eine politische Wissensgeschichte* (Berlin: Matthes & Seitz, 2021).

Ernaux, Annie, *A Girl's Story*, translated by Alison L. Strayer (London: Fitzcarraldo Editions, 2020).

Ette, Ottmar, 'Reiseberichte und Reiselandschaften', in *Roland Barthes. Landschaften der Theorie* (Konstanz: Konstanz University Press, 2013), pp. 95–120.

Fanon, Frantz, *The Wretched of the Earth*, translated by Constance Farrington (New York: Grove Press, 1963).

Fanon, Frantz, 'Rassismus und Kultur', in Fanon, *Für eine afrikanische Revolution. Politische Schriften* (Berlin: März, 2022), pp. 47–63.

Feichtinger, Moritz and Stephan Malinowski, '"Eine Million Algerier lernen im

20. Jahrhundert zu leben". Umsiedlungslager und Zwangsmodernisierung im Algerienkrieg 1954–1962', *Journal of Modern European History* 8 (2010), pp. 107–35.

Flaubert, Gustave, *Dictionary of Received Ideas*, translated by Gregory Norminton (London: Alma Books, 2010).

Foucault, Michel, 'La philosophie structuraliste permet de diagnostiquer ce qu'est "aujourd'hui". Entretien avec G. Fellous', *La Presse de Tunisie*, 12.4.1967; reprinted in Foucault, *Dits et Écrits, I: 1954–1975* (Paris: Gallimard, 1994), pp. 580–4.

Foucault, Michel, 'Intellectuals and Power' (1972), https://theanarchistlibrary.org/library/gilles-deleuze-michel-foucault-intellectuals-and-power.

Foucault, Michel, 'Des espaces autres', *Architecture, Mouvement, Continuité* 5 (1984), pp. 16–49.

Foucault, Michel, *The Archaeology of Knowledge*, translated by A. M. Sheridan Smith (London: Routledge, 1989).

Foucault, Michel, 'Des espaces autres', in *Dits et Écrits, IV: 1980–1988* (Paris: Gallimard, 1994), pp. 752–62.

Foucault, Michel, 'Entretien avec D. Trombadori', in *Dits et Écrits, IV: 1980–1988* (Paris: Gallimard, 1994), pp. 41–95.

Foucault, Michel, 'L'armée, quand la terre tremble', in *Dits et Écrits, III: 1976–1979* (Paris: Gallimard, 1994), pp. 662–9.

Foucault, Michel, 'Le problème des réfugiés est un prélude au grand mouvement migratoire du XXIe siècle', in *Dits et Écrits, III: 1976–1979* (Paris: Gallimard, 1994), pp. 798–800.

Foucault, Michel, *The Order of Things: An Archaeology of the Human Sciences* (London: Vintage, 1994).

Foucault, Michel, *History of Madness*, edited by Jean Khalfa, translated by Jonathan Murphy and Jean Khalfa (London and New York: Routledge, 2006).

Foucault, Michel, *Le Corps utopique, suivi de Les Hétérotopies* (Paris: Lignes, 2009), pp. 23–36.

Foucault, Michel, *Freedom and Knowledge* (Amsterdam: Elders Special Productions, 2012).

Fressoz, Françoise and Cédric Pietralunga, 'Apres le déconfinement, l'Élysée craint un vent de révolte: "Il ne faut pas perdre la jeunesse"', *Le Monde*, 10.6.2020.

Frisinghelli, Christine, 'Comments on the Photographic Documentations of Pierre Bourdieu', in Bourdieu, *Picturing Algeria*, pp. 201–14.

Gadant, Monique, *Parcours d'une intellectuelle en Algérie. Nationalisme et anticolonialisme dans les sciences sociales* (Paris: L'Harmattan, 1995).

Graff, Bernd, 'Makellos. Kein Fortschritt, dass gerade alle Relativierungen von Echtheit und Identität aufgegeben werden', *Süddeutsche Zeitung*, 12/13.9.2020.

Guillaumin, Colette, *L'idéologie raciste. Genèse et langage actuel* (Paris and The Hague: Mouton, 1972).

Gumbrecht, Hans-Ulrich, 'Lyotard: Eine Maschine ohne Körper kann nicht denken', *Neue Zürcher Zeitung*, 23.9.2019.

Gumbrecht, Hans-Ulrich, 'Jacques Derrida: Ein Abgesang', *Neue Zürcher Zeitung*, 15.7.2020.

Gündoğdu, Ayten, 'Disagreeing with Rancière: Speech, Violence, and the Ambiguous Subjects of Politics', *Polity* 49 (2017), pp. 188–219.

Habermas, Jürgen, 'Die Moderne – ein unvollendetes Projekt', *Die Zeit*, 19.9.1980.

Hafsia, Jalila, *Visages et rencontres* (Tunis: SAGEP, 1981).

Hafsia, Jalila, 'Quand la passion de l'intelligence illuminait Sidi Bou Saïd', *La Presse de Tunisie*, 6.7.1984.

Hajjat, Abdellali, *La marche pour l'égalité et contre le racisme* (Paris: 2013).

Hajjat, Abdellali, *The Wretched of France: The 1983 March for Equality*, translated by Andrew Brown (Bloomington: Indiana University Press, 2022).

Hall, Stuart, *Rassismus und kulturelle Identität. Ausgewählte Schriften 2* (Hamburg: Argument Verlag, 2012).

Hammoudi, Abdellah, 'Phenomenology and Ethnography: On Kabyle *Habitus* in the Work of Pierre Bourdieu', in Jane E. Goodman and Paul A. Silverstein (eds), *Bourdieu in Algeria: Colonial Politics, Ethnographic Practices, Theoretical Developments* (Lincoln: University of Nebraska Press, 2009), pp. 199–254.

Hamon, Hervé and Patrick Rotman, *Les porteurs de valises. La résistance française à la guerre d'Algérie* (Paris: Albin Michel, 1979).

Hanimann, Joseph, 'Wie philosophisch ist Emmanuel Macron?', *Süddeutsche Zeitung*, 1.2.2018.

Havercroft, Jonathan and David Owen, 'Soul-Blindness, Police Orders and Black Lives Matter: Wittgenstein, Cavell, and Rancière', *Political Theory* 44 (2016), pp. 739–63.

Heinze, Robert, 'Die Unterscheidungen sind das Problem', *Neues Deutschland*, 8.3.2022.

Heiter, Bernd, 'Immanuel Wallerstein: Unthinking Culture?', in Stephan Moebius and Dirk Quadflieg (eds), *Kultur. Theorien der Gegenwart* (Wiesbaden: Verlag für Sozialwissenschaften, 2011), pp. 708–21.

Hénin, Emmanuelle et al. (eds), *Après la déconstruction. L'université au défi des idéologies* (Paris: Odile Jacob, 2023).

Hiddleston, Jane, *Poststructuralism and Postcoloniality: The Anxiety of Theory* (Liverpool: Liverpool University Press, 2010).

Hilfrich, Carola, 'Unheim(at)liche Zugehörigkeiten: Algerien als Ort von Herkunft und Gedächtnis bei Jacques Derrida und Hélène Cixous', *Jahrbuch des Simon-Dubnow-Instituts* 10 (2011), pp. 389–403.

Honneth, Axel and Jacques Rancière, *Recognition or Disagreement: A Critical Encounter on the Politics of Freedom, Equality, and Identity* (New York: Columbia University Press, 2017).

Huffer, Lynne, 'Derrida's Nostalgeria', in Lorcin (ed.), *Algeria & France, 1800–2000*, pp. 228–46.

Huntington, Samuel P., *The Clash of Civilizations and the Remaking of World Order* (New York: Simon & Schuster, 1996).

Kalter, Christoph, '"*Le Monde* va de l'avant. Et vous êtes en marge". Dekolonisierung, Dezentrierung des Westens und Entdeckung der "Dritten Welt" in der radikalen Linken in Frankreich in den 1960er-Jahren', *Archiv für Sozialgeschichte* 48 (2008), pp. 99–132.

Kalter, Christoph, *Die Entdeckung der Dritten Welt. Dekolonisierung und neue radikale Linke in Frankreich* (Frankfurt am Main and New York: Campus, 2011).

Kerner, Ina, *Postkoloniale Theorien zur Einführung* (Hamburg: Junius, 2012).

Kleie, Stefan, 'Wer haftet für die "woke" Identitätspolitik?', *Frankfurter Allgemeine Zeitung*, 5.3.2021.

Knight, Diana, 'Barthes and Orientalism', *New Literary History* 24 (1993), pp. 617–33.

Knight, Diana, *Barthes and Utopia: Space, Travel, Writing* (Oxford: Clarendon Press, 1997).

König, Traugott, 'Flauberts Orient-Schock', *Die ZEIT*, 25.9.1981.

Koschorke, Albrecht, 'Die akademische Linke hat sich selbst dekonstruiert. Es ist Zeit, die Begriffe neu zu justieren', *Neue Zürcher Zeitung*, 18.4.2018.

Krais, Beate, 'Habitus und soziale Praxis', in Margareta Steinrücke (ed.), *Pierre Bourdieu: Politisches Forschen, Denken und Eingreifen* (Hamburg: VSA-Verlag, 2004), pp. 14–33.

Krais, Beate and Gunter Gebauer, *Habitus* (Bielefeld: Transcript Verlag, 2002).

Laermann, Klaus, 'Lacancan und Derridada. Frankolatrie: gegen die neueste Mode, den neuesten Nonsens in den Kulturwissenschaften', *Die Zeit*, 30.5.1986.

Lagasnerie, Geoffroy de, *La dernière leçon de Michel Foucault. Sur le néolibéralisme, la théorie et la politique* (Paris: Fayard, 2012).

Le Neve, Soazig, 'Polémique après les propos de Jean-Michel Blanquer sur "l'islamo-gauchisme" à l'université', *Le Monde*, 23.10.2020.

Le Sueur, James D., *Uncivil War: Intellectuals and Identity Politics during the Decolonization of Algeria* (Philadelphia: University of Pennsylvania Press, 2001).

Léger, Nathalie, 'Editor's Preface', in Barthes, *The Preparation of the Novel*, pp. xvii–xxiv.

Leggewie, Claus, *Kofferträger. Das Algerien-Projekt der Linken im Adenauer-Deutschland* (Berlin: Rotbuch Verlag, 1984).

Leggewie, Claus, 'Der andere 8. Mai 1945', *Frankfurter Allgemeine Zeitung*, 9.5.2015.

Leggewie, Claus, 'Roman nicht nur zur Stunde', *Frankfurter Allgemeine Zeitung*, 28.3.2020.

Leggewie, Claus, 'Papa, was hast Du in Algerien gemacht? Der Algerienkrieg in der europäischen Erinnerungskultur', *Merkur* 75 (March 2021), pp. 68–75.

Lévi-Strauss, Claude, *Tristes tropiques*, translated by John Russell (New York: Criterion Books, 1961).

Lorcin, Patricia M. E. (ed.), *Algeria & France, 1800–2000: Identity, Memory, Nostalgia* (Syracuse, NY: Syracuse University Press, 2006), pp. 228–46.

Lukács, Georg, *The Theory of the Novel*, translated by Anna Bostock (Cambridge, MA: MIT Press, 1971).

Lyotard, Jean-François, *Instructions païennes* (Paris: Éditions Galilée, 1977).

Lyotard, Jean-François, *The Postmodern Condition: A Report on Knowledge*, translated by Geoff Bennington and Brian Massumi (Manchester: Manchester University Press, 1984).

Lyotard, Jean-François, 'Rules and Paradoxes and Svelte Appendix', translated by Brian Massumi, in *Cultural Critique* 5, Modernity and Modernism, Postmodernity and Postmodernism (Winter, 1986–87), pp. 209–19.

Lyotard, Jean-François, *Peregrinations: Law, Form, Event* (New York: Columbia University Press, 1988).

Lyotard, Jean-François, *The Differend: Phrases in Dispute*, translated by Georges van de Abbeele (Minneapolis: University of Minnesota Press, 1988).

Lyotard, Jean-François, *La guerre des Algériens. Écrits 1956–1963*, edited by Mohammed Ramdani (Paris: Galilée, 1989).

Lyotard, Jean-François, *Phenomenology*, translated by Brian Beakley (Albany: State University of New York Press, 1991).

Lyotard, Jean-François, *Political Writings*, translated by Bill Readings with Kevin Paul Geiman (Minneapolis: University of Minnesota Press, 1993).

Lyotard, Jean-François, *Discourse, Figure*, translated by Antony Hudeck and Mary Lydon (Minneapolis: University of Minnesota Press, 2011).

Macey, David, *Michel Foucault* (London: Reaktion Books, 2004).

Macey, David, *The Lives of Michel Foucault* (London: Verso, 2019).

Mackenthun, Gesa, 'Essentialismus, strategischer', in Dirk Göttsche et al. (eds), *Handbuch Postkolonialismus und Literatur* (Stuttgart: Metzler, 2017), pp. 142–4.

Malabou, Catherine and Jacques Derrida, *Counterpath: Travelling with Jacques Derrida*, translated by David Wills (Stanford, CA: Stanford University Press, 2004).

Marty, Éric, 'Roland Barthes au Maroc', pp. 1–9, www.unige.ch/lettres/framo/application/files/4614/3705/8723/E_Marty.pdf.

Mbembe, Achille, 'Faut-il provincialiser la France?', *Politique africaine* 119 (October 2010), pp. 159–88.

Mokhtefi, Elaine, *Algiers, Third World Capital: Freedom Fighters, Revolutionaries, Black Panthers* (London: Verso, 2018).

Mokhtefi, Mokhtar, *I Was a French Muslim: Memories of an Algerian Freedom Fighter* (New York: Other Press, 2021).

Mölk, Ulrich, 'Gustave Flaubert am zweiten Katarakt: "Je l'appellerai Emma Bovary"', *Romanische Forschungen* 96 (1984), pp. 264–77.

Morgenroth, Claas, '1978. Roland Barthes. "Die Vorbereitung des Romans"', in Sandro Zanetti (ed.), *Improvisation und Invention. Momente, Modelle, Medien* (Zurich and Berlin: Diaphanes, 2014), pp. 149–59.

Naguschewski, Dirk, 'Politik im Diskurs. Roland Barthes und die "Afrikanische Grammatik"', in Mona Körte and Anne-Kathrin Reulecke (eds), *Mythen des Alltags – Mythologies. Roland Barthes' Klassiker der Kulturwissenschaften* (Berlin: Kulturverlag Kadmos 2014), pp. 132–41.

Nancy, Jean-Luc, 'L'indépendance de l'Algérie, l'indépendance de Derrida', in

Mustapha Chérif (ed.), *Derrida à Alger. Un regard sur le monde* (Arles: Actes Sud, 2008), pp. 19–25.

Naudier, Delphine, 'L'écriture-femme, une innovation esthétique emblématique', *Sociétés contemporaines* 44 (2001), pp. 57–73.

Neiman, Susan, *Links ist nicht woke* (Berlin: Hanser, 2023).

N. N., 'Un incendie criminel ravage l'université', *Le Monde*, 9.6.1962.

N. N., 'Den alten Volksgeist erwecken: Alain de Benoist über die "Verwurzelungs"-Ideologie der französischen Neuen Rechten', *Der Spiegel* 34, 19.8.1979.

N. N., 'Algérie-France. Regards croisés', *Lignes* 30 (1997).

N. N., 'Le 17/10/1961, le massacre des Algériens', *Le Nouvel Observateur*, 21.10.2004.

N. N., '"Racisme d'État": La plainte de Jean-Michel Blanquer contre un syndicat classée sans suite', *Libération*, 7.2.2018.

N. N., 'Appel de l'Observatoire du décolonialisme et des idéologies identitaires', *Le Point*, 13.1.2021, www.lepoint.fr/politique/appel-de-l-observatoire-du-decolonialisme-et-des-ideologies-identitaires-13-01-2021-2409523_20.php#11.

Nora, Pierre, *Les Français d'Algérie* (Paris: Christian Bourgois, 2012).

Oei, Bernd, *Flaubert: Die Entzauberung des Gefühls* (Berlin: LIT, 2010).

Ott, Michaela, *Welches Außen des Denkens? Französische Theorien in (post)-kolonialer Kritik* (Vienna: Verlag Turia + Kant, 2018).

Pantel, Nadia, 'Macron sollte die Proteste ernst nehmen', *Süddeutsche Zeitung*, 16.10.2020.

Peeters, Benoît, *Derrida: A Biography*, translated by Andrew Brown (Cambridge: Polity, 2013).

Péju, Paulette, *Ratonnades à Paris* (Paris: François Maspero, 1961).

Pérez, Amín, *Combattre en sociologues. Pierre Bourdieu & Abdelmalek Sayad dans une guerre de libération (Algérie, 1958–1964)* (Marseille: Agone, 2022).

Perroux, François (ed.), *L'Algérie de demain* (Paris, PUF: 1962).

Pinguet, Maurice, 'Les années d'apprentissage', *Le Débat* 41 (1986), pp. 122–31.

Plaetzer, Niklas, 'Universalismen zwischen Politik und Polizei. Jacques Rancière in der Postkolonie', in Mareike Gebhardt (ed.), *Staatskritik und Radikaldemokratie. Das Denken Jacques Rancières* (Baden-Baden: Nomos, 2020), pp. 191–208.

Pluckrose, Helen and James Lindsay, *Cynical Theories: How Activist Scholarship Made Everything about Race, Gender, and Identity – and Why This Harms Everybody* (Durham, NC: Pitchstone Publishing, 2020).

Precht, Oliver, 'Portrait of a Philosopher (Notes on a New Biography of Jacques Derrida)', *ZfL Blog*, 7.5.2021, www.zflprojekte.de/zfl-blog/2021/05/07/oliver-precht-portrait-of-a-philosopher-notes-on-a-new-biography-of-jacques-derrida.

Preciado, Paul B., 'Les leçons du virus', *Mediapart*, 11.4.2020, https://www.mediapart.fr/journal/culture-idees/110420/les-lecons-du-virus.

Postl, Gertrude, 'Eine Politik des Schreibens und des Lachens. Versuch einer historischen Kontexualisierung von Hélène Cixous' *Medusa*-Text', in Esther Hutfless et al. (eds), *Hélène Cixous. Das Lachen der Medusa zusammen mit aktuellen Beiträgen* (Vienna: Passagen Verlag, 2013), pp. 21–35.

Rajchman, John, 'Introduction: The Question of Identity', *October* 61 (1992), pp. 5–7.

Rajchman, John (ed.), *The Identity in Question* (New York: Routledge, 2014).

Ramdani, Mohammed, 'L'Algerie, un differend', in Lyotard, *La guerre des Algériens*, pp. 9–32.

Rancière, Jacques, *The Nights of Labor: The Workers' Dream in Nineteenth-Century France*, translated by John Drury (Philadelphia, PA: Temple University Press, 1989).

Rancière, Jacques, 'The Cause of the Other', translated by David Macey, *Parallax* 4:2 (1998), pp. 25–33.

Rancière, *Dis-agreement: Politics and Philosophy*, translated by Julie Rose (Minneapolis: University of Minnesota Press, 2004).

Rancière, Jacques, 'Our Police Order: What Can Be Said, Seen, and Done', *Le Monde Diplomatique* (Norway), 11.8.2006.

Rancière, Jacques, *Althusser's Lesson*, translated by Emiliano Battista (London: Continuum, 2011).

Rancière, Jacques, *Moments politiques: Interventions 1977–2009*, translated by Mary Foster (New York: Seven Stories Press, 2014).

Rancière, Jacques, *The Method of Equality: Interviews with Laurent Jeanpierre and Dork Zabunyan*, translated by Julie Rose (Cambridge: Polity, 2016).

Rancière, Jacques, 'Critical Questions on the Theory of Recognition', in Honneth and Rancière, *Recognition or Disagreement*, pp. 83–95.

Rancière, Jacques, 'Les vertus de l'inexplicable – à propos des "gilets jaunes"', *AOC*, 8.1.2019, https://aoc.media/opinion/2019/01/08/vertus-de-linexplicable-a-propos-gilets-jaunes.

Rancière, Jacques, 'Vorwort zur deutschen Ausgabe', in *An den Rändern des Politischen* (Vienna: Passagen Verlag, 2019), pp. 11–21.

Rancière, Jacques, 'Politics, Identification, and Subjectivization', in Marc James Léger (ed.), *Identity Trumps Socialism: The Class and Identity Debate after Neoliberalism* (London: Routledge, 2023).

Rancière, Jacques, *Uncertain Times*, translated by Andrew Brown (Cambridge: Polity, 2024).

Reed-Danahay, Deborah, 'The Kabyle and the French: Occidentalism in Bourdieu's Theory of Practice', in James G. Carrier (ed.), *Occidentalism: Images of the West* (Oxford: Oxford University Press, 1995), pp. 61–84.

Rehbein, Boike, *Die Soziologie Pierre Bourdieus* (Konstanz: UTB, 2006).

Reid, Don, 'Étienne Balibar: Algeria, Althusser, and Altereuropeanisation', *South Central Review* 25 (2008), pp. 68–85.

Rey, Terry, *Bourdieu on Religion: Imposing Faith and Legitimacy* (London: Routledge, 2007).

Ritter, Henning, 'Ins neue Leben schreiben', *Frankfurter Allgemeine Zeitung*, 25.6.2008.

Roldán Mendívil, Eleonora and Bafta Sarbo (eds), *Die Diversität der Ausbeutung. Zur Kritik des herrschenden Antirassismus* (Berlin: Dietz, 2023).

Ruz, Nathalie, 'La force du "cartiérisme"', in Jean-Pierre Rioux (ed.), *La guerre d'Algérie et les Français* (Paris: Éditions Fayard, 1990), pp. 329–36.

Said, Edward, *Orientalism* (New York: Pantheon, 1978).

Said, Edward, *Culture and Imperialism* (New York: Vintage Press, 1993).

Said, Edward, 'Diary', *London Review of Books*, 1.6.2000.

Salmon, Peter, *An Event, Perhaps: A Biography of Jacques Derrida* (London: Verso, 2020).

Samoyault, Tiphaine, *Barthes: A Biography*, translated by Andrew Brown (Cambridge: Polity, 2017).

Sarasin, Philipp, *1977. Eine kurze Geschichte der Gegenwart* (Berlin: Suhrkamp, 2021).

Sarasin, Philipp, 'Mit Foucault die Pandemie verstehen?', *Geschichte der Gegenwart*, 25.3.2020, https://geschichtedergegenwart.ch/mit-foucault-die-pandemie-verstehen.

Sartre, Jean-Paul, 'Jean-Paul Sartre répond', *L'Arc* 30 (1966), pp. 87–96.

Sartre, Jean-Paul, 'Colonialism is a System,' in *Colonialism and Neocolonialism*, translated by Azzedine Haddour, Steve Brewer, and Terry McWilliams (London: Routledge, 2001).

Sasse, Sylvia and Sandro Zanetti, '#Postmoderne als Pappkamerad,' *Geschichte der Gegenwart*, 11.6.2017, https://geschichtedergegenwart.ch/postmoderne-als-pappkamerad.

Schäfer, Hilmar, 'Pierre Bourdieus algerische Gründungsszene und das Konzept des gespaltenen Habitus,' in Sina Farzin and Henning Laux (eds), *Gründungsszenen soziologischer Theorie* (Wiesbaden: Springer VS, 2014), pp. 67–79.

Schep, Dennis, *The Autobiographical Effect: Writing the Self in Post-Structuralist Theory* (New York: Routledge, 2020).

Scheu, René, 'Das Spiel der Differenzen. Wie Jacques Derrida 1968 einen Begriff prägte, der rechts Karriere machte,' *Neue Zürcher Zeitung*, 18.7.2018.

Scholz, Anna-Lena, 'Hélène Cixous an der FU. Der Schrei der Literatur,' *Tagesspiegel*, 13.5.2016.

Schultheis, Franz, 'Algerien 1960: Zur Genese der Bourdieuschen Theorie der gesellschaftlichen Welt,' in Margareta Steinrücke (ed.), Pierre Bourdieu: *Politisches Forschen, Denken und Eingreifen* (Hamburg: VSA-Verlag, 2004), pp. 14–33.

Schwarzer, Alice, 'MLF wird 50: Allons les filles!,' *EMMA*, 24.7.2020, www.emma.de/artikel/50-jahre-mlf-337807.

Shatz, Adam, 'Not in the Mood,' *London Review of Books*, 22.11.2012.

Shatz, Adam, *Writers and Missionaries: Essays on Radical Imagination* (London: Verso, 2023).

Shepard, Todd, *The Invention of Decolonization: The Algerian War and the Remaking of France* (Ithaca, NY: Cornell University Press, 2006).

Shepard, Todd, *Sex, France, and Arab Men, 1962–1979* (Chicago: University of Chicago Press, 2018).

Simon, Catherine, *Algérie, les années pieds-rouges. Des rêves de l'indépendance au désenchantement (1962–1969)* (Paris: La Découverte, 2009).

Soulié, Charles (ed.), *Un mythe à détruire? Origines et destin du Centre universitaire de Vincennes* (Paris: Presses Universitaires de Vincennes, 2012).

Spivak, Gayatri Chakravorty, 'Criticism, Feminism and the Institution,' *Thesis Eleven* 10/11 (1984/85), pp. 175–87.

Spivak, Gayatri Chakravorty, 'Can the Subaltern Speak?' (1988), https://jan.ucc.nau.edu/~sj6/Spivak%20CanTheSubalternSpeak.pdf.

Spivak, Gayatri Chakravorty, *A Critique of Postcolonial Reason: Toward a History of the Vanishing Present* (Cambridge, MA: Harvard University Press, 1999).

Stangler, Cole, 'France is Becoming More Like America. It's Terrible', *New York Times*, 2.6.2021.

Steinfeld, Thomas, 'Schuld war nur der Poststrukturalismus', *Süddeutsche Zeitung*, 18.8.2020.

Steinmetz, George, 'Soziologie und Kolonialismus. Über die Geburt der Soziologie aus der kolonialen Erfahrung', *Mittelweg 36* 29 (2020), pp. 57–78.

Steinmetz, George, *The Colonial Origins of Modern Social Thought: French Sociology and the Overseas Empire* (Princeton, NJ: Princeton University Press, 2023).

Stoler, Ann Laura, *Race and the Education of Desire: Foucault's History of Sexuality and the Colonial Order of Things* (Durham, NC: Duke University Press, 1995).

Stoler, Ann Laura, 'Colonial Aphasia: Race and Disabled Histories in France', *Public Culture* 23 (2011), pp. 121–56.

Stoler, Ann Laura, 'L'éclat de Foucault dans les études (post)coloniales', in Jean-François Braunstein et al. (eds), *Foucault(s). La philosophie à l'oeuvre* (Paris: Éditions de la Sorbonne, 2017), pp. 107–23.

Stora, Benjamin, *La gangrène et l'oubli. La mémoire de la guerre d'Algérie* (Paris: Éditions de la Découverte, 1991).

Stora, Benjamin, *Appelés en guerre d'Algérie* (Paris: Gallimard, 1997).

Stora, Benjamin, *Les trois exils. Juifs d'Algérie* (Paris: Stock, 2006).

Stora, Benjamin, *Les clés retrouvées. Une enfance juive à Constantine* (Paris: Éditions Flammarion, 2015).

Stora, Benjamin and Alexis Jenni, *Les mémoires dangereuses* (Paris: Albin Michel, 2016).

Strauss, Simon, 'Lebensader in Gefahr', *Frankfurter Allgemeine Zeitung*, 21.7.2020.

Taguieff, André, *Force of Prejudice: On Racism and its Doubles*, translated and edited by Hassan Melehy (Minneapolis: University of Minnesota Press, 2001).

Thénault, Sylvie, *Histoire de la guerre d'indépendance algérienne* (Paris: Éditions Flammarion, 2005).

Thiel, Thomas, 'Die neue Lust am Büßen', *Frankfurter Allgemeine Zeitung*, 23.3.2022.

Thomä, Diether et al., *Der Einfall des Lebens. Theorie als geheime Autobiographie* (Munich: Carl Hanser, 2015).

Todd, Olivier, *Albert Camus: A Life*, translated by Benjamin Ivry (New York: Carroll & Graf, 2000).

Toscano, Alberto, 'The Name of Algeria: French Philosophy and the Subject of Decolonization', *Viewpoint Magazine*, 1.2.2018, https://viewpointmag.com/2018/02/01/name-algeria-french-philosophy-subject-decolonization.

Traoré, Assa and Geoffroy de Lagasnerie, 'Der Kampf Adama', in Daniel Loick and Vanessa E. Thompson (eds), *Abolitionismus. Ein Reader* (Berlin: Suhrkamp, 2022), pp. 288–315.

Truong, Nicolas, 'Emmanuel Macron, un intellectuel en politique?', *Le Monde*, 1.9.2016.

Véga-Ritter, Max, 'Un an d'enseignement de la philosophie entre docte Sorbonne et ravin du Rhumel', *Les bahuts du Rhumel. Les anciens des Lycées de Constantine* 60 (2012), pp. 4–5.

Vidal-Naquet, Pierre, *L'Affaire Audin, 1957–1978* (Paris: Éditions de Minuit, 1989).

Wade, Simeon, *Foucault in California. A True Story: Wherein the Great French Philosopher Drops Acid in the Valley of Death* (Berkeley, CA: Heyday, 2019).

Wallerstein, Immanuel, *The Road to Independence: Ghana and Ivory Coast* (Paris: Mouton, 1964).

Wallerstein, Immanuel, 'Fanon and the Revolutionary Class', in *The Essential Wallerstein* (New York: New Press, 2000), pp. 14–32.

Weber, Max, *The Protestant Ethic and the Spirit of Capitalism*, translated by Talcott Parsons (London: Routledge, 1992).

West, Patrick, 'In Defence of Postmodernism', *spiked*, 15.4.2023, https://www.spiked-online.com/2023/04/15/in-defence-of-postmodernism/.

Williams, Thomas Chatterton, 'The French Are in a Panic over *Le Wokisme*', *The Atlantic*, 4.2.2023.

Yacine, Tassadit, 'Pierre Bourdieu in Algeria at War: Notes on the Birth of an Engaged Ethnosociology', *Ethnography* 5 (2004), pp. 487–510.

Yacine, Tassadit, 'At the Origins of a Singular Ethnosociology', in Bourdieu, *Algerian Sketches*, pp. 13–34.

Young, Robert J. C., 'Foucault on Race and Colonialism', *New Formations* 25 (1995), pp. 57–65.

Young, Robert J. C., *Postcolonialism: An Historical Introduction* (Oxford: Blackwell, 2001).

Young, Robert J. C., *White Mythologies: Writing History and the West* (London: Routledge, 2004).

Zamora, Daniel, 'The Culture Wars Come to France', *Catalyst* 5 (2021), https://catalyst-journal.com/2021/12/the-culture-wars-come-to-france.

Zitzmann, Marc, 'Ein Überflieger mit Retro-Hauch zieht ins Elysée', *Neue Zürcher Zeitung*, 11.5.2017.

Films

Alger, la Mecque des révolutionnaires 1962–1974, dir. Ben Salama, France 2014, 55 mins.

Derrida, dir. Kirby Dick and Amy Kofman, USA 2002, 85 mins.

Derrida's Elsewhere, dir. Safaa Fathy, France 1999, 68 mins.

Ever, Rêve, Hélène Cixous, dir. Olivier Morel, France, USA 2018, 118 mins.

Intersecting Optics: A Dialogue on 'Race, Nation, Class' 30 Years On. A filmed interview with Étienne Balibar and Immanuel Wallerstein by Manuela Bojadžijev, dir. Charles Heller and Lorenzo Pezzani, France, Germany 2018, 43 mins, https://archiv.hkw.de/en/app/mediathek/video/62616.

'Simone de Beauvoir: Pourquoi je suis féministe', Télévision Française 1, 6.4.1975.

Vincennes, l'université perdue, dir. Virginie Linhart, France 2016, 90 mins.

Index